100 THINGS
JAZZ FANS
SHOULD KNOW & DO
BEFORE THEY DIE

Jody Genessy

TRIUMPH
BOOKS

Library of Congress Cataloging-in-Publication Data

Names: Genessy, Jody, author.
Title: 100 things Jazz fans should know & do before they die / Jody Genessy.
Other titles: One hundred things Jazz fans should know and do before they die
Description: Chicago, Illinois : Triumph Books LLC, [2019] | Series: 100 things...fans should know
Identifiers: LCCN 2018046926 | ISBN 9781629375816 (paperback)
Subjects: LCSH: Utah Jazz (Basketball team)—History. | Utah Jazz (Basketball team)—Miscellanea. | BISAC: SPORTS & RECREATION / Basketball. | TRAVEL / United States / West / Mountain (AZ, CO, ID, MT, NM, UT, WY).
Classification: LCC GV885.52.U8 G46 2019 | DDC 796.323/6409792258—dc23 LC record available at https://lccn.loc.gov/2018046926

This book is available in quantity at special discounts for your group or organization. For further information, contact:
   Triumph Books LLC
   814 North Franklin Street
   Chicago, Illinois 60610
   (312) 337-0747
   www.triumphbooks.com

Printed in U.S.A.
ISBN: 978-1-62937-581-6
Design by Patricia Frey

*To all Utah Jazz fans but especially my home team—
my mom, Patty (who's always been my biggest fan);
my dad, Tom (who instilled a love of sports in
me before passing away); my kids, Ethan, Sydney,
Aidan, and Jackson (my favorite fan club); and
my wife, Heather (the best teammate I've had).*

Contents

Foreword

I can remember sitting up in the office and lighting up a cigar at 9:00 on the Monday morning we got to Salt Lake City after moving the Jazz from New Orleans in 1979. I looked around. I looked at our staff, which was about nine people, and I said, "Well, what do we do now? Where do we go from here?"

I said to my wife, Barbara, "In all honesty, in three years here, I think, we will become very, very tough." We just didn't have a good team yet. We had an injured, wonderful asset in Pete Maravich, but he couldn't play anymore.

But that's where we were. I told then-owner Sam Battistone at the time, "I'd like to thank you for your faith in me. What I'm going to do is reward you by promising you and this organization to bring a world championship team to Utah next year. *Of course, it will be the Celtics or the Lakers.*"

Tom Nissalke was an excellent coach, but Johnny Wooden said, "A good coach is one who wins when he has good players; nobody can win with bad players."

The building of a team and the future relied on a few things. We needed finances. We needed people to step up and put money up ahead of time and we got pretty good support from the Battistones. We also needed to put the best possible people in place at all the positions. You have to hire the best coaches. You have to hire the best trainers. You have to hire the best strength coaches. You have to hire the best doctors. You have to hire the best ticket takers, the best ushers. You take care of the business, and then the players will come. But it takes patience.

We started getting excellent front-office people like Jay Francis and Dave Checketts. We started selling advertising. One other thing that was very successful and very helpful was starting the

Junior Jazz. That got kids and their families interested in basketball and in the team. We made a very key good investment in getting Adrian Dantley. A.D. gave us great credibility because he led the league in scoring. We had him and started to build around him and through the draft, getting guys like Bobby Hansen, Mark Eaton, Thurl Bailey and then we hit the mother lode with John Stockton and Karl Malone.

A lot of people say I was the first one who spotted John Stockton, but there were good basketball people—Neil McCarthy, Ladell Andersen, Jack Gardner—who had mentioned him. We heard whispers about this guard from Gonzaga and we also heard that the Portland Trail Blazers wanted him. We thought about taking him and trading him to Portland to maybe get two or three players, depending on how badly they wanted him. People were shocked when we took Stockton, and the rest is history.

Malone was the same thing. He got picked a little late, and I thought, *What do people know that we don't know?* We did our homework. My son Scott, Jerry Sloan, and I stayed in our cabin in Ogden Canyon and looked at film the weekend before the draft. We knew he was a tough guy. I said, "This guy is a wrecking crew! He won't be there when we pick." Lo and behold, he was.

All of a sudden, the pieces started falling into place. We found ourselves with a nice team—a very nice team. We had a wonderful attitude. Our players were all team-oriented, a characteristic that has carried on in this organization throughout the years.

I remember when we won the Midwest Division in 1984, which guaranteed us home-court advantage in the first round. It was the first time the Jazz made the playoffs, and we went and sat down in the locker room at the Salt Palace. You could still hear the noise outside, the people cheering. Dave Allred, who was in charge of public relations, came in and said, "Coach, they want the team to come out on the floor." We went out and walked around the base of the floor, shaking hands with the fans. That was very important for me because I thought, *Okay, we've arrived. Now nobody can say the Jazz aren't good.*

Even so, people wondered if we were going to stay that way. We had to be a little bit better every year. Coaching the All-Star Game that year was another highlight. Not only did I have Kareem Abdul-Jabbar and Magic Johnson, but I had Rickey Green and A.D. We had this great team. That was a big thrill. It was great to be there with Scotty and Phil Johnson, and my other son, Michael, was a ball boy.

Dick Motta, who should be in the Hall of Fame, suggested that Sloan was available and that we should hire him as a scout. That was a great hire. Sloan was so honest and such a good team person and he worked hard. He came at the right time. I felt we could get ourselves into the echelon of the top three or four teams, and that would be good enough for me and I'd pack it in. I'd put in a lot of years coaching—10 years in high school and college and 12 years in the pros. It was time for me to step aside and give Barbara a break and see my children more. If I have any regrets, it's that I spent a lifetime with other people's kids and not enough time with my own. It was an opportunity for Sloan, and he had an excellent coaching staff. They got along. They had fun. It worked out for everybody.

Another big thrill for me was getting inducted into the Utah Sports Hall of Fame in 2009. I made a lot of friends here and have a lot of respect for this area. I could live anywhere in the world, and we choose to live here in Utah, and basically it's because of the people. That's one of the reasons I was so excited when the Jazz made the NBA Finals. I wanted to see the fans be rewarded and certainly the players, some of whom were holdovers from my time.

As I said in a video for the Jazz's 40th season in Utah, "Who could have imagined all of this? In the summer of '79, the Jazz came to Utah, and people wondered, *Could it last? Would it work?* But over the years, this franchise has grown with the city. You became fans, the best fans, Utah Jazz fans. Win or lose, hope or heartbreak, this team was yours. You cheered for every rookie, every player, every coach. You listened to the voices on the sidelines. These trophies are your trophies. These jerseys are your jerseys. These records are your records. This is your history."

And this book, which spans the history of the Jazz franchise in an entertaining and enlightening way, is your book.

—Frank Layden
former Jazz head coach and general manager

Introduction

Being the Utah Jazz beat writer for the *Deseret News* was my identity for almost a decade from 2008 to 2017. It was a source of deep pride on personal and professional levels—for me and for others, especially my mom. It was an automatic conversation starter, a friend magnet, a spotlight for a former class clown who seeks attention (not sure that's a good thing), and a pretty awesome way to earn a living.

I'd never loved a job more than writing about the NBA team that I grew up cheering for. It was even better than getting free food as a McDonald's manager. Heck, I got free food in the press room and got paid to watch basketball. I remember attending a Jazz game that featured an America concert after the final buzzer in the early 1980s. The tickets were only $10. They'd do almost anything to get people in the old Salt Palace back then. A decade later, they didn't have enough seats in the new Delta Center to fit everybody who wanted to watch the Jazz play—even without a postgame show. Two decades later, I was earning a living by writing about Utah's favorite team.

It was rewarding and fun, going from hanging a Dr. Dunkenstein poster on my wall and emulating Adrian Dantley's ball spin on the free-throw line as a kid to remembering how my friends and I ended up at the airport after celebrating John Stockton's shot, to reporting on the end of Jerry Sloan's career, the interesting Ty Corbin era, and on the promising beginning of Quin Snyder's reign. I was in Springfield, Massachusetts, when Sloan, Stockton, and Karl Malone were inducted into the Naismith Basketball Hall of Fame in 2008 and '09. I was outside of the locker room when Sloan shockingly coached his last game, was in Dallas with the team when Utah traded away its franchise player (Deron Williams), and was wondering what to do with myself when the NBA shut down for part of the 2011–12 season. And, yes, I thought Jazz fans might throw me overboard when that series of events took place in my early days on this beat.

For nine years, I chronicled this franchise's every move for the *Deseret News*, and, man, was that an adventure. I was courtside when Paul Millsap—Miss Bettye's son, as his teammates called him—had his miracle in Miami. I was in the arena when Sundiata Gaines and Gordon Hayward dropped game-winning buckets on LeBron James. (I still kick myself for retreating to the press room moments before Gaines' memorable shot.) I was in Charlotte when Enes Kanter gave Al Jefferson arguably the greatest love letter ever written and in Chicago when the Turkish center informed Aaron Falk and I that he wanted to be traded.

I was there when D-Will made dazzling passes and clutch shots for the Jazz and then got lustily booed when he returned to his old stomping grounds after being traded to the New Jersey Nets. I was there when Hayward impressed Kobe Bryant as a rookie and then again when G-Time & Co. watched helplessly as the Black Mamba dropped 60 in his grand finale. I was in New York City to tease Hayward and rookie pal Jeremy Evans about eating at an Olive Garden in one of the world's culinary hotspots. I was there in Oklahoma City when Trevor Booker made his amazing back-to-the-basket volleyball trick shot and when a frustrated Raja Bell smacked the scorer's table and told Earl Watson, "We consistently do dumb [bleep]!" I was there when John Lucas III tried to fight Francisco Garcia in Houston and in Salt Lake City when the kind-hearted player thoughtfully brought pumpkin cheesecake for my kids to try for the first time. I was there when Sloan leaned on his garbage can outside of the Jazz locker room for interviews and when Corbin taught my oldest son, Ethan, how to properly shake some-one's hand (a firm grip and eye contact are important, he told him).

I was there when Rudy Gobert helped cancer-fighting Jazz superfan JP Gibson dunk the ball in a scrimmage, when the rising star's buzzer-beating tip-in saved the day in Sacramento, and when the big French center blocked his first shot in the Orlando Pro summer league, causing me to dub him "The Stifle Tower." I was there when Rodney Hood shimmied after his first ever game-winning bucket and when Old Man Joe Johnson defied the laws of nature and carried the Jazz to a fun playoff win in Los Angeles.

I was there when Larry H. Miller was memorialized after his death, when the team suffered through a miserable 25-win season, when the Jazz inexplicably lost at home to a shorthanded Los Angeles Clippers squad to hurt their playoff chances, when they came out on the short end of a grueling quadruple-overtime slug-fest in Atlanta, when Delonte West stuck his finger in Hayward's ear, when D-Will purposefully ran the wrong play that proved to be the last straw for Sloan, when Mehmet Okur's Achilles tendon snapped, when the Houston Rockets annihilated the Jazz by 45 in Utah, when the Golden State Warriors swept them en route to the 2017 NBA championship, and when Donovan Mitchell gave a mourning fanbase and franchise renewed hope with a strong summer league showing in the wake of Hayward's decision to bolt to the Boston Celtics.

I've been there for a lot of things with this team. However, I wasn't there for Al Jefferson's thrilling game-winning basket in Toronto. I watched that game from a Buffalo Wild Wings restaurant in, of all places, Buffalo because, well, let's just say I'll never live down leaving my passport on my nightstand before I left on that road trip. (I'll never forget UPS turning an overnight delivery into an over-three-nights-delivery mess either.)

I could keep reminiscing. I was there for a lot of good times, for a few excruciating and awkward experiences, for a number of incredible moments, and, honestly, for countless mind-numbing stretches of basketball and interviews. It wasn't easy, but it has been a fun and fulfilling experience to journey back to the beginning of the Jazz organization and dig up old stories way back to when a floppy sock-wearing Pete Maravich was dazzling audiences; to the Hall of Fame careers of Stockton, Sloan, and Malone; and all the way up to the entertaining beginning of the Mitchell era.

I often found myself smiling and even getting teary-eyed from nostalgia while researching and writing this book. After the obvious co-choice for the No. 1 chapter, picking—and rolling—out an order for the rest of the 100 Jazz stories wasn't nearly as easy. This franchise has had a lot of colorful characters and interesting moments. It's an honor to tell and retell stories about a team that means so much to the people and a state I love so much.

I hope you enjoy reading these 100 stories about the Jazz as much as I did telling them. On second thought, you will. As Hot Rod Hundley would say, "You gotta love it, baby!"

1 Stockton to Malone

Just as with peanut butter and jelly, hot dogs and baseball games, Adam and Eve, cookies and milk—not to forget fries and fry sauce for our Beehive State friends—two things are forever linked when it comes to the Utah Jazz.

John Stockton and Karl Malone.

They had statues erected in their honor on the arena plaza. They had streets—and oodles of babies—named after them. They were immortalized in the Naismith Basketball Hall of Fame, listed among the 50 greatest players in NBA history, and won two gold medals with Team USA.

They had thousands of highlight plays—you can almost still hear Hot Rod Hundley screaming "Stockton to Malone!"—including expertly placed passes and earth-shattering dunks and did for the pick-and-roll what Elvis Presley did for rock 'n' roll.

Not only that, but No. 12 (the all-time leader in assists and steals) and No. 32 (the second-leading scorer in NBA history) earned the adoration of generations of basketball fans in and out of the state of Utah for leading the Jazz to the playoffs 18 times, going to the Western Conference Finals five times, appearing in the NBA Finals twice, playing through countless injuries and illnesses, and combining to score what Stockton estimated to be a "zillion" points during their time together from 1985 to 2003.

That included the assist that gave Stockton the all-time record, surpassing Magic Johnson's mark of 9,221 on February 1, 1995. Though the bounce pass ricocheted higher than usual, Malone corralled the ball and then nailed a mid-range jumper for Stockton's 11th first-half dime and most historic assist. "He's been responsible for so many [of my assists], it does seem fitting," Stockton told reporters that night. "Like I've said all along, this isn't my record. These guys have had to make the shots, and Karl has made a zillion of them."

It only makes sense then that they share the top billing and first chapter in this book about the Jazz franchise.

Here's the neat thing: 15 years after they played their final basketball game together—in the 2003 playoffs against the Sacramento Kings—Stockton and Malone continue to be best of friends off the court. They even share a common bond of owning old-school flip phones when the rest of the technologically savvy world has jumped on the smartphone bandwagon. Though Stockton has settled back in his hometown of Spokane, Washington, and Malone returned to Rushton, Louisiana, the two occasionally get together to support family events or simply to hang out and reminisce. Malone even

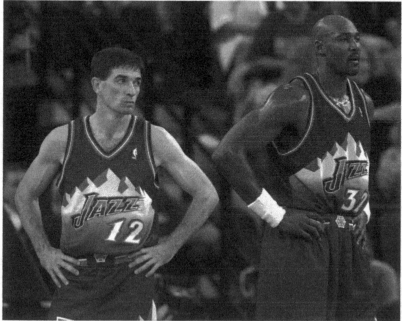

The epic pairing of John Stockton and Karl Malone led the Jazz to 18 playoff appearances. (AP Images)

made it out to Utah to watch Stockton's son, David, suit up for the Jazz in the spring of 2018.

Likewise, Stockton visited Louisiana during the 2017 football season to support The Mailman's son, KJ, play for LSU. That led to a classic story Malone told to a Los Angeles radio station that highlights the tenor of their relationship.

As the story goes, Malone and Stockton were visiting the Mississippi River levee in southern Louisiana, and the two of them decided, "Let's just go have a walk, bro." Though they're in their 50s and no longer professional athletes, the two Hall of Famers remain as competitive as ever. "I wasn't gonna tell him that my left knee was hurting," Malone admitted. "And he wasn't gonna tell me that his back was hurting, and we just walked each other there into the ground."

They walked up and down the levee three and a half times—"solving all the world issues"—when Malone finally looked at Stockton and said, "Bro, for real. What the hell? What the hell are we trying to prove at 54, 55 years old?"

One thing they did prove? They don't recover quite as quickly as they used to when they played 100 games a year. "When we got back, I don't think we moved for three and a half hours," Malone said. "Hell, I couldn't."

But Stockton made sure to move the ball to Malone during their distinguished careers. Considered by many to be the greatest pure point guard ever, Stockton played in 1,504 of a possible 1,526 games in 19 seasons. And Malone, a two-time NBA MVP, only missed 10 games in his 18 seasons with the Jazz. (Some Jazz fans will tell you he was cursed once he left for the Los Angeles Lakers, but that's another story.)

They couldn't quite get over the Michael Jordan and Scottie Pippen hump for an elusive NBA title, but this pair was certainly one of the greatest dynamic duos in sports for two fun decades.

Their competitiveness happened away from the basketball arena, too. Larry H. Miller, the late Jazz owner, once told the *Deseret News* a story that depicted how hard the two worked to fine-tune their bodies. "One day Karl told John that his body fat had been measured at 2.7 percent," Miller said. "John just kind of stood there, smirking. Finally, Karl asked him what that was about. John just said, '2.3.'"

During Stockton's retirement ceremony in June 2003, Hundley shared a fun anecdote that showed the good-ribbing nature of their friendship. Often a prankster behind the scenes, Stockton would jokingly get impatient while the team's idling bus waited for its final passenger, Malone. "We don't need The Mailman," Stockton would occasionally shout, as Hundley recounted in a *Deseret News* story. "We can win without him." As soon as Malone would board the bus, however, Hundley said Stockton would tell his favorite pass partner, "Hey, Karl—all the guys wanted to leave you. I said, 'We're not going anywhere without The Mailman.'"

For a couple of decades, that was the case on the hardwood. Former NBA All-Star Nick Van Exel joked that there was only one way to stop this competitive combo's pick-and-roll: "Yeah, I got a way to defend it. Bring a bat to the game and kill one of them."

Praising them in more positive terms, former Seattle SuperSonics star Shawn Kemp told The Players' Tribune that the Jazz duo inspired them. "'Stockton and Malone' is what me and Gary [Payton] used to always say in practice. They were the guys we looked at, first and foremost, when it came to trying to polish our game. And it's funny: those are the two guys where you can't mention one of their names without automatically thinking about the other."

Another old foe, Charles Barkley, jokingly told Jerry Sloan how good his teams would have been if he'd only had a power forward like him, but the legendary Jazz coach knew where his bread was buttered. "I thought I was a great coach until we lost these guys,"

Sloan said. "I was the most lucky guy in the world. I had the opportunity to coach two guys that's willing to pay the price of being good every day."

He also credits the two all-time NBA greats for helping him secure a spot in the Hall. "They could be [here] definitely without me. They would have made it on their own. There isn't any question about that," Sloan said. "I just happened to be here and have a chance to coach them."

Sloan took a quick second and rephrased that. "I don't think I really coached them," he said. "I just kind of watched them play [and] got a good seat every night."

2 John Stockton

Because of John Stockton's rare precision, great vision, generous pass-first mentality, and durability—not to forget sharing the court with talented guys like Adrian Dantley, Karl Malone, Darrell Griffith, and Jeff Hornacek—the longtime Utah Jazz point guard compiled more assists than any other NBA player even dreamed of dishing out.

The Picasso of the pick-and-roll also had defensive timing and tenacity that helped him set the league's steals record. His unflappable demeanor and competitive nature led to him never shy away from setting a hard pick on much-bigger athletes or back down to on-court bullies like Dennis Rodman. Then again, some considered him the physical aggressor (a nicer way to say dirty player).

Throw in his consistency, leadership, relentless pursuit, passion for winning, and loyalty, and it's no wonder why Stockton is arguably the most beloved sports figure in the history of Utah. Utahns, who booed in 1984 when the Jazz surprisingly used their No. 16 draft pick to select this relatively unknown playmaker from Spokane, Washington—a local kid who went to Gonzaga before Gonzaga was cool—will never admit their off-based judgment.

The eventual Hall of Famer also had admirers outside of the Beehive State. John Wooden was so impressed by the Jazz guard's style—of play, not fashion—that the legendary coach claimed Utah was the only NBA team he watched. "Well, let me put it this way: I watch John Stockton of the Utah Jazz. He's just my favorite player to watch in the pros," the late Wooden once said in an interview with the *Daily Press*. "The way he and Malone work that screen-and-roll, I've never seen at any time players work it quite as well as they do. And that's because of the abilities of each one."

Charles Barkley, Stockton's friend and Dream Team teammate, was also a big fan. In one visit to Utah in 1996, he jokingly interviewed Stockton's oldest son, Michael, and got the six-year-old to claim he was his favorite NBA player (after his dad, of course). Though the Round Mound teased the younger Stockton that his dad went to "Gorgonzola Cheese College" in an entertaining locker room exchange, Barkley also offered some free life advice: "Get 20 points and 10 rebounds [and] pass the ball like your dad and you won't have to worry about your education." He jokingly added, "Go to Auburn. They paid very well."

Barkley gave Stockton the highest of praise in an NBA.com article, saying, "John Stockton is the perfect point guard. There has never been a pure point guard who made better basketball decisions with the ball—ever."

You won't get Jerry Sloan to object. Around the time Stockton and Sloan were inducted into the Naismith Basketball Hall of Fame in 2008, the longtime Jazz coach thought New England Patriots coach Bill Belichick's description of retiring linebacker Tedy Bruschi as being "a perfect player" was a perfect way to articulate how he felt about Stockton. "I'd never heard that before, but

Big Spender

John Stockton is adored by Utah Jazz fans and admired around the sports world—and for good reason. He was a terrific athlete who overcame the disadvantage of being small in a big man's league, using his competitiveness, feisty on-court presence, unimpeachable work ethic, vision, determination, and basketball talent to carve out a two-decade-long Hall of Fame career.

But Stockton was so worried he wouldn't last in the NBA that he held out for an extra $5,000 in his rookie season. And in an era where cars and jewelry seem to be the norm for NBA rookies, Stockton's first purchase as a player didn't occur until he had been in Salt Lake for four months. The Spokane, Washington, native purchased a television for his one-bedroom apartment so he could watch the Super Bowl.

it certainly would represent John Stockton in almost every aspect of basketball," Sloan said. "When you say he's 'a perfect player,' [it was] the way he handled himself, the way he prepared himself to play, all those things."

Nobody saw that more than Sloan. Through an elite work ethic and impeccable conditioning, Stockton achieved an abundance of records, milestones, and success despite playing with a small-by-NBA-standards body and a deceptive choirboy appearance that looked anything but intimidating (scary Stockton glares notwithstanding). The 6'1", 175-pound athlete had durability and bounce-back ability, helping him play every game in 17 of 19 seasons for a total of 1,504 appearances in 1,526 regular-season contests. He was a productive player even up until he retired at the age of 41. His two trademark statistics are mind-boggling: 15,806 assists and 3,265 steals. He also scored 19,711 points, averaging 13.1 per game on 51.5 percent shooting.

Stockton's preferred length of uniform bottoms—his infamous Jazz-hued Daisy Dukes-style short shorts—were the, ahem, butt of many jokes, though some segments of the population weren't complaining about them. But his game sure wasn't made fun of. The only complaint some Jazz fans had was that he didn't shoot enough. That didn't stop Sloan from being as enthralled with Stockton as he was with tilling and tractors. "John's just an unusual guy. He loved to play. He loved to compete," Sloan said. "He's second to none as far as I'm concerned as far as wanting to play and proving that."

Wooden and Sloan might have really been impressed with another Stockton had they been in the family's backyard when No. 12 was growing up. Stockton said it took him about a thousand times of going mano-a-mano with older brother Steve before he finally came out victorious. He added with a laugh while telling that story at his Hall of Fame announcement ceremony, "One in 1,000 isn't a great record."

Stockton's record improved drastically after that. He started making name for himself with the Zags. After college he earned an invitation to try out for the 1984 U.S. Olympic team. It was at that camp where his pro career and friendship with Malone began to take off. Stockton didn't make the cut for that Olympic team, but he caught the attention of the Jazz who drafted him despite already having an All-Star point guard on their roster in Rickey Green.

Filip Bondy of hoopshype.com wrote about the Jazz's mysterious pick and TV announcer Al Albert's stunned reaction during a loaded draft that also included Barkley, Hakeem Olajuwon, and Michael Jordan. "Not many know about John Stockton," Albert said after the Jazz's surprise selection that received Bronx cheers back in Utah. "His name is certainly not on the lips of the fans here in New York…Frank Layden is certainly sticking his neck out."

Stockton got a kick out of his relative anonymity and the speculation some had about the Jazz snatching up a backup point guard in the first round. "The best thing about the draft," Stockton later said, "was watching the guys on TV flipping through their notes trying to find something on me."

Some might be surprised to learn that Stockton came off the bench for three years behind Green—a gradual progression and worthwhile experience he believes would benefit more young point guards—but he gave announcers plenty of material after that. In 1987–88, his first season as a starter, Stockton passed his way to an NBA single-season assists record, finishing with 1,128 to sneak past Isiah Thomas' previous mark by five assists. Stockton led the league in assists for the next eight seasons.

The Jazz won their second Midwest Division title in 1989, which was Stockton's second season as a starter and Sloan's first year as the team's head coach after replacing Layden a month in. The Jazz didn't always win their division, but they always made the playoffs during Stockton's 19 years. Many postseason appearances ended in frustration and early exits until Stockton hit a monumental three-pointer over the surging Barkley that sent the Jazz to their first NBA Finals in 1997. NBA.com's John Schumann claimed that basket in the Western Conference Finals in Game 6 at Houston is "easily the biggest shot in Jazz history."

Stockton and company couldn't clear the next hurdle—a 6'6" hurdle who happened to be the best player in the game—but that doesn't diminish Stockton's accomplishments. It's not like Stockton was the only player whose team couldn't overcome Air Jordan and the Chicago Bulls anyway. Danny Ainge even reportedly complimented Stockton for competing harder than anyone in basketball, including Jordan.

Sloan loved his will to win and work, too, and that Stockton faced his opponents. This skill put him in a position to break down his foe and make a play. He also marveled at how the mighty-mite would work his way out of double-team situations. "Now he's not 6'10", 6'9", or 6'8". He's kind of a small guy," Sloan admitted. "And to be double-teamed the way he was and to get out of it as well as he did is hard to imagine. But he had terrific hands, terrific eyes, and all those things are necessary."

3 The Mailman

It took thousands of hammer dunks—many with a trademark pose—and countless pick-and-roll plays, fade-away jumpers, and softly flicked free throws to score 36,928 points over the course of a career. And that's exactly what Karl Malone did en route to becoming the second-leading scorer in NBA history.

While punishing rims and snapping nets for a living, Malone led the small-market Utah Jazz to two NBA Finals, 11 50-win seasons, and six division titles. He made the All-Star Game 14 times, claimed residency on the All-NBA first team from 1989 to 1999, and was a three-time All-Defensive first teamer. His illustrious career also included multiple NBA records (including 11 straight seasons with 2,000 points), a pair of NBA MVP awards, two Olympic gold medals, and enough eye-popping statistics compiled during a 19-year career to fill up one of the diesels he owned back in the day.

Malone unquestionably played his way into hoops immortality in Springfield, Massachusetts. But it'd be more accurate to say he worked his way into the Hall of Fame. Malone was tireless in his efforts to get the most out of his massive, muscle-covered body. He routinely added new weapons to his basketball arsenal and refined his go-to moves in the offseason. And when he played, he played hard, at a high level, and often. While putting the power into the power forward position, this Mailman delivered in sleet, snow, rain, and pain—from Seattle to Salt Lake City to South Beach. "This guy didn't miss games," marveled ex-Jazz forward Matt Harpring, Malone's former hard-working teammate, who was equally impressed that he didn't skip practices either. "That's incredible in today's world...You don't find that. Talk about earning your money. You earned your money with [Malone], so I've got a lot of respect for him."

Malone wasn't without faults, of course. The 6'9", 256-pound specimen treated opponents in the lane like an angry bull in a china cabinet. He was a bruiser on the court. He even received the title of "dirtiest player" in a national vote and sent more than one opponent to the hospital. A physical specimen, who was jokingly called "The Hackman" by Charles Barkley, Malone never backed down or apologized for his tough and tumble style of play, even saying, "You hit me, I hit you. Volkswagen/Mac truck—who's going to get the worse of it?"

Malone was known for being outspoken, occasionally inserting his size 16 L.A. Gear high-tops into his mouth after contract disputes with the late Jazz owner Larry H. Miller and his vocal opposition to Magic Johnson returning with the HIV virus. Critics point out that he failed to win a championship, mock how he referred to himself in the third person—"Karl Malone gotta do what Karl Malone gotta do"—and tease him for being a Bayou redneck.

Nobody could fault him for the amount of work he put in, though. (Nobody dared point out his flaws in person either.) In 18 seasons with the Jazz, The Mailman delivered in all 82 games 10 different times and only missed 10 of 1,444 games. In one Ironman stretch, the power forward took to the court in 543 consecutive games—a streak that only ended because of a suspension. Malone's habit of hard work helped the Louisiana Tech beast blossom into a legend after being an overlooked 13th overall pick. (The Jazz wondered if they'd missed something when he dropped that low to them in 1985.) His coach, Jerry Sloan, loves guys who aren't afraid to roll up their sleeves and get dirt under their fingernails. It was rare to have someone with Malone's size, skillset, and drive. "He put as much into it as anybody I've ever seen off the floor," Sloan said.

Malone believed toiling for all those extra hours could give him an edge. That's why he was a regular in the Westminster College weight room with John Stockton. That's why he used the Wasatch Front mountains as his track and ran up and down the stairs of the University of Utah's Rice-Eccles Stadium twice a week. He still enjoys driving by the football field. "When I pass by that place, I smile because I touched every [step] in there training," Malone said. "When I would get to the top and I'd look around, [there wasn't] one person in there. No lights, no cameras, no fans."

Just a bunch of steps—and sweat.

Malone's Accolades

- Named one of the 50 Greatest Players in NBA history
- Two-time NBA MVP (1997, 1999)
- Only player in league history named to All-NBA first team 11 times (1989–99)
- Three-time NBA All-Defensive first-team selection (1997–99) as well as a second-team honoree in 1987–88
- Two-time Olympic Gold Medal winner as member of the 1992 Dream Team and 1996 U.S. team
- 1997–98 IBM Award honoring the player who contributed most to his team's overall success
- One of eight players to win All-Star game MVP honors twice, claiming honors in 1989 and 1993 (with co-MVP John Stockton)
- NBA Player of the Week 23 times and Player of the Month seven times
- Finished third to Patrick Ewing (36 points) and Xavier McDaniel (16.5) with 14.5 votes for 1985–86 Rookie of the Year
- Named to 1985–86 All-Rookie Team
- Picked in 1999 by *The Sporting News* as one of "99 Good Guys in Sports" for donating $200,000 worth of supplies to Navajo Indians and paying off a home mortgage for a family with four ill children
- 1998 Henry B. Iba Citizen Athlete Award, which recognizes athletes who do good deeds for others
- Named First Utahn of the Year in 1997 by *The Salt Lake Tribune*

Putting in that kind of work makes all the difference between being good and great. The grueling workouts were satisfying, addictive, and transformative. Pumping iron was Malone's not-so-secret weapon. It gave him arms that were as big as some guys' legs, legs strong enough to power through crowded lanes, and an intimidation factor. "Weight training was huge," Malone said. "If I wouldn't have trained like that, I think you could've took five years off of my career, five productive years."

In addition to his penchant for powerlifting, Malone used his personal pride, a commitment to himself and fans, and adrenaline to get through some of the roughest nights when his body wanted to stop long before his mind would allow it to. The crowds were almost like an anesthetic, numbing the pain and inspiring him to keep on keeping on. "You really sometimes forget how injured you are until after," he said.

For Malone, it wasn't just about suiting up and sucking it up in the regular season or playoffs. Every game, even the preseason, counted to him. He proved that in the first exhibition game in 1995 by returning after suffering a painful finger injury. He wanted to teach Joe Smith a lesson because he wasn't particularly fond of the hyped-up rookie—or any opponent, for that matter—so he attempted to block the Warriors forward's shot "to make a statement." Malone swatted at the ball but smacked his hand against the backboard. Instead of blocking the shot, he experienced a burning sensation in his still-bent middle finger and saw bone protruding through skin. "You ain't playing no more," Sloan told Malone.

The Mailman had other plans. He insisted on finishing out the preseason contest in Albuquerque, New Mexico. "I got a piece of tape, and taped it, and I played in a preseason game," Malone said. "But we were just like that."

The late Jazz owner, Larry H. Miller, enjoyed telling a story of the time the superstar sprained his ankle in a game against the Portland Trail Blazers. Malone's ankle swelled up like a balloon.

He just had it re-taped and then returned to action after the half-time break. "He could hardly walk," Miller recalled in 2006 when Malone was being honored with a statue, a street name, and a retired No. 32 jersey. "But he got on the court, he wouldn't let anybody know that he was hurt…the whole team was shocked that he was even out there."

Nobody really should have been shocked. Malone ended up with 24 points and 16 rebounds while showing how important it was for him to play through pain. "When he answered the bell in that kind of condition and played the way he did, I think the rest of the team felt they had to come to the party, too," Miller said. "That's what he did. He led. He inspired players by the way he played every night."

An unspoken friendly rivalry with his favorite pick-and-roll pal to not miss games pushed Malone to endure through agony. He knew Stockton had played with injuries, including not being able to move his neck, and that Jeff Hornacek kept plugging away despite not having cartilage in one of his knees. The prideful Malone knew he couldn't give them something to hold over him. "You think I'm going to let those two guys half my size outdo me?" The competitive player asked.

Malone was "personally kind of offended" whenever the NBA suspended him. He wanted to play for himself, his team, and the fans. You'll be disappointed if you're hoping to find a DNP-Rest in the box score next to Malone's name. That just didn't happen. That's how you end up playing 54,852 minutes, taking 26,210 shots (with a .516 shooting percentage), hauling in 14,968 rebounds, dishing out 5,248 assists, and scoring more points than anyone in NBA history but Kareem Abdul-Jabbar. "I took pride in playing," Malone said. "I took pride in when you walked up there to buy your season tickets…we're going to see Karl Malone and John Stockton on the floor every single night, trying to give it their all."

4 Jerry Sloan

When he was not doing chores, a young Jerry Sloan spent hours of his spare time shooting a basketball. The target was a bucket—breakaway rim not included—hanging outside of his grade school in McLeansboro, Illinois. Sloan and his brother had to borrow the ball to shoot hoops, and that ol' cowhide globe that hit home, borrowing Hot Rod Hundley's terminology, was a great-grandfather to the slickly designed, synthetic basketballs kids use in their driveways nowadays. Seven decades ago, basketballs were crafted with an air-filled bladder covered by wide straps of soft leather bound together by football-like laces with high ribs forming at the seams. You'd probably have to borrow a basketball from a museum to shoot one like that in the 21st century.

In a way those classic balls are almost as rare of an artifact as hard-nosed, lunch-pail-carrying, nose-to-the-grindstone coaches of yesteryear like Sloan. He banned headbands, made players tuck in their shirts, and had them wear similarly colored shoes. An "old-school coach" is how former Jazz player Matt Harpring fondly described him. "We don't play playground basketball," Harpring explained back in his playing days. "We pass, cut, move the ball, play tough defense. People think that's a lost art."

Deseret News columnist Doug Robinson aptly put it this way in 2003 after hearing a reporter ask if the game had passed up the John Deere-sporting, passenger-van-driving coach: "Sloan expects players to play hard every minute they're on the court. Silly man. That's the way he played—every game was like a knife fight for Sloan—so he expects today's players to play with the same intensity…Sloan coaches players to play as a team, not as individuals. How wacky is that? Today's player has to get his shots. Give him the rock and get out of the way. How else are you going to get endorsements and earn extra jack if you don't put up shots?"

It was with mixed emotions that Sloan took over for Frank Layden on December 9, 1988, after his Jazz coaching predecessor decided he'd had enough of the coaching grind and surprisingly resigned during the season. Sloan was as content as a barnyard dog chasing its tail as Layden's right-hand man. Layden had become a close friend with Sloan since hiring him as a scout for the Jazz in 1983. "Working with Frank was one of the best things that could happen to me," said Sloan, who'd been Layden's assistant for four years after a brief stint as head coach of the CBA's Evansville Thunder. "I wish he was still coaching. That's how much I enjoyed being his assistant coach."

Layden knew he left the franchise in good hands with Sloan, who had previous head coaching experience with Chicago. That happened to be the team the defensive-minded Sloan played for from 1966 to 1976, earning the honor as the first player to get his jersey retired by the Chicago Bulls. "The Original Bull," as Bulls fans called Sloan, became The Interminable Jazzman. From his former boss' resignation to his own shocking exit more than 22 years later, Sloan was the longest-tenured coach in major U.S. sports while tallying seven division titles, leading the Jazz to 20 playoff appearances, making two NBA Finals trips, and becoming the first coach in NBA history to win 1,000 games with one franchise.

Sloan took all the glory…and, of course, gave it to others, including Layden. "I replaced Frank and I always felt this was Frank's team. I just happened to be along at the right time and work with him," he said. "Even up until John [Stockton] and Karl Malone retired, I still felt like they were his people."

That was typical for Sloan. He'd often credit the late Jazz owner Larry H. Miller for keeping him around for so long, his longtime assistant Phil Johnson for his expertise and cool head, and his players for doing the work.

Sloan's impressive basketball resume also includes an undefeated 29–0 NCAA Division II championship season at Evansville as a player, a gritty 11-year career with the Baltimore Bullets and Bulls as a feared defender, stints as an NBA scout and an assistant coach, and his short stay as Chicago's head coach from 1979 to 1982. "I haven't accepted too many checks outside of basketball since I was a kid," Sloan said before his Hall of Fame induction in 2008. "Not many people get to do something they love to do and then get paid for it...I just feel like I've been lucky to be a part of basketball for as long as I have."

Sloan's gruff visage, chiseled with decades of triumph, tragedy, and everything in between, lights up when he shares stories of his grade-school club. Uncharacteristically, Sloan doesn't mind basking and bragging about the championship he won while attending a one-room school in his Illinois farming community for six years. "We played in a county tournament, played all the one-room schools," he recalled. "If you're good enough to beat the consolidated schools, you're pretty good. We were able to do that one time, so that was a tremendous thrill for me."

Sloan takes great pride about attaining perfect attendance for practice in high school. He lived 16 miles away from the school, didn't have a car, and practice began at 7:00 AM sharp. By the way, that was well before the school bus could get him there on time. He had three options: hoof it, hitchhike, or give up hoops. Sloan and his buddy, David Lee, became hitchhiking gurus. "I feel very good about the fact that I played basketball in high school and never missed a practice," Sloan said. "If you liked to play, you figured out a way to try to do it."

The passionate Sloan kept that inspirational attitude, commitment, and resourcefulness while helping Evansville achieve a perfect season and throughout his NBA career. He was drafted out of college by Baltimore and then got snatched up by Chicago the following year in an expansion draft. Coached by Johnny

"Red" Kerr, Sloan and the 1966–67 Bulls far exceeded expectations by making it to the playoffs in their inaugural season after being pegged as a team that wouldn't win more than 10 games. Kerr was among the coaches Sloan grew to admire and publicly thank over the years along with longtime Bulls coach and Utah native Dick Motta, Evansville's Arad McCutchan, Johnson, and Layden.

Sloan's decade-long run with the Bulls included two All-Star appearances and the retirement of his No. 4. It brought a smile to his face when he boasts about the "big check" the Bulls players received for earning that first postseason berth. "We got 440-something," he said, laughing. "We didn't even hardly know at the time we got paid to be in the playoffs. We were just happy to be there."

That's the mind-set he had about his lengthy stay with the Jazz. He figured naysayers thought he wouldn't last long in his second stint after Chicago exec Rod Thorn fired him during the 1981–82 season. "People said I probably wouldn't last very long in the beginning," he said, "because I would expect too much out of players and have a lot of problems." Sloan suffered no fools, so he'd occasionally have problems with players that he claimed "don't like to play," and his career ended after the well-publicized run-in with Deron Williams. But D-Will eventually grew up and apologized for his cocky, insubordinate behavior, and Sloan mostly earned the respect of those who played for him and against him. He even selected Charles Barkley to be his Hall of Fame presenter.

Sloan's appreciation for work—and insistence of it from his players—is deep-rooted. It came from his mother. "She said, 'Don't ever turn your back on your paycheck,'" Sloan said. "My father passed away when I was four. You had to learn to work."

5 The Shot

There are select moments that define Utah history. In 1847 Brigham Young entered the Salt Lake Valley after leading pioneers on a cross-country trek and declared, "This is the right place." In 2002 Salt Lake City hosted the successful Winter Olympics. Not to be overlooked, fast-food chain Arctic Circle invented a Utah culinary staple called fry sauce. And on May 29, 1997, John Stockton hit a buzzer-beating, game-winning three-pointer at The Summit in Houston that ranks right up there if you ask Utah Jazz fans. Jazz owner Gail Miller certainly thinks Stockton's heroic three-pointer that gave the Jazz a 103–100 Game 6 win and a 4–2 Western Conference Finals victory against the Houston Rockets belongs up there. "I think that was one of the highlights of Utah's history," Miller said.

"The Shot," as it's simply and fondly called, sent the Jazz to the NBA Finals for the first time in the franchise's 23 years of existence and sent Utah into a state of euphoria. Utah had come oh-so-close, getting to the Western Conference Finals three other times in five years, but now the Jazz finally punched their ticket to basketball's biggest stage.

Even more than two decades after the net-snapping swish, The Shot still sends shivers down the spines of fans, players, and team personnel as they recall how arguably the greatest passer in NBA history assisted his team's championship-winning hopes. During a 20-year reunion of the iconic moment in March 2017, Stockton and ex-teammate Bryon Russell humorously—and successfully—re-enacted the play in street clothes at the Jazz's practice facility. "You guys noticed it went in, right?" Stockton said while laughing after nailing the shot on the first attempt following an interview session. "Pretty ugly, though."

Twenty years earlier, it looked like the Jazz were headed to an ugly loss in Game 6 as the Rockets took a 13-point lead in the fourth quarter. Houston, which had a history of beating Utah in the playoffs, even led by 10 points with less than three minutes remaining that night. That's when Stockton, who holds the NBA assists record, took over. The Hall of Fame point guard led a furious rally and scored the game's final nine points, including a game-tying shot with 22.4 seconds remaining. Clyde Drexler's go-ahead attempt missed, and Karl Malone gave Utah a chance to win it in the final seconds by snaring his 11th rebound of the game. The Jazz called a timeout with 2.8 seconds remaining to set up a play and advance the ball past midcourt.

Many people remember The Shot, but they don't remember The Comeback. "We were known for execution and defense and setting screens," said Jazz center Greg Ostertag, who had a key block on a Hakeem Olajuwon shot during the rally. "We did what we needed to do to put ourselves back in position to win that game. That's what Utah Jazz basketball was all about."

The most memorable play in Utah Jazz history began with a picket fence formation at the top of the key. After the referee handed Russell the ball out of bounds, Antoine Carr raced into the lane and took Olajuwon with him. Jeff Hornacek curled around the perimeter toward the Jazz bench, clearing more space up top. Malone then set a pick on Drexler—"I was bear-hugged, not picked," Drexler told reporters—to neutralize the Rockets guard near midcourt. Charles Barkley, meanwhile, hesitated on a switch, and Russell inbounded the ball to a wide-open Stockton behind the arc. By the time "The Round Mound of Rebound" responded, Stockton had already taken a dribble, squared up, and elevated for the famous jump shot. "We ran that play a ton. There are 50 variables to it, depending on how the defense plays, where the pass comes. There's a lot of things that go into it," Stockton recalled at the reunion. "I was supposed to curl and try to get the ball fairly early on in the play, try to make a play, try to get into the paint, find a shooter, make a shot, whatever. I just remember as I started to curl, it felt like the whole Houston Rockets team was waiting over there for me just to curl right into them. I knew that wasn't going to work. Then Karl turned around and set a phenomenal pick on Clyde Drexler, and then the ball was in my hands."

And then it wasn't.

Viewers back in Utah—and everywhere else—heard NBC color analyst Bill Walton utter an infamous "Uh-oh" and play-by-play announcer Greg Gumbel say, "Stockton. Open. Three. YEAH! John Stockton sends the Utah Jazz to the NBA Finals!"

John Stockton shoots the three-pointer that gave the Jazz a 103–100 victory in Game 6 of the Western Conference Finals to send the Jazz to their first NBA Finals appearance in franchise history. (AP Images)

Jazz fans listening to the radio broadcast heard Hot Rod Hundley and analyst Ron Boone go bonkers. "Russell. To Stockton. For three," Hundley said. "Stock! Got it! Stock got it! Unbelievable! John Stockton!"

"NBA FINALS!" Boone exclaimed.

"John Stockton! It's over," Hundley continued. "The Jazz win it! We're on our way to the world championships."

Not surprisingly, Stockton dished praise to everyone else, including Russell for the inbound read and pass that set him up. "Guys like me, we don't have a beautiful jump shot," said Stockton self-deprecatingly, "so I wanted to make sure it snapped through straight, right up high."

Stockton had made similar shots in the driveway of his home and in gyms in Spokane, Washington. "You grow up and you're out there on the court by yourself and you're always saying, 'Three, two, one' like you see in the movies, and that's kind of how it is. I'd probably shot that shot 100 times in my head, maybe a thousand as a kid," Stockton said. "You don't really think about it at the time. It's quiet. The opportunity is there. All I could think of was, *Follow through, finish the shot.* That I did. Normally my shot's a little quirky and weird anyway, but that one followed through and snapped through. It found its mark, so it was a good day."

The reaction to The Shot was pure joy in motion. Stockton, Malone, and Hornacek embraced at midcourt and jumped up and down before the rest of the team, including Sloan and faithful assistant Phil Johnson, rushed to celebrate with them. "Coach's knees looked pretty good," Stockton said while seated next to Sloan at the reunion press conference. "You were bouncing up and down on that court, Coach."

"My leg felt a lot better after you made it," Sloan replied.

"I was just running around like a chicken with my head cut off," Russell recalled. "It was super-duper exciting just to see everybody. I can replay it in my mind, everybody jumping and hugging, and Sloan coming with his arms wide open hugging Karl. It was real nice."

Ostertag might have been the only one to miss The Shot. He'd just fouled out and was kind of sulking at the end of the bench with his head in a towel. Greg Foster and Stephen Howard were blocking his view, too. "I was disappointed I'd fouled out," he said, "so I was sitting there, and all of a sudden I heard everybody screaming and hollering, and it got real quiet so I knew something good had happened, so I just jumped and ran out."

Hours later, the celebration ramped up again when the Jazz's charter flight landed at the Salt Lake International Airport and the team was greeted by 20,000 screaming fans at 3:00 AM. Sleep could wait for the offseason. Twenty years later, members of that Jazz team are still touched by that showing. "Obviously, when you come back from there, and the airport's packed, just driving through the crowd to see that many people," Hornacek said, "that's something else."

As fate had it—Michael Jordan had a say, too—the Jazz played well but couldn't defeat the mighty Chicago Bulls in those Finals or the next year. Utah has only returned to the Western Conference Finals once—in 2007—since then, too. All of which makes The Shot even more special to Jazz faithful. The struggle to get to the championship round had been an arduous challenge.

But Stockton earned even more respect from a fellow Hall of Famer that night. "Obviously, the best player in this series was John Stockton, and he finished it off the way a star should finish it off," Barkley said in his postgame remarks. "I've said it many times: he's just awesome. He made all the plays down the stretch, all the plays, all the big shots. Karl Malone deserves MVP, but he would never get MVP without John Stockton. He's the best pure point guard ever. To score [nine] straight points in a crucial situation, that's not easy to do. He made all the shots."

6 The 1997 NBA Finals

John Stockton hit a three-point jumper on the night of May 29, 1997—just as he did 955 other times in his career. But this was no ordinary shot. This shot over Charles Barkley sent the Utah Jazz to the NBA Finals for the first time in the franchise's 23-year history. It was "The Shot" and it opened the floodgates of emotion, immersing the Jazz and their fans into a deluge of jubilation from the court in Houston to the streets of Salt Lake City. "That was a big deal obviously for the whole state and for us," Jeff Hornacek said of Stockton's shot, which clinched the Western Conference Finals win against the Houston Rockets in Game 6. "As players, none of us had gotten there."

An impromptu wild night of partying—wild by Utah standards, at least—didn't end until after an estimated 15,000-20,000 fans converged at Executive Airport in Salt Lake City to welcome their hoops heroes home in the middle of the night. "Utah's first conference title was not going to go unnoticed—or without accompanying fan celebration," the *Deseret News* noted. "The crowd was raucous but not unruly, if you overlook the two teenagers sprinting around in only their underwear."

Fans, most wearing more than underwear, cheered and held "Show me the title" signs. Bryon Russell waved a purple Jazz flag on top of a slowly driving truck. Tears streamed down Antoine Carr's cheeks. "It was unbelievable. It was unreal," Karl Malone told the *Deseret News*. "Three o'clock in the morning and they didn't seem like they were sleepy at all. I didn't see one yawn."

Two days later, the moment they'd all been waiting so long for finally arrived. The Utah Jazz were in the NBA Finals. Making it all the more fun, they were facing one of the greatest players and dynasties in history—Michael Jordan's Chicago Bulls.

Game 1—No Deliveries
Michael Jordan's epic jumper at the end of the 1998 NBA Finals is what most sports fans remember, but he drained a shot at the buzzer to begin this championship series with a win at the United Center. Karl Malone had a chance to give the Jazz the lead with the score tied 82–82 with 9.2 seconds left, but he missed both attempts. Scottie Pippen might have foiled a special delivery after walking up to Malone and delivering an infamous line. "I just whispered in his ear that The Mailman doesn't deliver on Sunday," he said
Final: Bulls 84, Jazz 82, Bulls lead series 1–0.

Game 2—Classic MJ
This was just a rough showing for the Jazz, who fell behind by as many as 21 points in the fourth quarter on a night when Karl Malone missed 14-of-20 shots and John Stockton only dished out seven assists. Malone wouldn't use having a floor burn on his shooting hand as an excuse, telling reporters, "Obviously, I'm stinking it up right now. I kind of wish people would stop talking about [my hand]. I don't have an excuse. I'm just not getting it done."
Final: Bulls 97, Jazz 85, Bulls lead series 2–0.

Game 3—A Statement
As the series shifted to Utah, so did the momentum for the Jazz. With chatter about Karl Malone not deserving his NBA MVP award after two rough outings, The Mailman powered his way to 37 points and 10 rebounds. "I think he felt comfortable at home," Michael Jordan said. "He came in to make a statement inside."
Final: Jazz 104, Bulls 93, Bulls lead series 2–1.

Game 4—The Pass

The Chicago Bulls appeared as if they were going to leave SLC with a win, using a late 10–1 run to seize a 71–66 lead with 2:42 left. Enter John Stockton, who willed the Jazz to a series-tying victory with big shots, free throws, and perhaps the most famous of his assists—a full-court touchdown strike to his tight end who'd gotten behind the coverage. Karl Malone caught "The Pass" and rumbled in for an easy go-ahead layup. Seconds later, The Mailman found himself at the free-throw line again, and Scottie Pippen tried to approach him but was blocked by Jeff Hornacek. Malone then hit the first free throw—"I guess he delivers on Sundays here," Pippen joked—and Bryon Russell sealed the win with a dunk after Malone rebounded Michael Jordan's missed three-pointer.

Final: Jazz 78, Bulls 73, NBA Finals tied at 2–2.

Game 5—Lost Opportunity

This was Michael Jordan's famed Flu Game, in which he carried the Chicago Bulls by firing in 38 points with seven rebounds and five assists after battling a stomach ailment throughout the day. It was the Jazz who felt nauseous afterward. Regardless of how he got sick—bad pizza, bad bug, bad alcohol, or bad luck, depending on who you believe—His Airness reached deep to rally his team out of a 16-point deficit and the series. John Stockton, Karl Malone, and Jeff Hornacek all struggled for the Jazz, who were outscored 23–16 in the fourth quarter. "They should be lucky getting out of here with a win like that because we gave it up," Jazz backup center Greg Foster lamented to the *Deseret News*. "That was our game."

Final: Bulls 90, Jazz 88, Bulls lead series 3–2.

Game 6—So Close

Once again, the Jazz took the Bulls down to the wire. Three of Utah's losses in this series were by a combined eight points. "They came here with a lot of heart, a lot of desire," Finals MVP Michael

Jordan said. "They gave us a run for our money." Jerry Sloan called 34-year-old M.J. "the greatest player I've ever seen play" after the Finals MVP scored 39 points with 11 rebounds and four assists to clinch a fifth NBA crown in seven years. Steve Kerr hit the game-winner in this one, and the Jazz's final hope fizzled when Bryon Russell's crosscourt pass was tipped and batted away by Toni Kukoc and Scottie Pippen. Karl Malone averaged 23.8 points on 44.3 percent shooting compared to 27.4 on 55 percent in his MVP season. "I'm disappointed, but it's not the end of the world," he said.

Final: Bulls 90, Jazz 86, Bulls win series 4–2.

"Utah would give neither this game nor that title away, and that is what's important to remember here," *Chicago Tribune*'s Skip Myslenski wrote. "It's also the reason the Jazz emerged as the greatest challenge the Bulls have faced in their long and distinguished reign and why their series, which initially looked so one-sided, eventually evolved into a taut affair that seemed to suck the air from all who observed it."

About 10,000 Jazz fans greeted the team at the airport upon their return from Chicago. "And while a championship would be a wonderful thing," Frank Layden told the crowd and Jazz at the gathering, "I wouldn't trade this team for the championship team."

7 Larry H. Miller

When Larry H. Miller thought about his legacy later in life, the successful entrepreneur and philanthropist had one thing he wanted younger generations to discover and older generations to remember. Miller hoped people would say, simply, "He was a man who loved Utah."

That deep love took root in his Salt Lake City childhood neighborhood where he played marbles and baseball with his Capitol Hill buddies. It germinated as he attended West High School, where he met his lifelong sweetheart Gail, and continued growing stronger as the business mogul's Utah-based empire blossomed. He started out as a stock boy in an auto parts store and kept working and working and working until he'd become a self-made billionaire.

Miller leveraged buying a Toyota car dealership on May 1, 1979—something he did on a whim while visiting an old friend during a vacation in Salt Lake City—into becoming the 10ᵗʰ largest dealer in the nation with 42 auto lots and $2.3 billion in sales in six states. By the time he passed away at age 64, Miller had 80-plus ventures, ranging from movie theaters and restaurants to sports apparel stores, a financing company, and philanthropic organizations. He also bought a minor league baseball team (Salt Lake Bees); built a racetrack (Miller Motorsports Park); and owned real estate ventures, an insurance company, his own arena (Delta Center), and, of course, a basketball team (Utah Jazz). That helps 7,000 employees earn a living.

And he did all that—and much, much more—while generously giving back to the community. Among his charitable contributions: donating $50 million to the Salt Lake Community College campus, paying for BYU's baseball and softball complex, buying a scoreboard for the University of Utah, and gifting about 300 college scholarships each year. "He felt like the community was his to take care of, to do good things for," Gail Miller said. "He spent his life in making things better wherever he went."

Miller had never seen a Jazz game in person but decided he needed to buy half of the franchise in 1985 as a "gift to Utah." Though the NBA team had lost $17 million in 11 years since its 1974 New Orleans beginning, he was able to quickly convince six lending institutions to loan him $8 million so he could purchase 50 percent of the team from owner Sam Battistone. That decision hadn't been easy to make. As he chronicled in his book, *Driven*, Miller even conferred with a high-ranking LDS Church leader, Gordon B. Hinckley of the First Presidency, before finally committing to the process while driving on I-15 and telling Gail, "The Jazz can't leave. We have to do everything we can to keep them here."

A year later, Miller actually had the pen in his hand and the contract on his desk to sell his half of the Jazz for a lofty $14 million, which would have been a significant return on investment and doubled his personal net worth. The deal, however, would have resulted in the team moving to Minnesota. "I bent over the desk to sign, but then I froze," Miller wrote. "Thoughts were racing through my mind. What would I do with that much money? What does it mean to me? What would Salt Lake City be without the Jazz? What kind of hole would that leave in the community? And how could I face the fans who would be upset by this?"

Miller insisted that he'd never bought the Jazz to turn around and flip the organization for a profit. Rather, he wrote, "Gail and I always viewed the Jazz as the grand gift we could give the city and state." It's for that same reason why he never seriously entertained offers to buy the team—even for as much as $400 million. Four years later Miller found enough investors to finance the Delta Center construction, which cost $93 million, including a $20 million bond from the city, to keep the Jazz entrenched in SLC. "Larry Miller became a fixture in my life in 1985 when he began the rescue of the Utah Jazz," Hall of Fame guard John Stockton wrote in the foreword for Miller's book. "The move was bold and risky for him and his family, but his love for the Salt Lake City community and desire to keep the Jazz in Utah trumped his fears."

Miller was one of the most hands-on NBA bosses. He shagged balls and defended players in warm-ups, sat in a visible courtside seat, joined the team in the locker room, occasionally yelled at the team and referees louder than Jerry Sloan, teared up in press conferences, made fashionistas tear up over his standard sneakers and polo shirt, and poured his heart and soul into a team that became his passion until he breathed his final breath after succumbing to complications from diabetes on February 20, 2009. "I don't think anybody could be as fortunate as I've been to have him as an owner and keep me here as long as he did," Sloan said after Miller died. "We lost 56 games (in 2004–05), and I'm still here."

A night after his death, Miller's courtside seat was left empty as one of several heartfelt gestures and tender tributes the Jazz made to honor the man responsible for the sold-out building and for the successful franchise that had been to the playoffs in 22 of his 25 years as owner. Prior to tip-off, all the arena lights were turned off except for two spotlights that glowed down onto his usual seat, which had a white rose placed on it. Following a pregame moment of silence—a poignant and paradoxical way to honor an always outspoken and opinionated man—a fan loudly yelled, "We love you, Larry!"

At his viewing the following week, some guests couldn't help but smile when seeing Miller's casket. It was painted blue and decorated to look like one of his favorite cars. It had two thick white stripes down the middle and a Ford Cobra emblem on the hood. Even the stunning white bouquet on top inscribed with the words "Dear Husband" included a black-and-white checkered ribbon for the car lover.

Inside of the Jazz locker room, there is a plaque that displays a quote the late owner required of his team: "NOBODY LAID DOWN, NOBODY QUIT, NOBODY LEFT ANYTHING IN THE LOCKER ROOM. IT WAS ALL OUT THERE ON THE FLOOR...

"I'VE ALWAYS SAID TO OUR GUYS 'I'LL NEVER ASK YOU TO WIN, BUT I WILL ASK YOU TO GIVE US EVERYTHING YOU'VE GOT.'"

8 Frank Layden

If you ask Jerry Sloan, it's quite appropriate that the No. 1 jersey was retired in Frank Layden's honor. "I always say this," Sloan said at his retirement press conference in 2011. "I could have still been with Frank as his assistant coach 'til the day I retired."

The sentiment is nice and all, but that wasn't in the cards for Layden. When he stepped down early in the 1988–89 season, he was done being an NBA coach. Knowing he had a worthy replacement in Sloan on his bench helped make the decision easier. Upon the recommendation of legendary coach Dick Motta, Layden hired Sloan as a scout a few years earlier and then promoted him to coach before calling it quits. "It was time," he said, "for me to be looking to step aside and give [my wife] Barbara a break and my children."

Layden had spent the better part of three decades up to that point coaching—for about 10 years in high school, almost a decade in college at his alma mater Niagara, and then for 12 years in the NBA as an assistant at the Atlanta Hawks and as the second head coach of the Utah Jazz (1981–88).

Layden began his tenure with the Jazz as the general manager when the franchise relocated from New Orleans to Utah in 1979. Speaking of then-owner Sam Battistone, Layden told the *Deseret News*, "I'd like to thank him for his faith in me. What I'm going to do is reward him by promising him and this organization to bring a world championship team to Utah next year. *Of course, it will be the Celtics or the Lakers.*"

Jokes aside, Layden knew the Jazz were nowhere near that level. "I can remember sitting up in the office and lighting up a cigar at 9:00 on the Monday morning we got here," Layden said. "I looked around. I looked at our staff, which was about nine people, and I said, 'Well, what we do now? Where do we go from here?'"

To the bottom of the standings turned out to be the answer. In their inaugural season in Utah—with Layden as GM and Tom Nissalke as the head coach—the Jazz went 24–58. They only averaged 27.7 wins over the next three seasons.

Battistone opted to make a coaching change two seasons into the Utah era, and Layden, who'd opted to take the job as GM over head coach a couple years earlier for job security purposes, was tabbed as the bench boss early in the 1981–82 season. With Layden in place, the Jazz began to stockpile talent around Adrian Dantley, drafting the likes of Darrell Griffith, Thurl Bailey, Mark Eaton, and Bobby Hansen, and acquiring guys like John Drew and Rickey Green. That crew essentially saved the franchise in Utah in the 1983–84 season by winning the Midwest Division and advancing to the second round of the Western Conference playoffs to jazz up the Wasatch Front. "We were a team that was tired of losing. Frank put together the right formula, and it just clicked for us that year," Griffith said. "We went from the bottom to winning the Midwest Division. It originated with Frank. Frank gave us this attitude of, 'Have fun, relax, don't take the game too serious, even though it is serious.'"

Layden's uncanny sense of humor was what he best became known for on a national level—he'd often make fun of his weight, among other things—but he was the all-important bridge between the shaky New Orleans days and the Stockton-to-Malone era. He was also a staunch supporter of community arts and the Junior Jazz program. "Frank played such a key role in holding this franchise together with sticks and glue for the better part of 11 years," the late Larry H. Miller said. "He actually loosened me up a little bit in that game, too, when he combed his hair [famously teasing Pat Riley]. That's what he's about—he's bigger than life. He knows that basketball is important. He works very hard at it, but you've got to enjoy your life somewhere, and sometimes even during the course of basketball games, he can crack smiles on a lot of people's faces. There were not many men in this profession that had the dignity and integrity that Frank Layden has."

Added Sloan: "The Utah Jazz, in my mind, will always be recognized as Frank Layden's basketball team."

In other words, Layden's contributions—including his role as community ambassador and team president (through 1999)—greatly overshadowed his less-than-spectacular record of 277–294 as the Jazz's head coach. Layden also brought in his son, Scott, who played an integral role in the franchise's history for more than two decades as an assistant and eventually as general manager.

Thanks to the Jazz's breakout season in 1983–84, Frank Layden coached the Western Conference team in the '84 All-Star Game, which he jokes was the second-best moment of his life after his honeymoon. He was later named NBA Coach of the Year and Executive of the Year after Utah improved its record by 15 games to finish 45–37. The Brooklyn native, who was inducted into the New York City Basketball Hall of Fame in 1998, was also given the J. Walter Kennedy Citizenship Award in 1984.

His Coach of the Year award led to a classic quip that was delivered about Layden, not by him. During the awards ceremony, former NBA executive Pat Williams roasted Layden with this line: "I'm convinced that when the great list of coaches is finally read, Frank Layden is going to be right here listening." Never one to let a good joke go to waste, Layden poked fun of himself about his decision to call it quits and let Sloan take the reins in 1988: "Being realistic, it wasn't like Johnny Wooden was stepping aside."

John Stockton was grateful for the trailblazing crew that Layden assembled before he joined the organization in 1984. "Maybe one of my most recurring thoughts is how thankful I am to that group that came before me with Rickey and Thurl and Adrian and John Drew, all these guys that changed the culture of the Utah

Jazz," Stockton said. "I give a lot of that credit to Frank Layden. He found a way to reach these guys and get them to play as a team."

9 Pistol Pete

In 2017 Hugh Jackman and Zac Efron starred in *The Greatest Showman*, a movie musical based on the inspirational story of P.T Barnum. That title would have been a perfect one for a movie inspired by the career of another entertainer who dazzled audiences with his version of a circus act: Pete Maravich.

While the Jazz were in New Orleans from 1974–79, the wildly entertaining Maravich was easily the team's main attraction. The way he dribbled, passed, shot, and played with pizzazz, razzle, and dazzle, Maravich didn't need lions, trapeze artists, or a bearded lady with a voice like an angel to mesmerize audiences with his show. He flamboyantly played basketball like it was a H-O-R-S-E game.

Rick Barry said Maravich was the greatest ballhandler he'd ever seen, a talent that the *Los Angeles Times* said came about as a result of the Pennsylvania native dribbling through his house blindfolded, in movie theaters, and while hanging out of the window of his family car as his dad slowly drove around the neighborhood. He won $5—and lost skin off of his fingertips and knuckles—after accepting a friend's challenge to spin the ball for an hour straight.

Bill Walton compared him to a master chess player who "saw things that nobody else did," which helped Pistol Pete dish out sweet-looking assists from an early age. As a 12-year-old, he zipped a behind-the-back bounce pass through an opponent's legs to a teammate for a layup. "Oscar [Robertson] was the best guard I've ever played against," former Los Angeles Lakers great and ex-Jazz coach Elgin Baylor once said. "Jerry West was the best I've ever played with, and Pete was the best I've ever seen."

Playing for his father, Press Maravich, at LSU, Pistol Pete became a major hit with his flair and prolific scoring. He averaged 44.2 points in college and led the NCAA in scoring as a sophomore, junior, and senior. His scoring undoubtedly would have been much higher if he'd come around after the three-point line and if freshmen were allowed to play varsity ball at the time.

During his six seasons with the Jazz, Pete Maravich was a magician on and off the court.
(USA TODAY Sports Images)

Maravich wasn't as prolific in the NBA, of course, but he still carved out a Hall of Fame career with the Atlanta Hawks, Jazz, and then finally the Boston Celtics before injuries thwarted his charismatic talent. Maravich averaged 24.2 points, 5.4 assists, and 4.2 rebounds in his pro career.

Before it even got its own name, the NBA's 18th team got a big name. Knowing things would be tough as an expansion franchise, the New Orleans organization paid a king's ransom to acquire Maravich two months before adopting its Jazz name. Not only did he have local ties from his LSU days, but Pistol Pete was an exciting player, who was worth the price of admission even if his team wouldn't be. "Not only did he love the game," former Jazz general manager and coach Frank Layden said, "but he knew the game."

Sporting shaggy hair, his lucky gray floppy socks, the No. 7 jersey, and John Stockton-approved shorts, Maravich averaged 25.2 points in 330 games with the Jazz from the inaugural season in 1974 until he was waived early in the team's first year in Utah in 1980. He was the franchise's first All-Star (five times overall, including three with New Orleans) and the first All-NBA first-teamer (1976 and '77). The 6'5" guard, who had the flashy style of a Jason Williams and the shooting and dribbling abilities of a Steph Curry, averaged an NBA-high 31.1 points in the 1976–77 season. That remains a franchise record, as does the 68-point game he had that year against New York. "Nobody could stop him," Clyde Frazier, who entered the Hall of Fame with Maravich in 1987, told the *New York Post*. "I couldn't stop him, [Butch] Beard couldn't stop him. I was just happy there wasn't a three-point line because he would've gotten 100."

In his column about Maravich, *Los Angeles Times* writer Scott Ostler described him as being "a misunderstood genius, a Vincent van Gogh of the hardwood." Pistol Pete had the reputation of being a ball hog, even though he averaged more than five assists over a 10-year career. Some didn't care for his showboating ways either.

When he played for the Hawks, a banner hung up in Philadelphia. It read: "Pistol Pete, why do hot dogs cost $2 million in Atlanta and 35 cents in Philly?"

Maravich struggled with knee injuries in the final year before the franchise relocated to Salt Lake City in 1979. He moved with the team but just never regained his Pistol Pete feel for the game again and only lasted 17 games in Utah. Layden, then the Jazz GM, later offered Maravich a job as an assistant coach after they parted ways. When he referred Maravich to his friend Red Auerbach in Boston, the Jazz exec told the Celtics GM, "Get him a ring." Boston claimed him five days after Utah waived him on January 17, 1980, but Maravich's knee was shot, and he retired at the age of 32.

Tragically, Maravich died of a heart attack at age 40 in 1988 while playing a pickup basketball game at a church in Pasadena, California. Five years later, Pistol Pete, the first player to have his jersey number retired by the Jazz, was honored by Utah in a banner-raising ceremony. "Pistol was so head-and-shoulders above the rest of us," Hall of Fame guard Calvin Murphy told NOLA.com.

10 Hot Rod Hundley

Rodney Clark Hundley—better known by basketball fans as Hot Rod Hundley—showed a wide range of emotions when the Utah Jazz honored him and his colorful 35-year broadcasting career with the franchise in January 2010. During moments of this night—with an appropriate "You gotta love it, baby!" theme—Hundley acted giddy, probably similar to when Hot Rod pulled off a fancy behind-the-back pass as a two-time All-American showboating star at West Virginia, did some other fun basketball trick to entertain the Los Angeles Lakers crowd, or after calling all of those "Stockton-to-Malone!" highlights in the heyday of the Jazz franchise. This night was special enough that it brought out deep emotions in a man who was deeply flawed, lovable, and loved, and certainly not in that order. "Thank you," Hundley said with a soft, broken voice at a press conference on the day a banner was raised in his honor at Utah's arena. "I can't talk."

Hot Rod Hundley can't talk? That's how much this recognition meant to a silver-tongued man who never lacked for a phrase, even if he occasionally had to borrow one from a legend like Chick Hearn. Not surprisingly, the highly entertaining Hundley, who had a way with words, wasn't speechless for long. Flooded with memories and emotions, he managed to string together a few sentences.

Hundley fondly recalled flying into Salt Lake City after the team relocated from New Orleans—he was there from the beginning in 1974—and saying how the snow-capped mountains were "so beautiful" on that June day in 1979. The city's cleanliness and wide streets stunned him. Hundley quickly fell in love with Utah, and Utah people quickly fell in love with him—and together they fell in love with their Utah team as it transitioned from Pete Maravich and Adrian Dantley to John Stockton and Karl Malone to Andrei Kirilenko and Deron Williams before he finally hung up the microphone for good in 2009. He'd called all but 14 games in a three-and-a-half-decades-long Jazz journey, including five years in the Crescent City, 25 years as the simulcast voice of the Utah Jazz, the final five in a radio-only position, and more than 3,000 games overall.

Hundley was there for the New Orleans Jazz's first ever game in New York on October 17, 1974. He was there for all those games, in which Pistol Pete looked like he had as much fun playing as Hot Rod, the No. 1 overall pick of the 1957 NBA Draft by the Cincinnati Royals. He was there for the exciting surge of the heart-filled 1983–84 Jazz team, when Stockton's shot sent the Jazz to their first NBA Finals in 1997, and every night all the way through to his final call when the Lakers eliminated Utah from the first round of the playoffs in 2009.

Thanks to the colorful way he described the action playing out in front of him in his distinctive style, Jazz fans felt like they were there with him in the arena. It didn't matter if they were driving their cars on State Street or lounging in their living rooms. Hundley had a way of making the game play out in listeners' minds. "He called the game like he played—with excitement, color, and flair," former Jazz president Randy Rigby said.

Since that banner-raising moment in 2010, sportswriters have written their articles and columns in Utah from the Hot Rod Hundley Media Center. From 2010 to 2017, the press room featured a 60-foot-long memorial with photos and pieces of memorabilia along with his most famous message inscribed in huge letters: "YOU GOTTA LOVE IT, BABY!"

The press room still bears his name, even though the sharp and detailed display and the timeline of his successful hoops career was taken down or covered up in the massive arena remodel. A scan of the beautiful mural took you on a visual journey from Hundley's college days at West Virginia in the 1950s, to his NBA playing time with the Lakers, to a broadcast career that spanned from 1967 to 2009 and included stints with the Lakers, Phoenix Suns, Jazz, and CBS in Los Angeles, Phoenix, New Orleans, and Utah.

Professionally, Hundley's broadcasting career was as good as it gets. He even earned a spot in the Naismith Basketball Hall of Fame. Personally, though, it's been well-documented that Hundley, whose father abandoned him as a young child, chose a womanizing, party lifestyle over being a family man with his wife, Flo, and their three daughters. They settled in Phoenix. He chased broadcasting glory, among other things. "[Flo] is a great woman," Hundley told the *Deseret News* in a candid interview about his life and leaving his family. "It's all my fault. It was me being me. I try

Fifteen Hot Rod Hundley Calls to Remember

"With a gentle push and a mild arc, the old cowhide globe hits home!"
"Yo-yo dribble"
"Leapin' leaner"
"Hippity-hop"
"Good if it goes"
"Frozen rope"
"Belt-high dribble"
"It's in the ol' refrigerator!"
"Looking down the barrel"
"Cal Korver"
"No harm, no foul"
"From the parking lot"
"Stockton to Malone!"
"You gotta love it, baby!"

to make up for it with money. I failed as a husband and a father. That haunts me. It leaves an empty spot. That bothers me. The other side [basketball] is wonderful."

Two years after the Jazz honored him in 2010, Hundley was diagnosed with Alzheimer's disease. He passed away at age 80 on March 27, 2015, surrounded by family members at his home in Phoenix. *Deseret News* columnist Brad Rock wrote: "He never showed up at EnergySolutions Arena, aka the Delta Center, without signing autographs, never walked in the pressroom without someone stopping him to talk. Stockton. Malone. Sloan. And Hot Rod—the Big Four of the Jazz's glory years. Fans loved Jerry Sloan for his work ethic and passion. They loved John Stockton for the same things, as well as their on-court brilliance. And they loved Hot Rod, who passed away on Saturday, because he brought it all home. He was as much a part of the show as the players and coaches. As much a part of families as a good piece of furniture, treasured over the years. And just like the furniture, he'll be a part of Utah families for generations."

11 1983–84: The Team with Heart

The fact that the Utah Jazz organization held a special reunion for the 1983–84 team three decades later, even making player trading cards, gives a glimpse of the importance of this season in franchise history. Frank Layden, the architect of that squad's roster and the bench boss, put it this way: "It saved the franchise. Without a doubt."

Multiple key figures from that historic Jazz team—Griffith, Mark Eaton, Thurl Bailey, Rich Kelley, Jerry Eaves, Frank Layden, and Phil Johnson, among others—were introduced and given a standing ovation. Purple posters with detachable trading cards of players such as Griffith (aka Dr. Dunkenstein), Adrian Dantley, Eaton, Bailey, Rickey Green, Bobby Hansen, Kelley, and John Drew were given away. Hundreds of autographs were signed before tip-off of this Orlando Magic-Utah Jazz game.

And a life's worth of memories were rekindled from a season that included a 45–37 regular season record and a trip to the Western Conference Semifinals after a first-round win against the Denver Nuggets.

Layden, the coach from 1981–88 and general manager at the time, marveled at how the stars aligned that year. He rescued Green from Billings, Montana, and the CBA a couple of years earlier and proudly watched "The Fastest of Them All" blossom into an All-Star point guard. The gritty Hansen was discovered while Layden watched film of Joe Barry Carroll. Eaton's game transformed from an auto mechanic with raw potential into a defensive powerhouse quicker than anyone could've guessed. Bailey contributed as a rookie after helping North Carolina State win a national title. Dantley's unique offensive skillset helped him become an All-Star and the

NBA's leading scorer. The Jazz were the first team in league history to have four separate players win statistical titles: Dantley (scoring, 30.6 points per game), Eaton (blocks, 4.3 shots per game), Griffith (three-point percentage, .361), and Green (steals, 2.66 per game). "It was just the perfect combination for us to win," Layden said.

The Jazz took some lumps on their way up, though. They went 30–52 the previous season and 107–221 in their first four seasons in Utah. The difference in 1983–84? "They matured," Layden said. "With a little coaching, we probably would have won 55 games."

That's a funny line, but Bailey and Griffith firmly believe that Layden's sense of humor was seriously an essential part of the Jazz's success. Players had fun and felt comfortable and thrived under his leadership. Layden even allowed them to wear casual clothes on flights instead of suits like players on other teams. Griffith says that improved team chemistry. "We were a team that was tired of losing. Frank put together the right formula, and it just clicked for us that year," Griffith said. "We went from the bottom to winning the Midwest Division. It originated with Frank."

Assisted by son Scott and Phil Johnson, Layden tried to simplify things. "We had three rules: be on time, play hard, and play smart," Layden said. "That's almost like you tell your kids. If they do those things, then you're going to be successful."

Success ensued after that 1984 team—from the Jazz challenging the powerhouse Lakers in an epic seven-game playoff series in 1988 to the NBA Finals trips in 1997 and '98, the sweet-but-short-lived Deron Williams and Carlos Boozer era, and unexpected first-round victories against the favored Los Angeles Clippers in 2017 and Oklahoma City Thunder in 2018.

None of that happens without the success of the 1983–84 Jazz team. The Jazz weren't just devoid of success on the court. They lacked steady ownership, a long-term place to play, and a sense of security in the community. "This was groundbreaking. This was trailblazing in a way," Bailey said.

The following summer, the Jazz drafted John Stockton. A year later, the organization lucked out and snatched Karl Malone late in the lottery. And continuing a three-year run of offseason fortune, Larry H. Miller became the outright owner in 1986 and added much more stability to the franchise.

Layden takes great pride in the fact that the Jazz went from being an instable organization that held 11 home games in Las Vegas during the 1983–84 season to one that was approached about its secrets to success from pro sports teams like the Pittsburgh Steelers, Dallas Cowboys, and Los Angeles Dodgers. Over the next five years, Utah won more games per dollar spent than any team in any professional sport. "We were ahead of Moneyball," Layden said.

The pinnacle of the 1983–84 season was outlasting the Nuggets in that riveting playoff series that earned them the nickname of "The Team with Heart" after Denver columnist Woody Paige suggested otherwise in an inflammatory column. "We all came together then. We believed in each other. The community was just starting to rally, too," Bailey said, recalling Jazz billboards. "That was kind of the beginning of the Jazz fans…It really solidified that this organization was on its way."

12 The 1998 NBA Finals

Utah fans shouldn't look too closely at the deeper wrinkles staring back in the mirror, but it's been a while since *Saving Private Ryan* was on the big screen, *E.R.* ruled the small screen, gas cost $1.15 a gallon, and the Jazz last played in the NBA Finals. For what it's worth, the Chicago Bulls haven't returned to basketball's biggest stage since 1998 either.

Time flies when you're having, well, feverish flashbacks and wondering what might've been had Michael Jordan not pushed off of Bryon Russell...or if Dick Bavetta hadn't called off Howard Eisley's three-pointer, Ron Harper's shot-clock violation had been called, the Jazz had won Game 2 at home and not been blown out 96–54 in Game 3, Dennis Rodman hadn't clutched up on the free-throw line in Game 4 after missing practice to attend a wrestling match before Chicago went up 3–1, Utah could've taken advantage of an injured Scottie Pippen's absence, or John Stockton had not missed a last-second deep shot in Game 6.

Sloan balked at the notion he might reminisce about the NBA Finals with old Jazz guys. Fans still lament over lost opportunities, which is what fans in tough-luck places like Salt Lake City, Buffalo, and Minnesota tend to do. Sloan? He moved on and wasn't about to sulk over the stinging setback to The Worm & Co. "There's not much to think about," Sloan said. "We lost and went home. That's what happened."

Surely, though, there has to be a Finals experience that stands out? Maybe how Stockton scored 24 points with eight assists in a Game 1 victory as the Jazz knocked off rust from a 10-day sabbatical after sweeping Shaq, Kobe, and the Los Angeles Lakers in the Western Conference Finals? Or how Utah forced a Game 6 by winning at the United Center when Karl Malone (39 points) and Stockton (12 assists) stepped up to extend the series and foil Phil Jackson and crew from smoking cigars in Chicago? Or Malone struggling for only 16 points on 5-of-16 shooting in that pivotal Game 2 loss at the Delta Center? Or simply just losing to Jordan and Pippen for a second straight June? "It's painful to still be alive," Sloan said, laughing. "That's part of sports. You couldn't ask for guys to play any harder. They made some mistakes. That's what basketball is about—a game of mistakes."

Jazz mistakes, the Bulls' championship-caliber execution, and forgotten plays be darned, one sweet memory remains. "The fact," Sloan convincingly said, "that we were there."

The Jazz showed resolve in 1998, going 62–20, and losing just three times in the Western Conference playoffs while earning a rematch. "A lot of people talk about winning a championship, and that's an amazing thing," Sloan said. "But the more amazing thing is to lose and then come back and try to do it again, which our guys did. They put everything they could in to try and have a chance to win, and that takes a tremendous amount of concentration and desire to even get to that point again."

Sloan, the gritty man who coached the Jazz from 1988 to 2011, was mostly impressed because his stars were supposedly over the hill. Stockton was 36 years old, Jeff Hornacek was a year younger but without one of his knees, and Malone was a month from turning 35. "It had been reported that we needed to get rid of Stockton and Malone because they were getting too old," Sloan recalled. "And that's when they pushed up and made it to the Finals a couple of years in a row. I don't think they showed any signs of being too old to play whenever we got there."

Instead, the Jazz and Bulls duked it out until the end of arguably the greatest NBA Finals game ever—to be commemorated for eternity thanks to Jordan's iconic push-off-aided, game-winning jumper with 5.2 seconds left in Game 6 at the Delta Center.

Sloan might be the only one who hasn't seen basketball's most famous shot over and over again. Jazz fans have definitely watched it—a maddening amount of times. Utah had a chance to go to Game 7 at home and beat the best player who's ever stepped on the court. Basketball's big prize—the golden Larry O'Brien NBA Championship Trophy—was…oh…so…close. A parade down State Street was two wins away. Blame it on fate, Jordan, conspiracy theories, pressure-packed shortcomings of Utah's stars, or whatever. "We're lucky to have that opportunity," Hornacek said. "Things fell into place for us; we just couldn't beat the Bulls."

Call it bad timing to be among the upper echelon of teams in NBA history. "Our players played hard," Sloan said. "I thought we got beat by a great player."

He learned to live with that fact years ago. "Whenever you've done the best you can do and you feel like you put everything you had into it, I don't think you can ask for any more from people," Sloan said. "That's like asking a guy to be alive when he's dead."

Or to be Michael Jordan when you're not.

"We're not the champs," Stockton said almost 20 years later, "but we're proud of what we accomplished."

13 Adrian Dantley

The Utah Jazz didn't have much success at first after being transplanted out West from New Orleans, but they did have two things going for them: a curious new fanbase and Adrian Dantley. From the time they arrived in Salt Lake City in 1979 until they drafted Karl Malone, A.D. *was* the Utah Jazz. "If it wasn't for him," former Jazz coach Tom Nissalke said, "the franchise wouldn't be here."

Having been with three previous teams—the Buffalo Braves, Indiana Pacers, and Los Angeles Lakers—in his four previous seasons, Dantley was traded to Utah. In Salt Lake City, he finally found a stable home at the same time the franchise did.

It paid off nicely.

The Notre Dame product consistently put up huge scoring numbers in Utah, averaging between 26.6 and 30.7 points from 1979 to 1980 through 1985–86, including NBA scoring titles in

1980–81 (30.7 points per game) and 1983–84 (30.6 points per game). He made the All-Star team in six of his seven seasons with Utah and was the face of the fledgling franchise. Kids around the Beehive State tried to duplicate how No. 4 slowly spun the ball in his hands at the free-throw line and scored in a variety of creative ways.

Dantley led Utah to its first Midwest Division title in 1983–84 despite being an undersized 6'4" power forward who wasn't blessed with explosive athleticism or lightning speed. Instead, he used dead-eye marksmanship, a silky smooth shot, crafty moves, precise footwork, and imposing strength as his weapons to get to the free-throw line and backboard. Over the course of his 15-year Hall of Fame career, Dantley averaged 24.3 points on 54 percent shooting. "We love him," Jazz coach Frank Layden told *The Salt Lake Tribune* during the team's breakout season of 1983–84. "He's our piranha. He'll eat you alive. He would score in a raging storm at sea."

Despite a prolific career at every level—from his All-American days at legendary DeMatha Catholic High School and Notre Dame to winning a gold medal in 1976 as Team USA's leading scorer and consistently performing throughout a prolific NBA career with the Jazz and six other teams during which he scored 23,177 points—it took Dantley seven times as a Hall of Fame finalist to earn an entry ticket into hoops immortality.

In some ways Dantley was slighted his whole life. As an oft-told story shared by NBA.com goes, Dantley got a 99 on a history test in the ninth grade while no other students scored above 80. Morgan Wootten, a teacher and legendary basketball coach at DeMatha, was suspicious that the teenager had cheated on the exam, so he made the freshman stand up and answer questions in front of the entire class. Dantley aced the quiz a second time, answering every question correctly. Wootten was stunned. "I never should have underestimated you," he told Dantley.

Getting his No. 4 jersey retired by the Jazz in 2007—a move that might have helped him finally get the deserved Hall of Fame recognition—was another honor that fit in the better-late-than-never-but-still-too-late category. Nissalke, his first coach in Utah, put it this way: "For years, when you thought of the Utah Jazz, you thought of three people—John Stockton, Karl Malone, and Adrian Dantley."

Nissalke admitted he "lost interest" in the Hall of Fame when Dantley went so many years without induction. "To me, he was everything you want in a player—a competitor, a hard worker, trained hard, practiced hard," Nissalke said. "He was just an absolutely amazing player and also a very, very tough guy."

Nissalke wasn't the only one puzzled at what took so long for Hall of Fame voters to honor Dantley, whose career took off after the Lakers traded him to Utah for Spencer Haywood in 1979. "Adrian Dantley is a historical-level figure who changed the course of basketball at every level—high school, Notre Dame, professional NBA basketball," Bill Walton told Tim Buckley of the *Deseret News*. "You look at the numbers, you look at the success, you look at the way he absolutely dominated every level of basketball—this guy is what the Hall of Fame is all about."

"If you ever had to play against Adrian Dantley, you knew right away he's one of the best players you've ever faced. [You] could not guard the guy. No one could," Clyde Drexler said. "He was consistent, he was durable, he was a winner. He had a great collegiate career, an incredible NBA career."

Some were critical of Dantley for being selfish, claiming he put his own stats ahead of his team's success. While he put up gaudy offensive stats with Utah, the Jazz only qualified for the postseason in three of his seven seasons there. He was also derided for defensive deficiencies. Dantley's feuding with Layden—and a short holdout during a contract dispute in 1984—and his reputation for being surly didn't help his cause either.

Rick Barry said it was silly to downplay the impact of someone who scored 23,177 points because he wasn't a defensive stopper. "I mean, how many guys are? He was an offensive machine," the eight-time All-Star told the *Deseret News*. "He wasn't a big guy and yet he'd take you inside and embarrass you. He was a great player."

Dantley averaged 29.6 points in 461 games with the Jazz. He eventually was traded to the Detroit Pistons after his relationship with Layden deteriorated. By then, it was determined that The Mailman was ready to carry the offensive load on his broad shoulders. "We made a very key good investment in getting Adrian Dantley," Layden said. "Adrian Dantley gave us great credibility because he led the league in scoring. I felt when we started the game we started with 30 points. It was 30–0 when we started. He played hard and he was a great, great scorer. We had him and we started to build around him."

14 The 1988 Western Conference Semifinals

Regardless of when it happens—summer league, preseason, or the 37th game of the year—Utah Jazz fans love beating the Los Angeles Lakers. Give them an NBA superstar who's recognizable by one name—Kobe, Shaq, Magic, Kareem, LeBron, Mailman (oops, sorry)—and it's even better. Do it in the playoffs, and, well, that's euphoria.

That was the case when the Jazz crushed the Lakers in the Western Conference Semifinals (4–1 in 1997) and in the conference finals (4–0 in 1998) en route to the NBA Finals. Kobe Bryant & Co. avenged those losses by eliminating Utah three years in a row between 2008–10.

But one of the most satisfying playoff experiences in Jazz history was a 4–3 series loss to the Lakers in 1988. This was the first time the two franchises had met in the postseason. It was a battle of polar opposites: the Showtime Lakers from Tinseltown vs. a blue-collar bunch from a small mountain town; Glitz vs. Grit; a fashion-conscious, carefully coiffed *GQ*-looking coach (Pat Riley) vs. a bespectacled bench boss who was pushing 300 pounds and preferred jokes over gel (Frank Layden). "He buys his clothes; I find mine," Layden once joked about Riley. A team that was only in the playoffs for the fifth time with a couple of up-and-coming stars (John Stockton and Karl Malone) faced off against a star-studded powerhouse franchise that had already won 10 NBA championships and featured established Hall of Famers Magic Johnson, Kareem Abdul-Jabbar, and James Worthy in their prime.

The series followed the script in Game 1 with the heavily favored defending NBA champions cruising to a 110–91 win at the Forum. Layden took the pressure off his guys with his self-deprecating humor. "I don't think we can beat the Lakers," he said in a postgame press conference that Utah didn't exactly love. "If we could do that, I'm wasting my time. I should really be beatified."

Saint Layden knew his team wasn't as overmatched as he made it sound, which the Jazz proved by shocking the basketball world with back-to-back wins 101–97 in L.A. and 96–89 at the Salt Palace. Mark Eaton gave the Lakers fits down low, and The Mailman delivered on both ends as the Jazz stunningly went ahead 2–1. "He's 7–4 and wide as a city block," Lakers guard Michael Cooper described Eaton to *Sports Illustrated*. "You can't go over him, you can't go around him. He can be devastating."

With everybody wondering what was going on with the Lakers—from Riley calling out Magic to Abdul-Jabbar's mom calling to ask if he was sick—the champs did what champs do in Game 4. Their three biggest stars shined brightly in a 113–110 win in Utah with Worthy scoring 29, Johnson 24, and Abdul-Jabbar

20. Said Riley after tying the series 2–2: "The obituary that was written for the top three was obviously premature."

Game 5 was a heartbreaker for the Jazz. They rallied out of a 10-point fourth-quarter deficit to seize a late lead only to witness Michael Cooper hit a game-winner with seven seconds left to give the Lakers a 111–109 victory and a 3–2 series lead. Stockton had an amazing performance—24 assists, 23 points, and five steals—but told reporters it was for naught. "The world's full of satisfied losers," he said. "It comes down to whether you win or lose—who cares what your numbers were?"

Layden didn't allow reporters into the Jazz locker room after Game 5, willingly incurring a fine because he was afraid he'd go off on the refs, but Malone made headlines after making a guarantee

The Combover

Even with the incredible performances by players from both sides, the lasting memory of this Lakers-Jazz series came in Game 4. Late in the third quarter of a tight nationally televised game, the two coaches were at the scorer's table trying to settle an issue. When the summit ended, Frank Layden retreated to the Jazz bench, grabbed a comb, and, with dramatic flair, exaggeratingly ran it through his hair to poke fun at his friend and his famously slicked-back hairstyle.

Pat Riley was a good sport and laughed. Layden took a bow, and then the game continued. The Jazz coach added to the playful mockery by giving Riley a large Salt Lake City-branded comb he'd found at a souvenir shop.

The Lakers went on to repeat as NBA champions, outlasting the Dallas Mavericks and Detroit Pistons in ensuing seven-game series. The Jazz, meanwhile, had let the league know their fun was just beginning even if their coach wasn't in it for the long haul. After Layden resigned early in the next season, Riley made an admission about the oversized grooming device to the *Los Angeles Times.* "I dumped it," he said. "I mean, it was pink!"

Decades later the two former coaches and friends still get a good chuckle out of it. "He still talks about it," Layden said.

heading into Game 6 in Utah. He called the Lakers' Game 5 win a "miracle" and wondered how many more miracles they had left. "We're going back to L.A.," Malone stated. "That's a guarantee."

The Mailman delivered on the promise, scoring 27 points with 11 rebounds in a series-tying 108–80 blowout, setting up an enticing Game 7 in L.A. But despite huge outings from Stockton (29 points, 20 assists) and Malone (31 points, 15 rebounds), the Lakers finally put the Jazz away with a 109–98 win at the Forum. "I said to Pat Riley after it was over that two things came to mind," Layden said. "The better team won, and it was a lot of fun."

15 Jeff Hornacek

Everything about Jeff Hornacek was a perfect fit for Utah when the Jazz pulled off an all-time great trade to acquire him in February 1994—his style of play that symbiotically meshed with John Stockton and Karl Malone; his ability to tickle the twine with floaters, mid-range jumpers, tricky off-balance, and flip-off-the-glass shots and quick-release bombs from outside; his screens and the way he moved around the court; his gritty and underrated defense despite limited athleticism; the calmness he brought to the locker room and court; his coach-on-the-floor approach; his camaraderie with Jerry Sloan; and his down-to-earth personality and family-oriented lifestyle that instantly won over fans.

A 30-something white man with a bum knee, a short haircut, an average build, and a darling family, this Jeff even looked like he could've been the accountant down the street who played pick-up hoops at the church on the corner every Thursday night.

There was perhaps one exception to an otherwise perfect pairing. His nickname: Horny. While it was catchy and assisted people uncertain whether to say Horn-a-check (no) or Horn-a-sec (yes), it also raised some eyebrows. Utah, home of The Church of Jesus Christ of Latter-day Saints' headquarters, is known for conservative values yet there he was with a nickname that sounded like dirty-minded Austin Powers gave it to him. Then again, some thought having an edgy moniker in a religious state made it even better. Whether you called him Hornacek or Horny, the fit was a match made in hoops heaven. "We were missing something," Jerry Sloan told the *Deseret News*, "and that something was Jeff Hornacek."

Though the Jazz gave up a nice scorer in Jeff Malone in the deal with Philadelphia, things clicked with Hornacek taking that shooting guard spot. The Jazz made the Western Conference Finals that year, and his sharpshooting and contributions were integral to the team getting over the hump and into the NBA Finals twice in the next four years. During his time in Utah, the Jazz's winning percentage was stellar: .719 (59 wins per 82 games) compared to .639 (52.4 wins per 82 games) in the same amount of time before he arrived. He scored a career-high 40 the season after joining the Jazz and always provided a steady third option to the Hall of Fame pair. "He was beyond impactful when he came to us," Stockton said.

A 1992 All-Star with the Phoenix Suns, the 6'4" guard averaged 14.4 points and 4.0 assists in Utah. The two-time NBA three-point contest champion hit a franchise-record 42.8 percent of his threes, including an 8-for-8 night from beyond the arc early in the 1994–95 season. He also drained a franchise-record 89.7 percent of his free throws with Utah, hitting 67 in a row and leading the NBA with a 95 percent clip in his final season. "He's not the fastest guy or the best jumper," former teammate Adam Keefe told the *Deseret News*, "but if you had him play the bar sports, nobody would touch him. Pool. Ping-pong. Darts. I've seen it. We play those games when we get together, and he beats the snot out of everybody. His hand-eye coordination is amazing."

So was his ability to endure pain and essentially play with one good knee. Though he was missing cartilage that acts as a cushion in his left knee—leaving him with painful bone-on-bone rubbing—Hornacek was nearly as reliable as Stockton and Malone. He played in 477 of a possible 487 games in seven years with the Jazz. That was especially impressive later in his career when he hobbled around like a man who needed a knee replacement. "You see him walk down the hallway," Jazz general manager Kevin O'Connor said, "and you think, *How does he play?*" In that same *Deseret News* article, the team's physician, Dr. Lyle Mason, said a colleague saw knee X-rays hanging up in his office. The doctor said to Mason, "'Looks like you have a total knee to do.' I said, 'No, that's Hornacek's knee.' He said, 'That's *Hornacek's* knee?'"

Well, at least what remained of the joint.

Dealing with the agony of his knee wasn't what ultimately led to Hornacek retiring in 2000. He was tired of the hurt in his heart he'd feel when missing his kids' little league games, science fairs, school plays, and daily lives during the travel-intensive NBA seasons. The travel and grind also got to him. Sloan and teammates hoped to convince him to play at least one more year, but Hornacek hung up his sneakers after the 1999–2000, so he could spend more time with his wife, Stacy, and their three young kids, Ryan, Taylor, and Abby. He used to famously say hello to them on TV by swiping his left cheek three times during his unique free-throw routine. Stacy and the kids made a pillowcase with their pictures on it for him to take on trips. While some NBA players lived it up on the road, Hornacek would occasionally call Stacy 12 to 15 times a day. He once told his kids over the phone how to make a French toast breakfast to serve to their mom in bed. After 14 years in the NBA, he was more interested in driving the carpool than driving the lane, more excited to chase children around the house instead of chasing a championship. "As the kids got older," Hornacek later told *Newsday*, "I just felt I was missing out on so much."

Hornacek was unofficially a player/coach while with the Jazz. Stockton said he'd coach them on the plane and in huddles. He'd track opponents' stats and share the intel with teammates so they would know who was hot or not and he'd offer suggestions for the Jazz offense. "He would draw plays in his hands," Stockton recalled, smiling. "That would drive me crazy."

Both Stockton and Karl Malone expected Hornacek to eventually make the transition from player to Mr. Mom to coach. "You could see it when we were playing together. He was going to be a coach," Malone said. "I knew that time was coming."

That process began in 2007 when the Jazz pleaded with Hornacek to help a struggling Andrei Kirilenko with his wayward shot. He continued helping Jazz players smooth out their strokes on a part-time basis—most notably a young Gordon Hayward—while traveling up from Phoenix once a week before Tyrone Corbin convinced him to join his coaching staff on a full-time basis after Sloan's surprising mid-season resignation in February 2011. His kids were mostly grown up. It was time.

Two years later, Hornacek was hired as a head coach by the Suns, his first NBA team. He finished second behind the San Antonio Spurs' Gregg Popovich for 2013–14 Coach of the Year honors after the Suns made a 23-win improvement and finished 48–34 in his first season. Knicks president Phil Jackson hired him as New York's head coach on June 2, 2016, after Phoenix fired him earlier that year.

It's crazy to think Hornacek nearly didn't have an NBA career. After graduating from Lyons Township High School in the Chicago suburb of La Grange, the teenager worked in a Sweetheart paper cup factory rolling paper, hoping to earn enough money to enroll at Cornell because Western Michigan was his only scholarship offer. His dad, John, a high school coach at a different school in the Windy City, helped arrange a tryout at Iowa State. Hornacek played well enough for the Cyclones to give the 145-pound walk-on a scholarship after a semester, and they eventually retired his No. 14 jersey in Ames—as it was at the Delta Center.

But he interviewed for accounting jobs with firms in Des Moines, Iowa, because it didn't look like NBA teams were going to draft a comparatively slow and unathletic guard who couldn't jump even if he was the Big 8's all-time assists leader. He has his dad to thank again for arranging another tryout—this time with Phoenix after Coach Hornacek called in a favor to Bob Knight, who convinced Suns GM Jerry Colangelo to bring him into a pre-draft camp. Impressed, Phoenix put Hornacek's accounting ambitions on a permanent hold by selecting him in the second round in 1986.

Though Hornacek is effusive in his praise for the coaching he received from Cotton Fitzsimmons and Sloan en route to becoming one of 20 players to total more than 15,000 points and 5,000 assists, it was actually his wife who helped him correct a flaw in his shot early in his NBA career. While shagging shots for him on a regular basis, Stacy noticed the side spin and suggested that he point his index finger at the basket instead of flicking it to the right. *Voila!* He no longer needed to tape his left thumb to his hand either. He went from shooting 45.4 percent as a rookie to 50.6 percent the following year. Combined with his versatility, that consistency kept him in the league for a long time.

The only thing he regrets missing in his career was winning an NBA title when the Jazz made the NBA Finals in 1997 and '98. "We're lucky to have that opportunity," he said. "Things fell into place for us. We just couldn't beat the Bulls."

16 Dr. Dunkenstein

Lee Benson, the *Deseret News* sports editor when the Utah Jazz retired Darrell Griffith's jersey in 1993, eloquently summed up how important No. 35 had been for the organization since the Jazz selected him second overall in 1980. "Griffith smiled...the same smile he used for the 11 years, from 1980 through 1991, that he was the Jazz's equivalent of the sun coming up. As the franchise struggled for legitimacy, then for respectability, and then with prosperity, there was Griffith, always reporting for duty, always doing his job, and always, above all else, keeping loose. He got along with Adrian Dantley and then he got along with Karl Malone. He got along with Frank Layden and then he got along with Jerry Sloan. He got along with Sam Battistone and then he got along with Larry Miller. He was a player's player, a coaches' player, and an owner's player...and he never met a maple court he didn't like. The only hard part was the ending."

Before the sun set on his NBA career, Griffith lit up his opponents' and his fans' imaginations with his flashy style, dazzling dunks, array of offensive skills, and a dependability to come through in various roles.

After capping his NCAA Player of the Year senior season by leading Louisville to the 1980 national championship, Griffith enjoyed a splendid career in Utah over the next decade. The 6'4" athlete was quick, agile, and could seemingly jump over the Wasatch Mountains; dribbled around opponents with ease; controlled the ball well with both hands; developed a shot from distance; and used floaters, finger rolls, tricky maneuvering, and athleticism to score in high volumes from everywhere on the court—or from the parking lot, as announcer Hot Rod Hundley often stated. And, man, could he dunk with flair and power, which explains why so many young Utahns had Dr. Dunkenstein posters hanging on their walls in the 1980s.

During his 11-year NBA career—all with the Jazz—Griffith averaged 16.2 points on 46.3 percent shooting. The 1981 NBA Rookie of the Year averaged between 19.8 and 22.6 points his first five seasons before missing all of 1985–86 with a broken foot. When paired with Adrian Dantley for those first five years, Griffith gave the Jazz a potent 1-2 scoring punch. As he developed a well-rounded offensive arsenal, his Hot Rod Hundley-created nickname "Golden Griff" was a better description than the fun Dr. Dunkenstein moniker he'd previously been given.

Griffith wasn't the All-Star on the team, but, as Benson aptly wrote, he shined like the sun for a team coming out of a dark period. The beginning of Griffith's tenure with the Jazz was bleak in ways. Sure, it's fun to fill up a stat sheet, but it's even more fun to do that while filling up the standings with wins. Utah wasn't doing that. In fact, the struggling franchise only won 28 games his rookie year and 25 his second season. A 30–52 record in 1982–83 offered a bit more hope, but the Jazz were still considered one of the worst, if not the worst, teams in the league going into 1983–84. Then everything changed.

Griffith had played in about 300 games as a pro, but he still distinctly remembers being in the Salt Palace before one particular tip-off in the spring of 1984. "My first two years with the Jazz were my worst years in sports," Griffith said. "It didn't reflect on the Jazz itself. It's just that we [weren't] winning, and that's rough."

This night was different, just as the season was. Ten years after the Jazz debuted in New Orleans, they were about to make their first playoff appearance after slogging through nine straight losing seasons. Before that first-round series against the Denver Nuggets tipped off, Griffith and teammates stood on the Salt Palace court and watched as a Midwest Division championship banner was raised into the rafters. It commemorated a season of firsts: a winning record (45–37), a Midwest Division title, playoffs. "That was a big moment for me as a player," Griffith said, "because you want to be able to leave a legacy of winning. In a short period of time to make that change, it was very fulfilling."

Four years earlier, Frank Layden had gushed on draft day about being able to pick Griffith up with the No. 2 pick. Coming off of a consensus All-American season, the Louisville star knew he was in for a challenge with a team that had been a perennial doormat for most of its existence. Just after being drafted, Griffith told Channel 5, a Salt Lake City TV station, "You've got to start somewhere."

Like the Jazz, Griffith also evolved for the better. In his first two seasons, he only made 25 total three-pointers. That increased to 38 in Year Three. In his Channel 5 interview, Griffith recalled a chat with Layden. "He told me, 'Hey, that line is out there for a reason. We're going to take advantage of it.'" Griffith did just that, even leading the league with 91 threes on 36.1 percent shooting in 1983–84. Griffith's high-arcing rainbow threes were a nice new weapon and a thing of beauty. Teammate Thurl Bailey joked with KSL-TV, "You look at your watch and you count the seconds it took for his shot to get to the rim shooting from the parking lot."

When Griffith returned from his foot injury, his role shifted as the Jazz started relying on a couple of guys named Karl Malone and John Stockton to carry more of the offensive load. But he kept contributing until the 1980s faded into the 1990s and the brilliance of his game dimmed into the twilight of his career.

Nearly three decades after his retirement, Griffith still shines in the franchise's record book. He ranks in the Jazz's all-time top 10 in seasons played (10, fourth), games played (765, fourth), minutes (21,403, fourth), points (12,391, fifth), three-pointers made (530, fourth), steals (931, fifth), and field goals made/attempted (5,237/11,305, third). John Stockton (19) and Mark Eaton (11) are the only other players with at least 10 seasons whose entire careers were with the Jazz. "He had one agent, one team, and one position for his entire career," Benson wrote. "They don't make them like that very often."

17 Donovan Mitchell

After the Utah Jazz made a trade to acquire him with the No. 13 pick of the 2017 NBA Draft, Donovan Mitchell said he had two things he wanted to accomplish in his rookie season. "My goal," he said, "was some solid playing time and average eight points a game."

Done.

And, yeah, done.

Solid playing time was an understatement for both the amount of time the guard out of Louisville played and the way he actually played—and this from a 6'3" shooting guard whom some doubted could handle either and/or both guard positions in the NBA. But reminiscent of Louisville/Utah predecessor Darrell Griffith, Mitchell had one of the most electrifying Jazz debuts in franchise history.

Utah's love affair with Mitchell began in the summer of 2017, shortly after the team traded for him. Curious about this athletic kid out of Louisville, Jazz fans went gaga over Mitchell after back-to-back plays against No. 3 pick Jayson Tatum of the Boston Celtics. First, Mitchell picked the highly touted Celtics rookie's pocket and raced toward the other end of the court. Upon being fouled by a frustrated Tatum, Mitchell turned around and walked up to confront him before wisely backing up. But it showed he was not to be intimidated. On the next play, Mitchell brilliantly pulled off a spin move that resulted in Tatum losing his balance and falling while the Jazz guard dished a crisp assist to a teammate for a dunk. It was just a preseason game, but Mitchell mania began in full earnest that day at the Huntsman Center during the Utah Jazz Summer League. "It kind of all happened so fast, but it was just in the flow of game and it was definitely a spark," Mitchell told reporters. "We really didn't have energy in the first half so I just wanted to make my presence felt."

His presence only felt bigger from there. Before games during the ensuing regular season, Mitchell tweeted out a simple message a few hours before tipoff: "Let's go!"

And then did he ever.

In what would have been his junior season at Louisville had he not entered the NBA early, Mitchell averaged 20.5 points, 3.7 rebounds, and 3.7 assists in 33.4 minutes in the 2017–18 season. But he didn't just put up nice stats for a rookie—he was daring, dazzling, an instant leader for a team that desperately needed one. The 21-year-old was a major factor in helping the Jazz defy odds by turning a 19–28 start into a shocking 48–34 record, a first-round upset against the star-studded Oklahoma City Thunder and a second-round date with the Houston Rockets.

The athletic guard with a 6'10" wingspan won the NBA Slam Dunk Contest in style and displayed his high-flying aerial show in pregame layup drills and most impressively in the heat of action during games, too. He scored 41 points in a game in December and followed that up with a 40-point outing two months later. He ignited a Jazz team that began 19–28 to finish with a 42–32 record and advance to the second round in a year no one figured they'd even make the playoffs.

He was the runner-up of an entertaining and controversial Rookie of the Year race with Philadelphia 76ers guard Ben Simmons, a 2016 draftee who sat out what would have been his first NBA season with an injury. "It's special to see a rookie be able to do what he's doing out there," Blazers star guard Damian Lillard said of Mitchell.

Oh, and Mitchell was a pretty darn good defender, too. In fact, that aspect of his game is what led Jazz coach Quin Snyder to predict that he'd get some of the solid playing time he sought. "We like that he likes to defend," Snyder said during the 2017 offseason. "The competitor in him will allow him to play early in his career."

Wearing a Darrell Griffith jersey, Donovan Mitchell throws down a dunk, which helped him win the 2018 Verizon Slam Dunk Contest title. (USA TODAY Sports Images)

Perhaps most of all, Mitchell re-injected life, hope, and pizzazz into a Utah hoops scene that had been demoralized by the loss of Gordon Hayward during the 2017 free-agency period.

Things went so well for Mitchell that his "Spida" nickname even earned an official entry in dictionary.com. And his No. 45 jersey—even if it was a nod to eternal Jazz enemy Michael Jordan—became a popular sight around the Wasatch Front.

This was just the beginning for Mitchell, who has his eyes on even bigger prizes than the Rookie of the Year trophy that evaded him. "I want to be Defensive Player of the Year, I want to be an All-Star, hopefully MVP," Mitchell said. "You can say those things…but now it's like I see what type of work you have to put in. I feel like I can do it. You can taste it a little more. You can feel it."

One of the neatest things Mitchell did his rookie season was develop a rare personal relationship with Jazz fans. He bought tickets for a college student hoping to take a girl in his class on a date. He paid for a new phone for another fan in need of some financial assistance. He made surprise visits to Fourth of July BBQ parties. He attended a BYU basketball game and a University of Utah football game. He visited a high school in a low-income part of the Salt Lake Valley and rewarded high-achieving students with a personal greeting and backpacks. And the list goes on. In other words, he was as good at "giving back to the community"—a phrase he repeated—as he was at making acrobatic dunks and gravity-defying, twisting layups. "I just wanted to come by," Mitchell said during a 3-on-3 tournament in July of 2018. "If I was a kid, I would die if my hero came to this. I want to be a part of the community and I love it here."

Mitchell Mania became so big midway through the 2017–18 season that nearly 1,100 fans lined up outside to meet him at an autograph signing in the Fashion Place Mall in late December. He ended up signing 500 autographs.

Snyder loved that Mitchell was all about the team even while he was thrust into the spotlight with his dunking, heroics, and Rookie of the Year race. "The biggest thing you could say about Donovan is to talk about our team," Snyder said. "I think our guys, they've said it, 'The strength of the team is the team.' He's been a team-first guy, and sometimes the team needs a guy to take things on his shoulders."

More often than not, Mitchell—the son of a New York Mets executive who has a pretty wicked fastball—delivered during a dazzling debut campaign while taking the team on his shoulders. Because of his work ethic, respectfulness, gregarious nature, and unlimited potential, Mitchell quickly earned the respect of coaches and some of the top stars in the league. There's no way he'd fall to No. 13 in a redraft of the 2017 prospects. "He's another guy that I think people looked at and just thought he was undersized," Dallas Mavericks coach Rick Carlisle said. "To me the question was, 'Could he be a full-time point guard in the NBA?' His college coach believed that he could. I saw evidence of it. But there just weren't a lot of believers out there. While he's not the starting point guard on their team, he does play the point position a lot and does a lot of playmaking from the two spot. He's proving that he can do that. He's got a unique combination of dynamic athleti-cism and compact skill, very tight game, great range, efficient shot, and a knowledge player. Mitchell's a rare rookie that can create for himself and create for teammates and really has a good sort of beyond-his-years knowledge of the game."

Mitchell worked with Chris Paul in the summer before his rookie year, became friends with Lillard, and often received friendly advice and postgame hugs from the likes of LeBron James, Dwyane Wade, Russell Westbrook, Paul George, and James Harden. "It's pretty surreal. There are a bunch of times where I try my hardest not to smile or to show that I'm in awe," Mitchell told Louisville, Kentucky's NBC affiliate. "That's been the biggest thing, when

LeBron first talked with me [and] DWade, you see me like covering my mouth just because I was so excited. At the end of the day you want to beat those guys. After the first initial [meeting] it was like, 'Okay, now I'm coming for you.'"

Though he fully embraced the fun of the ROY race—even playfully mocking eventual winner Simmons, a second-year player but technical rookie, by wearing a T-shirt with the definition of rookie on it during the playoffs—the New York native is focused on bigger and better things in his new home. "At the end of the day, I'm not worried about that one," he said of the Rookie of the Year race. "I can never win that award again. We've got MVP and try to win the Finals and other things we can win multiple times that I'm going to focus on."

In the meantime, Mitchell's status grows. He further ingratiated himself early in the 2018 season by soaring to block a Hayward dunk attempt from behind in Utah's 98–86 win at Boston. Hayward only scored seven points for the Celtics, while Mitchell finished with 28 points, six assists, three steals, and a play that will be cherished for years to come.

18 Hall of Famers

Hot Rod Hundley's quick wit is on display in big vinyl lettering on the glass door of the Naismith Basketball Hall of Fame's Center Court entryway: "My biggest thrill came the night Elgin Baylor and I combined for 73 points at Madison Square Garden. Elgin had 71 of them."

While Baylor carried the bulk of the scoring load that night—setting an NBA scoring record in the Los Angeles Lakers' 123–108

win against the New York Knicks on November 15, 1960—
Hundley's two points were necessary for the duo to reach the
73-point mark.

That feat and quote aren't the only reasons why the pair earned
spots in the Hall of Fame, of course. They're among 12 enshrinees
with ties to the Utah Jazz—some ties being much stronger than
others—who were immortalized in hoops history after their basketball careers. Their shrines are worth checking out:

Walt Bellamy: The 6'11" big man, a four-time All-Star,
finished with 20,941 points (20.1 points per game) and 14,241
rebounds (13.7 rebounds per game) between 1961 and 1974. Only
six points and five rebounds came in a Jazz uniform, though. He
was on the first team in New Orleans but was waived after playing
only one game. Bellamy was also inducted into the Hall of Fame
with the gold medal-winning 1960 U.S. men's basketball team.

Sam Jones: Only Bill Russell (11) has more NBA championships than this shooting guard, who won 10 titles with the Boston
Celtics during a career that spanned from 1957 to 1969. His Jazz
connection: the five-time All-Star nicknamed "The Shooter" was
an assistant coach for New Orleans during the inaugural season in
1974–75.

Pete Maravich: Though he made the trek west to Utah with
the Jazz—the legend described as "perhaps the greatest creative
offensive talent in history" in his Hall bio—Pistol Pete had his
best days when he played in the South. Maravich averaged 44.2
points per game and scored 3,667 points at LSU—both NCAA
records—and was a five-time All-Star with the Atlanta Hawks and
New Orleans in the 1970s before injuries cut his career short.

Spencer Haywood: He wasn't with the Jazz for long, logging
just 34 games in the team's final season in New Orleans (1978–79)
before being traded to the Los Angeles Lakers in the deal that
sent Adrian Dantley to Utah. Haywood was a gold medal winner
(1968), a four-time All-Star with the Seattle SuperSonics, and an

NBA champion with the Los Angeles Lakers after taking the ABA by storm with the Denver Rockets his rookie year.

Elgin Baylor: The talented small forward, an 11-time All-Star, spent his entire playing career with the Los Angeles Lakers and was known later in his life for being the general manager of the Los Angeles Clippers. What some Utahns might not realize, however, is that Baylor was a coach with the Jazz in New Orleans—first as an assistant (and one game as interim head coach) in 1974–75 and then as the main man from 1976–79. He was fired before the team relocated to Salt Lake City after his teams went 86–135.

Gail Goodrich: This point guard is best known for his playing days with the Los Angeles Lakers, including being a part of the record 33-game winning streak in 1971–72. He wrapped up a stellar 1,000-plus-game career with the Jazz in the Crescent City from 1976–77, but he only averaged 14.2 points in New Orleans after putting up between 17.5 and 25.9 points the previous eight seasons with the Phoenix Suns (1968–70) and Lakers (1970–76).

Hot Rod Hundley: Some might say Hundley deserved to be inducted into the Hall of Fame for his Baylor quote alone, but it was his love for the game, his charming and colorful on-air personality, and his ability to bring basketball to life over the airwaves as the Jazz's play-by-play broadcaster that led to him receiving the Curt Gowdy Media Award from the Hall of Fame in 2003. Hundley was the only former player to be honored with the coveted distinction, which has been awarded to one member of the print media and one member of the electronic media since 1990.

Bernard King: His time in Utah was a mess. King pleaded to a misdemeanor of attempted forcible sexual assault charge and received treatment for substance abuse while with the Jazz, but he sorted his life out and went on to accomplish great things elsewhere in the NBA. After 19 forgettable games with the Jazz in 1979–80, he became a four-time All-Star, led the NBA in scoring in 1985, and finished with an average of 22.5 points thanks to successful stints with the Golden State Warriors, New York Knicks, and Washington Bullets.

Adrian Dantley: It took a while for A.D. to be recognized by the Hall of Fame—and the Jazz organization, frankly—but both of those overdue moments came in back-to-back years long after his splendid career ended. In April of 2007, Dantley and the Jazz officially made amends as his No. 4 jersey was retired by the organization. A year later Dantley was enshrined—and some believe the team recognition spurred that to happen. Dantley was deserving of both honors, having made six All-Star teams, winning two scoring titles and averaging 24.3 points over a 15-year career.

John Stockton: The Gonzaga great's first-ballot induction was a no-brainer. A pass-first point guard, the 6'1" playmaker finished his 18-year career (all with the Jazz) first in NBA history with assists (15,806) and steals (3,265). Stockton was a 10-time All-Star and formed one of the best duos in league history with The Mailman. Stockton was also a two-time gold medalist and member of the 1992 Dream Team.

Jerry Sloan: He was a feisty player, earning two All-Star trips and getting his jersey retired as "The Original Bull" in Chicago, but Sloan's excellent run as head coach of the Jazz earned him a spot in the Hall of Fame. His Jazz teams racked up 1,223 wins, made the NBA Finals twice, and qualified for the playoffs 15 years in a row and 19 times overall.

Karl Malone: He came into the NBA with The Mailman nickname and he made a habit of delivering terrific performances throughout a 19-year career. Considered the greatest power forward to play the game by some, Malone remains the No. 2 all-time scorer in NBA history behind Kareem Abdul-Jabbar with 36,928 points (25 points per game). He was a 14-time All-Star, first-team All-NBA 11 times, a two-time NBA MVP, and, like Stockton, a player on two gold medal-winning U.S. Olympic teams.

Others with Utah ties in the Hall of Fame include: Jack Gardner (University of Utah coach), Roger Brown (Utah Stars), Moses Malone (Utah Stars), Bill Sharman (Utah Stars coach), Zelmo Beaty (Utah Stars), and Kresimir Cosic (BYU).

19 The Jazz Nickname

For years, a group of clever and boisterous New Orleans fans chanted, "There ain't no jazz in Utah" when the franchise returned to play in its city of origin. It was a funny jab. To their point, nobody would argue that there's as much jazz in Salt Lake City as the French Quarter offers. And, let's be real, the Utah Osmonds or Utah Mormon Tabernacle Choir weren't great options even if more fitting.

The Jazz nickname was far from being a clear-cut choice in 1974 when the NBA awarded New Orleans an expansion team. That spring, a naming contest was held, and more than 6,500 names were submitted, but only three contestants entered the Jazz name. The eight semifinalists: Blues, Cajuns, Crescents, Deltas, Dukes, Jazz, Knights, and Pilots. Jazz emerged as the winner after deliberation, and the city known for being the undisputed "jazz capital of the world" embraced the name. As the team's media guide still notes, this was the second time Jazz had been born in New Orleans. "Jazz is one of those things, for which New Orleans is nationally famous and locally proud," co-owner Fred Rosenfeld said at the time. "It is a great art form, which belongs to New Orleans and its rich history."

The purple, gold, and green Mardi Gras color scheme and musical J-Note logo added to the symmetry of the selection.

Unfortunately for New Orleans, Jazz looked—and sounded—a lot better than the team actually played basketball. Five years after it debuted, this Jazz show hit the road.

Another contest was held in Utah after owners Sam Battistone and Larry Hatfield relocated the franchise to a place that was home to a completely different brand of Saints, which, of course, was one of the top suggestions for a rebranding. New Orleans' NFL team might have had something to say about that. Other submissions included the Stars—to carry on the defunct ABA team's success in Utah—as well as Bees, Crickets, and, of course, Briny Shrimp. "But once the contest was over, Battistone concluded that none of them sounded better than Jazz," *Deseret News* columnist Brad Rock wrote. "That was his story, and he was sticking with it. So what if Utahns didn't know Count Basie from Count Chocula."

This topic has come up several times over the years—from those early debates about whether the franchise should pick a name with local ties, then again in 2002 when the Charlotte Hornets relocated to New Orleans, and most recently in 2012 when owner Tom Benson decided to give his team a new identity more reflective of Louisiana than a flying pest. Benson openly lobbied for Utah to return the Jazz name. He even pleaded with NBA commissioner David Stern to help facilitate the request. Stern awarded the city the 2014 NBA All-Star Game, but made it clear the city would have to find a less jazzy nickname. "It belongs to Utah," Stern told NOLA.com. "I wouldn't make it such an important point. There are many things that are indigenous to the area. I'm sure there will be some wonderful nicknames."

Jazz CEO Greg Miller weighed in via his blog: "The window of opportunity to change our name closed shortly after we moved to Utah from NOLA. We are Utah Jazz. And we always will be."

New Orleans went with the state bird, Pelicans, over fellow finalists Mosquitoes, Rougarou, Swamp Dogs, and Bull Sharks. Louisiana native Karl Malone expressed his gratitude for Benson keeping the team in New Orleans but admitted the name didn't come off the tongue very easily. "It took me a while to say Pelicans. It had to grow on me."

The same thing happened in Utah after the Jazz arrived in a relocation process that didn't allow for an immediate name change. The organization got serious about it in 1983 when Jay Francis, now a Larry H. Miller Group executive vice president, helped conduct market research that revealed how fans just weren't connecting with the Jazz name, colors, and logo that all screamed New Orleans, but not Utah. According to *The Salt Lake Tribune*, the Jazz brass let the league know they wanted to change the name and logo. That plan was thwarted by the success of the 1983–84 team, though. Suddenly, the Utah Jazz and their merchandise were as popular as Neil Diamond's "The Jazz Singer" and as hot as Jazzercise workouts. "For the first time when I traveled," Francis told *Trib* writer Aaron Falk, "people didn't ask me if I was with a musical group."

Although you can reasonably argue that the organization should've changed when it arrived in Utah, the Jazz and their fun J-Note logo have continued to strike a chord with Utahns ever since. This Jazz harmoniously blends together athletes and residents from a wide variety of ethnicities, religions, races, and backgrounds and provides a pulsating beat that helps move the community forward through good times and bad.

Those chanting New Orleans fans, understandably miffed that their perfectly fitted name and team left in 1979, have a point if they're comparing the amount of jazz in the Big Easy to the availability of that style of music in Salt Lake City. But there most definitely is Jazz in Utah now.

Just as the Lakers' nickname has taken hold in an area with far fewer than the 10,000 lakes in its first home (Minnesota), the seemingly misappropriated New Orleans-created nickname now has deep roots in a place settled by religious pioneers. There might not have been some jazz in Utah back in the 1970s, but there certainly is now, and the Jazz in Utah have become an integral part of the community's identity—even if the name sounds like an oxymoron.

20 Sloan's Resignation

For years during his lengthy career, Jerry Sloan was asked how long he was going to continue coaching the Utah Jazz. And for years, his answer remained the same. "Maybe," he'd tell inquiring minds, "I'll wake up tomorrow and say, 'This is the time to get out of it.'"

The tomorrow he warned about—and that Jazz management and supporters dreaded—arrived at an unexpected time. A day after an argument with Deron Williams convinced him that it was time to ride off into the sunset on a John Deere tractor, Sloan informed management of his decision and made his shocking mid-season resignation official on February 10, 2011, in a press conference that included tears, words of gratitude, and heartfelt speeches. "My time is up," Sloan said, "and it's time for me to move on."

That time as the Jazz's head coach began on December 9, 1988—when predecessor, friend, and former boss Frank Layden had his own surprising midseason resignation—and lasted 22-and-a-half years. It was a tenure filled with highs of two NBA Finals appearances, lows of multiple early playoff exits, an unprecedented 1,127 wins with the same organization, and a spot in the Hall of Fame. Sloan's eyes watered, and his voice cracked as he bid farewell and passed the coaching torch off to assistant Tyrone Corbin, a hire the Jazz made for continuity. Corbin called it "a bittersweet moment" to replace a legend whom he played for and coached with in Utah. "This," Sloan lamented, "is a little bit tougher than I thought it would be."

Phil Johnson, his longtime right-hand man, resigned with Sloan after the two had coached together for 22-plus years. "Twenty-six years is a long time to be in one organization," said Sloan, who started in Utah as a scout in 1983.

During his remarks, Sloan offered a lot of thanks—to Layden, whom he often said he would've been happy coaching under his whole career, and to former Jazz owner Sam Battistone for originally hiring him. He thanked the late Larry H. Miller and his family for standing by his side through the death of his first wife, Bobbye, and showing faith in him even after a 56-loss season, fans who supported him, and the media for being "fair" to him. "I've been blessed. But today's a new day," Sloan said. "If I get this over with, I know I'm going to feel much better."

Jazz management did all it could to change the mind of the longest-tenured coach in U.S. professional sports—a rock who'd outlasted 245 coaching changes in the NBA since taking over for Layden in 1988.

The beginning of the end happened at halftime of the Jazz's home game against the Chicago Bulls, the team with whom Sloan began his playing and coaching careers, and revolved around his contemptuous relationship with the equally strong-headed Williams. Utah's franchise player and All-Star point guard, Williams defiantly ran a wrong play late in the first half, and Sloan called him out in the locker room for freelancing.

Jazz CEO Greg Miller was with the team during the break and said Utah's coach told his star something along the lines of, "Hey, if you're going to change the play, it would be nice if you'd let the rest of the team know so we have a chance to score."

"My bad," Williams responded, indignantly.

The contentious moment didn't end after that exchange. Miller still believes Sloan might not have left if Williams would have let it be at that. Instead, he said Williams continued to mouth off. Center Al Jefferson tried to ease tensions by telling his teammate, "C'mon now."

"We had an argument. We've had them before," Williams said the next day. "Am I the reason coach resigned? I highly doubt that. Never once did I say, 'It's me or him.' It's never happened."

This argument, however, was the final straw for Sloan, who told Miller, "I don't have anything else." The 68-year-old head coach then requested to speak to Miller after the game. Williams had followed them and told the Jazz CEO he wanted to be in the meeting as well. "Jerry said, 'Do you want me to just quit right now?'" Miller said.

Everybody who heard Sloan say that was shocked. Miller even pledged his support to the coach, telling him the Jazz would side with him over a player "a hundred times out of a hundred" if it came to making a choice.

Sloan again told him he didn't know how much he had left in him. He was worn out on the inside. The coach ended up coaching the rest of the game—the Jazz lost to the Bulls 93–89—and the conversation continued in the coaches' office for about an hour after the game. Media members, who normally speak to Sloan 10 minutes after the final buzzer, waited for the postgame interview without knowing what was going on behind closed doors. Miller hoped to convince Sloan to coach the rest of the season or at least until the All-Star break. "He said, 'You know, Greg, I'm going to be 70 years old. I've been at this a long time, and there's nothing left in the tank. I think I'm done,'" Miller recalled.

"Jerry, c'mon. I understand…"

Sloan interrupted him: "I'm serious. I'm out of gas."

Miller warned Sloan that his midseason departure would be a "PR nightmare" and said the organization would have a tough time managing that. Sloan conceded to sleep on it and reconsider his decision in the morning. A meeting was set for 11:00 AM, but news broke before that even began. Sloan's tank was truly on empty. "Going into the meeting, I was convinced that I was going to turn him around," Miller said. "He came in and he just said, 'I stand by what I said last night.' And we were done."

Jazz owner Gail Miller also pleaded with Sloan to reconsider resigning, but the coach's mind was made up. So was Johnson's. And just like that, an amazing era ended. "We had to respect Jerry. He's a professional. He'd given us 23 great years, and you can't hold somebody there against their will," Miller said. "As difficult as it was, we had to let him go. I had to say, 'Okay, I respect you. Good luck.'"

Though ESPN reported otherwise, Williams was adamant that he hadn't told the Jazz it was either him or Sloan. General manager Kevin O'Connor and Sloan backed that claim. "I would never force Coach Sloan out of Utah," Williams said in an interview with the team-owned radio station, 1320 KFAN. "He has meant more to this town, more to this organization than I have by far. I would have asked out of Utah first."

Less than two weeks later, Williams was traded to New Jersey, though management denies that it was related to Sloan's departure. Sloan insisted the same was true about Williams supposedly trying to push him out. "I've had confrontations with players since I've been in the league," Sloan said. Simply put, he told KSL-TV, "I forced myself out."

Seven years after a heated locker room exchange with Williams ended up being the impetus to Sloan's shocking midseason resignation, the former Utah Jazz player and coach sat down for a long-overdue heart-to-heart discussion about their rocky relationship.

In the summer of 2018, Williams got a chance to apologize multiple times for his part in his rocky relationship with Sloan during a conversation at the legendary coach's Utah home. Sloan got to sternly make some points of things that had bothered him for years before eventually shaking the hand of a relieved Williams, who admitted that his stubbornness and being "young and stupid" led to him poorly handling the situation prior to Sloan's resignation in 2011. "I got a chance to apologize for how things went down," Williams told Aaron Falk of utahjazz.com. "He got to voice his opinion about all the times I was a little s--- to him and was a pain in his ass and for him to get things off his chest. I think it was good. There was nothing bad about it. It was only positive."

The meeting was arranged by Jazz president Steve Starks and former CEO Greg Miller. They both attended along with Sloan's wife, Tammy, before the three of them gave Sloan and Williams time to clear the air in private. Starks wanted to get the two strong-willed men together to help them reconcile before it was too late. Sloan's health is deteriorating as he battles Parkinson's disease and Lewy body dementia. "The thought of Coach Sloan passing away at some point before this meeting took place to me was terrible," Starks told utahjazz.com. "As Deron's career started to wind down and Coach's health declined, enough time had passed—and now it was time to come together. I really believe if the meeting didn't take place, both of them would regret it."

21 Mark Eaton

As the NBA legend goes, a junior college basketball coach was in an auto repair shop in Southern California when he spotted the legs of a rather large human being protruding from underneath one end of a sports car with his head poking out the other end. It's a fun story, especially considering how that mechanic—Mark Eaton—went on to become one of the most dominant rim protectors in NBA history.

Though an entertaining anecdote, it's not fully accurate. It's also not true that the 7'4" center reached into the Delta Center rafters to hang up his banner when his No. 53 jersey was retired in 1996. But the Jazz would have never benefited from Eaton's presence in the paint from 1982 to 1993 had the tall mechanic—that part is true—not been seen by an assistant basketball coach from a nearby junior college who spotted him while driving by the Orange County tire shop, where Eaton was working. That Cypress College coach, Tom Lubin, turned his car around for a better look at Eaton, who was helping someone. "The customer," Lubin told *The New York Times*, "was hardly up to his belt."

Eaton went through a growth spurt at Westminster High School, going from 6'3" to 6'11". He wasn't that interested in basketball, describing himself as an uncoordinated benchwarmer. He was a pretty good water polo goalie, played the trumpet, helped his dad repair boat engines, became an Eagle Scout, and then took a year-long course in Arizona to become a certified mechanic following his 1975 graduation. Eaton really had no intention of doing anything other than fix cars at this point, but Lubin had once discovered a diamond in the rough in Swen Nater. He saw big potential in Eaton, so he tried to persuade him to come play for Cypress. Eaton resisted, Lubin persisted, and more resistance and persistence happened until they agreed on a workout. Eaton eventually enrolled in the college—three years after high school—and then moved on to UCLA for a rather uneventful two seasons.

The best thing that happened to Eaton at Westwood was a five-minute conversation he had with Wilt Chamberlain during a pick-up game. "Wilt said, 'The only way you're going to survive is to think of yourself as the last line of defense,'" Eaton told *Sports Illustrated* during his 1989 All-Star season. "It was like a lightbulb going off over my head and it's how I've approached the game ever since. My job is to protect the basket."

Now a motivational speaker for corporations and an author of the inspirational book *The Four Commitments of a Winning Team*, Eaton still shares that story to help motivate people to focus on their strengths. Although he developed a nice left-handed hook shot and set some mean picks, defense was always his forté. He probably had a bigger impact on an NBA team than any other player in league history who only averaged six points.

Utah took a flier on him in the fourth round of the 1982 draft after he'd averaged less than four minutes a game at UCLA. By the middle of his first season in the NBA, though, he became Utah's starting center. Two years later, Eaton earned Defensive Player of the Year honors after setting a still-standing NBA record of 456 blocks (5.56 per game) in the 1983–84 season. He went from repairing autos to destroying offenses. Jerry Sloan told *SI* that the Eaton-led Jazz defense played "basketball I feel proud of," which is as big of a compliment as you can get from the Hall of Fame coach.

Offensive-minded fans were sometimes flustered by Eaton, but, then again, so were offensive-minded opponents. Former Philadelphia 76ers coach Jim Lynam told *Sports Illustrated*, "Whatever his blocks are, square them. That's how many intimidations he has."

Eaton finished with 3,064 blocks—grab your calculator to square that for the intimidation count—and still has the fifth most rejections since the NBA began tracking that stat in 1974. Management had the defensive giant's back until his back went out, ending his career just as the Jazz were gearing up for their NBA Finals run. Without his contributions in the 1980s—when opposing players entered the key at their own peril—that might have happened elsewhere. "If Mark Eaton had not played for the Utah Jazz, we would now be the Toronto Jazz or the Minnesota Jazz," Frank Layden said at Eaton's jersey retirement ceremony. "All I have to say to you, Marcus, is, 'I love you, man.'"

Eaton is a fixture at Jazz games all these years later and continues to serve the Utah community—in a philanthropic sense through his Standing Tall for Youth organization and in a culinary sense at his popular Italian restaurant, Tuscany, just southeast of Salt Lake City. He and his wife, Marci, live on a golf course near Park City.

Lex Hemphill wrote for the team website that it was poetic justice that a banner for Eaton was raised to the rafters after his career: "Eaton deserves the honor of having his number retired for many reasons, but for one in particular: more than any other player's story, his rags-to-riches basketball odyssey most closely parallels the success of the NBA's smallest-market franchise."

22 Gordon Hayward

With the help of his parents and Butler coach Brad Stevens, Gordon Daniel Hayward decided to enter the NBA draft in 2010. Utah plucked him ninth overall. Nearly three decades after some Jazz fans responded to the selection of an unknown Gonzaga guard with a smattering of Bronx cheers, the same thing happened at the draft party when the team used a rare lottery pick to bring a skinny computer engineering major from a small school into the fold.

The lukewarm reaction was a good omen for Hayward just as it turned out to be for John Stockton. Hayward said all the right things about Utah—as he always did—and general manager Kevin O'Connor tried to convince him the boos weren't personal. Some fans just expected the team to draft a big man. O'Connor told him, "You go out and play like we think you're capable of playing, and there won't be any more issues."

That was true until, well, he parted ways in 2017, bolting for Boston to reunite with Stevens.

After his initial tepid welcome, Hayward was optimistic he could "change some of their opinions" through his hard work and play. Over the next seven years, O'Connor and Hayward both proved to be right. Though he was frustrated at times during the rebuilding process, Hayward continued to work on his game as management worked on the roster and coaching staff. Eventually, his No. 20 jersey became the hot item in Utah, and deservedly so. Early on, NBA veterans saw something special in Hayward. At the end of Hayward's rookie season—when he scored 22 points and had a highlight dunk at Staples Center—Los Angeles Lakers star Kobe Bryant said he was "very, very fond" of the Jazz wing. "He's a very skilled, all-around player. I think he's going to have a bright future in this league," Bryant said. "He reminds me of a more talented Jeff Hornacek. Jeff couldn't put the ball on the floor as well as he can."

Incidentally, Hornacek helped propel Hayward's progression as his shooting coach before joining the Jazz staff on a full-time basis. Shooting inconsistency was an issue for the first few years of his career, and he'd often either defer to teammates or look to officials to bail him out on drives. But as he continued to work on his game and body and develop a tougher mentality, his confidence, versatility, and skillset grew. Remarkably, Hayward's scoring production increased every year for the first seven seasons of his NBA career, going from 5.4 points a game as a rookie to a team-best average of 21.9 in his seventh season. In 2017 Hayward was named an All-Star—the Jazz's first in five years—and finished the season shooting 47 percent overall and 40 percent from three-point range. He also contributed 5.4 rebounds and 3.5 assists—and often drew the toughest defensive assignments—while lifting Utah to 51 wins, the Northwest Division title, and the playoffs for the first time since 2012.

The Jazz envisioned him paired with 7'1" center Rudy Gobert as an indelible tandem for years to come. They had good chemistry, played off of each other's strengths, and made teammates better on both ends of the court. Utah general manager Dennis Lindsey said he'd pinch himself because it seemed too good to be true.

While Gobert was a defensive beast and was proving to be very efficient on offense, Lindsey lauded Hayward for the offensive component he provided, including joining Kevin Durant as one of only two players in the NBA to amass 1,500 points, 350 rebounds,

One-time fan favorite (before leaving for the Boston Celtics) Gordon Hayward drives to the basket against Paul George during a Jazz victory in 2015. (AP Images)

250 assists, and fewer than 140 turnovers in a season. Going back to 1983–84, only James Worthy in 1990–91 had a similar year. "My hope," Lindsey said, "is that it will be the modern-day version of John and Karl—that Rudy and Gordon will be that synonymous with the Jazz as well in the next eight to 10 years."

Coach Quin Snyder called Hayward's final season in Utah "a special one." The small forward surged past Deron Williams—who'd no longer get away with throwing the ball at Hayward's head, which happened during Hayward's rookie year—for the No. 8 spot on the Jazz's all-time scoring list. He also moved into eighth for career assists. Opposing coaches loved him, too. "I have a man crush on that guy," Los Angeles Clippers bench boss Doc Rivers said. "He's really good."

Hayward grew up playing a lot of different things: basketball, soccer, baseball, tennis, video games. You name it, he played it. As an 11-year-old, he tried football and was the quarterback for his team's option offense. His dad described him as being a "toothpick." That made him nervous because toothpicks tend to snap rather easily, and Hayward got hit every time he touched the football. "Every time he went down, I was just cringing because I was like, 'Oh my goodness, this guy, he's going to get hurt,'" said his dad, Gordon Scott Hayward. "At that time, he was traveling AAU nationally. If he had any basketball future, it was going to go down the drain."

The end of Hayward's gridiron days—and any chances to end up on the Indianapolis Colts' roster—came after he made a painfully honest admission. "He said, 'Dad, you know, I really like football. It's a lot of fun. But it doesn't hurt nearly as much when you watch it on television.'"

The Haywards had established a neat father-son tradition in which the older Gordon would give the younger Gordon a personal performance analysis after every game. It began inside of their minivan when he played hoops at age four. The postgame chats became a ritual—evolving into detailed texts, as Hayward moved up through the ranks from Brownsburg High to Butler to the Utah Jazz. They called the tradition "Van Talk," and whether over a mobile phone or in a minivan, it has kept the Haywards tight over the years in spite of distances.

Hoping to avoid "Ambulance Talk," younger Gordon quit football and eventually focused on two sports in high school: tennis and basketball. And he was really good at both. For a time in high school, Gordon and twin sister Heather were mixed doubles partners with dreams of playing tennis at Purdue, their parents' alma mater. He was only 5'11" as a high school freshman and didn't have high hopes for a college career in basketball—let alone harbor NBA aspirations. Some inspired "Mom Talk" from Jody Hayward convinced him to not quit basketball as an underclassman guard.

From there, Gordon experienced a shocking growth spurt and hit the 6'8" mark as a senior. That changed everything. He became part of Indiana's rich basketball history, finishing his heralded prep career with a Hollywood-esque last-second, game-winning layup to lift Brownsburg to an Indiana state championship on the Pacers' home court in 2008. He then blossomed into an NCAA poster boy after enrolling at nearby Butler. As a sophomore he helped the Bulldogs get into the championship game—after qualifying for the Final Four in Salt Lake City—and came one half-court heave away from upsetting Duke.

Years later, some Jazz fans, perhaps even ones who booed his selection seven years earlier, tried to convince Hayward to stay in Utah with a popular #STAYWARD billboard campaign. They'd seen the growth of a fresh-faced kid out of Butler, one who seemed to get picked on and wasn't aggressive enough to be the go-to guy early in his career, evolve into someone who bulked up and did the bullying seven years later. Hayward was the basketball version of wimpy Steve Rogers transforming into Captain America. Even his hair got better. The Jazz were so enamored with his progression and overall package they talked about him getting his own statue someday. "Regardless of where Gordon decides to be, I think Gordon knows how much he's appreciated here and how the fit's been," Snyder said the day after the team was eliminated from the second round of the 2017 playoffs. "It's been great for him. We certainly want him to continue here. There's lots of good things happening here."

Not surprisingly, Hayward's first visit back as a Celtics player in November 2018 was met with more boos—far more—than on draft day. Jazz fans, though, had something to cheer about that night—a 123–115 victory against his Celtics. (Hayward didn't come to Utah with Boston in 2017–18 after suffering a gruesome, season-ending leg injury in his first game with his new team.)

23 All-Stars

For a long while, it would have been easier to list the years the Utah Jazz weren't represented in the All-Star Game instead of detailing which years they were. Between 1977 and 2004, only three All-Star Games didn't include at least one Jazz player in the mix. (The NBA didn't host an All-Star Game during the shortened 1999 season.)

Between 2005 and 2018, however, the Jazz have only had All-Stars in five of 14 years. Gordon Hayward's inclusion as a Western Conference reserve in 2017 snapped a six-year drought for the rebuilding franchise.

Here are some of the franchise's All-Star highlights:

- Twelve different players have received a seat at the All-Star table (through 2018): Pete Maravich, Truck Robinson, Adrian Dantley, Rickey Green, Karl Malone, John Stockton, Mark

Eaton, Andrei Kirilenko, Carlos Boozer, Mehmet Okur, Deron Williams, and Gordon Hayward.

- Karl Malone leads the franchise with 14 of the team's 43 All-Star appearances. John Stockton was a 10-time All-Star, Adrian Dantley made it six times, and Pete Maravich earned three invitations. Carlos Boozer and Deron Williams are the only other players who went multiple times with the Jazz (twice each).
- Pete Maravich was the Jazz's first All-Star in 1977. He scored 10 points with four assists and four steals in the first All-Star Game after the NBA and ABA merged.
- Adrian Dantley led a West team in 1980, which included Magic Johnson and Kareem Abdul-Jabbar, in scoring with 23 points, but MVP George Gervin carried the East to a 144–136 overtime win.
- Darrell Griffith never received an All-Star invitation, but in 1985 he was one of eight participants in a loaded Slam Dunk Contest that included the likes of Dominique Wilkins (winner), Michael Jordan, and Julius Erving.
- In 1989 the Jazz had their biggest contingent with three players at the All-Star Game: Karl Malone, John Stockton, and Mark Eaton. The Mailman was named MVP after totaling 28 points and nine rebounds in a 143–134 West win. Stockton was MVP runner-up with 11 points and 17 assists. In his only All-Star Game, Eaton contributed five rebounds and two blocks but didn't score in nine minutes.
- Karl Malone and John Stockton put on quite the show for their hometown fans in 1993, earning co-MVP honors in the only All-Star Game in Salt Lake City. Stockton dished out 15 assists with nine points, while Malone amassed 28 points and 10 rebounds. The weekend had more local flavor as Jeff Malone won the All-Star Shootout, and 58-year-old Hot Rod Hundley (four points), Ron Boone (four points), and Thelmo Beaty (two points) each played in the Legends Game.

- Though not an All-Star, Jeff Hornacek had quite the All-Star Weekend in 2000 by winning the three-point contest over Dirk Nowitzki and Ray Allen and then teaming up with Utah Starzz forward Natalie Williams to win the 2Ball championship. Karl Malone played three scoreless minutes and caused a stir by skipping the first two days of festivities in the Bay Area to spend time with family in Arkansas.

- In 2002 Karl Malone was honored as an All-Star for the 14th time, but he remained in Salt Lake for personal reasons, including having the opportunity to carry the torch at the Winter Olympic Games.

- Mehmet Okur was named as Carlos Boozer's replacement after a knee injury kept the Jazz power forward from participating in the 2007 game.

- Carlos Boozer had a strong showing the following year in New Orleans with 14 points and 10 rebounds. Deron Williams had another highlight as he edged out Chris Paul, Jason Kidd, and Dwyane Wade in the Skills Challenge.

- The Jazz didn't have an All-Star in 2012, but Jeremy Evans rose to the challenge and won the Slam Dunk Contest, getting some help from best buddy Gordon Hayward.

- Utah was well-represented in the 2015 Rising Stars Challenge with youngsters Trey Burke, Rudy Gobert, and Dante Exum. Burke teamed up with Damian Lillard to win the Skills Challenge competition.

- In 2017 Gordon Hayward became the Jazz's first All-Star since 2011. He scored eight points in a gritty defensive battle won by the West 192–182, but he had one very impressive stat: four steals. Hayward also was the Skills Challenge runner-up behind Kristaps Porzingis.

- Rookie Donovan Mitchell wasn't named an All-Star, but he wowed the audience with some jaw-dropping dunks, including one using two backboards, en route to winning the 2018 Slam Dunk championship.

24 Deron Williams

Much ado was made about the fastball Deron Williams threw that might have left a Spalding-size hole in Gordon Hayward's midsection had the rookie not caught the missile of a missive sent his way early in the 2010–11 season. Obviously frustrated in Utah's TNT-televised home blowout loss to the Phoenix Suns, D-Will lacked discretion with his frustration over the fact Hayward didn't run along the baseline like he was supposed to do. Williams reacted—overreacted?—to the mistake made by a rookie in his second game by throwing a 102 MPH two-seamer at Hayward.

That play, however, was part of what the Jazz got with Williams while he was with the team for nearly six seasons. His demeanor was a blessing and a curse. You got the uber-competitive and surly-at-times player, but you also got a teammate who was supportive and sensational. He smiled. He growled. He barked. He made terrific passes, cross-overs, and an occasional rim-rattling dunk. He dominated Chris Paul. He got overlooked. He loved attention, didn't love media. You followed his lead, and he'd make you a better player. You didn't, and he'd let you know about it. The Illinois product was as stubborn as his Illinois-born coach—bickering behind the scenes but performing on the court. Somehow, they made it work—until they couldn't anymore. One thing you knew about Williams: he cared. He was a perfectionist who wanted teammates to perform, execute, and care at his high level. But if they didn't, they'd better keep their eyes glued to him in case he threw some high heat their way.

Williams' time with the Jazz was like dumping gasoline on a fire—a scorching hot ball of flames erupted impressively before eventually flaming out after getting too hot for its own good.

It became clear after John Stockton retired in 2003 that for various reasons Raul Lopez, Carlos Arroyo, Mo Williams, Howard Eisley, and Keith McLeod were not the long-term answer as the Hall of Fame point guard's replacement.

In 2005 the Jazz made an aggressive draft day move, jumping up three spots to the No. 3 position in what turned out to be a lopsided trade with the Portland Trail Blazers, who ended up with Martell Webster (sixth) and Linas Kleiza (27th) from that year's first round and Joel Freeland (30th) the following year. Utah got its choice between two enticing playmakers—a quick, nifty passer, and tricky dribbler in Chris Paul or a big, powerful, and athletic Deron Williams. The Jazz picked Williams because of his size and the belief he'd be more durable in Jerry Sloan's system. It was a move they didn't regret even as Paul, picked fourth by the New Orleans Hornets, breezed to Rookie of the Year honors while Williams worked his way off the bench into a starting position midway through the season. (Williams was bothered by not starting—he believed the Jazz would've made the playoffs that year if he had started all season—and by occasionally playing shooting guard.)

"I won't compare him to anybody, but I know…he under-stands basketball probably as well as anybody I've ever coached, for a young guy," Sloan said of Williams in an interview with the *Deseret News*. "You can run an offense, and he knows exactly where all five guys are going to be, what's going on in a game, and he can adjust to situations. I haven't seen a guy able to do that."

No need to remind Sloan about that No. 12 guy, by the way. Williams was just that good (while playing for Sloan, at least). In his second season, D-Will finished second in the league in assists (9.3 per game) and helped the Jazz win 51 games, a 10-game improvement, and reach the Western Conference Finals. In

2007–08 Williams (18.8 points and 10.5 assists) and Carlos Boozer (21.1 points and 10.4 rebounds per game) looked like a 2000s version of Stockton and Malone. Though Paul still received the bulk of the publicity, Williams quietly joined Magic Johnson and Kevin Johnson as the only three players to record more than 1,500 points, dish out 800 assists, and shoot better than .500 from the field in a season. He was named second-team All-NBA after not being named to the All-Star team. Williams was snubbed again from All-Star honors in 2009 despite career highs of 19.4 points and 10.7 assists.

The recognition finally came Williams' way in his final two seasons with Utah. In 2009–10 he became the first NBA player since 1996–97 to record nine-plus assists in 21 straight games and averaged 18.7 points and 10.5 assists. Fittingly, D-Will made his All-Star debut that year in his hometown of Dallas. Williams was again an All-Star in 2011, but he couldn't hide his frustrations that season after the Jazz tried to retool after Boozer and Kyle Korver left for Chicago. Hayward wasn't his only target, by the way. Williams was becoming more vocal behind closed doors—sometimes butting heads with Sloan—and openly grumbled about teammates not understanding the offense, spacing, and timing. "We had a better chemistry," Williams said in January of 2011. "I don't want to say better players to fit the system but a better mesh of guys…You start thinking that [negative] way and start pointing the blame. I've just got to do a better job of playing and not getting frustrated."

One month later, Sloan did the unthinkable, calling it quits after 22-plus seasons as the Jazz's coach. Suddenly, a Jazz community full of No. 8 jerseys, fans who idolized him as Stockton's heir apparent and supporters who'd vehemently argued that D-Will was a better point guard than CP3—he did have a 12–4 head-to-head record against him while in Utah—found themselves distraught after learning that a locker room dispute between their favorite player and favorite coach was the impetus to a decision that ended an era.

A week and a half later, another era came to an abrupt ending as Williams was traded to New Jersey—not because of his part in Sloan's resignation, management said, but rather because they weren't willing to risk losing him in free agency the following year. "There's no need to make him a villain out of this," then-Jazz CEO Greg Miller said. "I would like to thank Deron for five-and-a-half seasons with the Jazz. I'd like to wish him well for the balance of his NBA career. I consider Deron a friend and I have no hard feelings toward him."

With the way things played out, Williams went from being one of the most respected players in Jazz history to one of the most reviled. Before his first game in Utah as a visitor the next season, Williams took the high road when asked about the franchise that picked him over Paul and gave him a $70 million max contract. All things considered, Williams had the best years of his career in Utah, averaging 17.3 points on 46.6 percent shooting, 9.1 assists, and 3.2 rebounds. "I have no hard feelings. I have nothing but great things to say about the organization," he said. "They gave me my first chance in the NBA. They gave me my first big contract in the NBA...They're a well-run organization. I just thank them for everything they've done for me."

Williams said winning Game 7 against the Houston Rockets en route to the 2007 Western Conference Finals was his favorite memory, but he cherished friendships, rattling off movie one-liners with buddies C.J. Miles and Paul Millsap, setting up Boozer dunks, and assisting on Korver threes, and sharing other basketball moments with teammates. Williams left a positive impact in the community, having devoted time and money to autistic kids and diabetic children, low-income families, and families of deceased and injured military members through his Point of Hope Foundation.

Asked what he missed most about being with the Jazz, Williams said "playing in front of the fans"—the 19,911 who filled the arena with a loud, unmatched passion. "We ..." Williams caught himself and laughed after saying "we" and continued. "They have the best fans in the NBA, I believe, game in and game out. They support the Jazz, no matter what the record is, how we're playing, who we were going up against. They just always had our back."

Until they didn't, but Williams understood that. He never stopped loving them or the state, though. In fact, Williams and his family—wife Amy, his childhood sweetheart, and four children—bounce back and forth from homes in Park City and Dallas. "I definitely had my best years in Utah," he told Bleacher Report in 2017, "and the most fun playing the game of basketball."

And Jazz fans might be more accepting of Williams after knowing he apologized multiple times to Sloan at the Hall of Fame coach's house in the summer of 2018. "There are a lot of things I could have handled better, but I was stubborn," Williams told utahjazz.com. "I was young and stupid. I could have just come in there and shut up, which would have been the smart thing to do, the right thing to do. He's the coach. But at the time, how I was—my competitiveness, my stubbornness—sometimes it just got the best of me."

25 2004: Overachievers

From the time Adrian Dantley, Darrell Griffith, Mark Eaton, and Rickey Green gave Utah its first taste of the NBA postseason in 1984 until John Stockton and Karl Malone bowed out of the first round in 2003, the Jazz made it to the playoffs for 20 consecutive years. It remains the third-longest streak in NBA history.

That '03 offseason proved to be a painful one for Utah. Stockton retired on May 2. Malone signed with the Lakers in search of an elusive championship in Los Angeles. It was the end of one heck of a run for Utah.

(Cue dramatic music.)

Making matters even worse—plenty of salt in these parts to pour on the wound—the Jazz's leading scorer at the beginning of the 2003–04 season, Matt Harpring, suffered a season-ending injury a few days after Christmas. Not surprisingly, the new-look Jazz registered their first playoff DNQ—Did Not Qualify—in two decades. It was not surprising because Utah could no longer count on consistent production from its Hall of Fame pick-and-roll duo, endured Harpring's knee injury, and included a ragtag group of basketball misfits who lacked star power and depth. "If this team wins 20 games, I'll be surprised," one scout told *Sports Illustrated* before the season tipped off. "This is probably the least talented club in the league."

Though his Jazz team looked like it was assembled from a group of kids not picked for a pick-up game, Jerry Sloan arguably had the best coaching season of his career. Of the multiple seasons in which Sloan deserved to be honored with the NBA Coach of the Year, this ranked way up there. Even with daunting challenges and major losses, this Jazz team finished 42–40—just one game shy of a playoff spot. It was Utah's 19th straight winning season and 21st year in a row at .500 or better. Sloan was runner-up for the Red Auerbach Trophy behind Hubie Brown, who helped the Memphis Grizzlies improve from 28 wins to 50. Sloan was named COY by *The Sporting News*.

Only 17,306 fans attended the first game of the post-Stockton-to-Malone era, leaving more than 2,500 seats empty during that late October night in 2003 at the Delta Center. Those spectators went home happy after the new Stockton (Carlos Arroyo) and the new Malone (Andrei Kirilenko) rallied past the Portland Trail Blazers in the fourth quarter for a rousing 99–92 win. "We never gave up," the Puerto Rican point guard told reporters after totaling

18 points with 13 assists. "That's the most important thing…We kept on fighting."

The late Larry H. Miller made a guarantee to Jazz fans about that massive rebuilding project: "I can promise you one thing—we're gonna be a lot of fun to watch." Even without The Mailman, that promise was delivered. AK-47 had an All-Star season, leading the Jazz in oodles of statistical categories. Newcomers Arroyo, Raja Bell, and Gordon Giricek (an in-season trade acquisition for DeShawn Stevenson) became important pieces. Veterans Greg Ostertag and Jarron Collins chipped in. And Sloan even guided the Jazz to a winning season with guys like Sasha Pavlovic and Raul Lopez playing roles.

Sloan also dealt with an enormous trial in his personal life that season as his wife of 41 years, Bobbye, battled cancer for the second time in seven years. She passed away at age 61 two months after the season ended. Sloan considered leaving that season to be by her side after the malignant tumor was discovered in her pancreas in January—not related to the breast cancer she'd survived—but Bobbye insisted he finish coaching that season. "Last year should have been fun for him because it was about everything he stands for, but it couldn't be," Jazz general manager Kevin O'Connor told *The New York Times* later in 2004. "When he came, he worked. He was concerned he would let his team down, his coaches down, but we had an agreement that he could leave any time he needed to."

In true Sloan fashion, the 62-year-old only missed three games, heroically managing to divide his attention while still giving his full heart and energy to his wife and his team. Sloan needed basketball as much as his young team needed him. Sloan didn't see it this way, but the whole season was a touching, inspiring story even if it lacked a happy ending. "People told me what a great year we had," he said in a speech to sponsors. "We didn't even make the playoffs."

The Jazz just missed the playoffs—a 5–12 rough stretch in January and February certainly hurt—but it was a minor miracle they were even in the race. Sloan helped a group add up to more than the sum of its parts. Like their coach, the scrappy and resilient Jazz kept fighting all season just as they had on opening night.

26 Miracle in Miami

If you refer to the "Miracle in Miami," the catchy phrase will conjure up images of Doug Flutie tossing a game-winning Hail Mary touchdown pass. Utah Jazz fans fondly remember another sports figure. LeBron James, Dwyane Wade, and Chris Bosh were all on the AmericanAirlines Arena court on November 9, 2010, during a classic NBA game.

But all anybody could talk about afterward was Miss Bettye's son, Paul Millsap. As described in the *Deseret News* recap that night, he was "also known as…the former NCAA rebounding champion, the current Miami Heat-killer, the new 2011 three-point-shooting contest frontrunner, Carlos Boozer's more-than-capable replacement, and, on this night, the man, the myth, the legend."

This, mind you, was before Millsap elevated his status to that of a four-time All-Star with the Atlanta Hawks, but on this night he certainly played like one. Millsap—or Miss Bettye's son, as his teammates jokingly called him—had a performance so epic that it overshadowed Miami's title-winning trio. The latest, greatest Jazz power forward out of Louisiana Tech scored a career-high 46 points and fueled a comeback fire as Utah rallied from down 22 to outlast and shock the Heat with a thrilling 116–114 overtime victory.

The Jazz trailed by eight with 37.3 seconds remaining when Millsap really turned the heat on—or off, if you will. After scoring 31 points in three quarters before leaving with a bruised hip, Millsap saved his best for the end of regulation when he drilled a trio of three-pointers in a 26-second span and then sent the game to overtime with a save-the-day put-back at the buzzer. "We just kept chipping away, chipping away," Jazz point guard Deron Williams said. "Miss Bettye's son—that's Paul Millsap, if y'all don't know—just carried us, put us on his back. Just the way he played was great. It was brilliant. His back's going to be hurting tomorrow from carrying us."

Millsap's mouth might've gotten sore from smiling, too. "It is speechless to be down like that to a team like this in a hostile environment and come out with a win," Millsap said. "We clawed our way out of there. But that says a lot about our team."

It said a lot about Millsap as well, Jazz coach Jerry Sloan pointed out. "He shows you what he's about. That's one of the things: when it gets tough, he doesn't quit working," Sloan said. "That's why he's gotten to be better and works at the game to make himself better. How many people…would've thought three years ago or four years ago he would be able to make three three-point shots in a row?"

Teammates said they knew. They saw him hit threes in practice against them every day. Anybody who witnessed his sizzling shooting from outside in this one also became a believer. "It takes some special plays in order for us to be in the game," Jazz guard Ronnie Price said, "and Miss Bettye's son was special tonight."

Jazz players didn't always refer to Millsap as Miss Bettye's son, but they had fun calling him that over and over on this particular night. It looked like the Jazz were going to get blown out by King James & Co. early on. Utah trailed 22–7 after a 15–0 Miami run. That Heat lead expanded to 22, and the visitors went to the halftime locker room down 19 after shooting 31 percent and scoring just 32 points. Some probably wondered how much fun the Jazz players had the night before at South Beach. "They pushed us around," Sloan said. "We settled for shots. Our guys looked like we were going to quit a little bit. We had a tough time getting going."

Strangely, Utah's comeback push began with struggling leading scorer Al Jefferson on the bench—he didn't play after the third quarter—and with Deron Williams, C.J. Miles, Kyrylo Fesenko, Price, and, of course, Millsap on the court. Miami responded to Utah's surge, which saw the Jazz take a brief two-point lead, and Wade gave the Heat a seemingly safe eight-point advantage after hitting two free throws with 37.3 seconds to go. Millsap later smiled about how he "shocked them" with what happened next.

The 6'8" power forward—who was not really used as a stretch four in Utah—drained his first three-pointer and then watched Williams follow his lead seven seconds later. Miami still held a five-point lead with 19.3 seconds left, but then Millsap stunned just about everyone by sinking two more three-pointers—one to cut the lead to 101–99 and the other to bring the Jazz within one after Miami scored.

Wade split a pair of free throws in the final seconds, and then a lucky bounce and quick thinking by Millsap sent the game to overtime. Miles missed a game-winning three-point attempt, but Millsap snatched the offensive rebound and flung the ball back into the net at the buzzer. "It fell right in my hand," Millsap said. "And my thing was just to put it up quick and put it up in the basket."

Backup big man Francisco Elson was the unlikely hero at the end of overtime. He was fouled late and coolly sank a go-ahead free throw. It only figured on what seemed like a night of destiny for Utah that Elson's attempted miss on the second free throw banked off the backboard and dropped in. "Paul Millsap just rubbed off on me. I couldn't miss," Elson said. "He wasn't missing, so I couldn't miss them."

Eddie House badly missed his game-winning three-point attempt. At that point, you could have heard a pin drop. Big Al said it "definitely" ranks on the top of his all-time great games list, even though he was in a front-row seat instead of playing in crunch time. "[Paul] went on a rampage. I was on the bench watching like, 'Wow,'" Jefferson said. "We were down eight points with [30] something seconds. He's hitting threes. They're missing free throws, going into overtime, and win it. It was amazing to watch that."

Ty Corbin, Sloan's assistant at the time, later said this game was why coaches tell their players to not give up. "There are examples all the time in this league that you get and you try and teach and tell the guys, 'Look, you've got to play it out,'" the third-year coach said. "'If there's time left on the clock, you never know what can happen.'"

27 Paul Millsap

Elijah Millsap loves telling a story about the time his older brother was bit by a dog. Paul Millsap, a popular former Utah Jazz player, spins a yarn about the same Bayou biting, but his tone and tale are different. If you believe Elijah's take on the controversial family story from their childhood, it wasn't just any ordinary pooch that sank its teeth into Paul down the street from their home in Grambling, Louisiana. "He got bit," Elijah said, "by a three-legged dog."

Elijah laughs when he says that. Paul? Not so much. He only grins the grin of a sibling who's plotting payback and who wants to set the story straight after getting teased about this for years. "It's not true. The dog wasn't three-legged," Paul insisted. "Everybody wants to make fun and say that. It was a four-legged dog."

Though this type razzing is what brothers do to each other, Paul is used to getting disrespected and having his name misspelled. He's been called Ronnie Milsap—like the famous country western singer. "He's a good singer—from what I hear," Millsap said, chuckling. "People either compare or get it mixed up." Adidas, the NBA's former uniform provider, accidentally spelled out "Milsap" on the back of his jersey when the Atlanta Hawks took on his former team in 2014. The Jazz also ended up with an "L" that night in large part because Milsap/Millsap amassed 30 points and 17 rebounds.

Because he's undersized compared to many power forwards, people used to discount the 6'8" player's ability to produce at a high level, too. They learned better. Millsap led the NCAA in rebounding for three straight years at Louisiana Tech, consistently produced as Carlos Boozer's backup and then as a starter during a seven-year stint in Utah, and after the Jazz casted him aside because management thought Derrick Favors and Enes Kanter provided a better chance for long-term success, the grinding hard worker used that slight as motivation en route to making himself a four-time NBA All-Star with Atlanta.

If only the three-legged dog could see him now!

Millsap admitted he was surprised after the Jazz went in a different direction when he became a free agent in 2013. Drafted 47th overall out of Karl Malone's old college in 2006, Millsap had a huge motor, was relentless and crafty in the paint, and evolved into a valuable but underused asset on the perimeter. He'd made Utah his home and wanted to remain. Millsap tore it up on the court, too, averaging 12.4 points over seven seasons—and as many as 17.3 in 2010–11 as the post-Boozer starter—and 7.0 rebounds. No Jazz fan will ever forget the Miracle in Miami when he scored 11 points in 28 seconds to force overtime of a come-from-behind win for Utah. "I don't hold grudges. I don't hold nothing against them because without them I wouldn't be here," Millsap said. "They drafted me. They took a chance on me. I'm grateful for the years that I've been there. But with all good things, things come to an end. I can understand what happened, so I'm not mad about it."

As for his brother, well, that's another matter. Elijah clearly delights in sharing Paul's painful memory or a doggone good story, depending on your point of view. "When we was growing up, me and him, we was walking to the Candy Lady's house down the street," Elijah said. "I seen the three-legged dog before he did…I was shocked and I took off running."

The brothers can agree that all parties scurried in a hurry. One went fast. One went faster. And the other didn't go fast enough. In order, that'd be the dog, Elijah, and unfortunate Paul. "He took off running and the dog started chasing us," Paul explained, blaming his brother. "I'm like, 'What are you doing?'" By then, though, Elijah was already gone. Paul, further accusing his brother of desertion, said, "By the time I realized it and I took off running, the dog had caught me, bit me in the leg. I was small, though."

Paul, now with the Denver Nuggets, didn't bite back. "I kept running," he said. "I didn't feel it until I got home."

At this point, Paul's former Jazz teammate, an eavesdropping Kyrylo Fesenko, asked if the dog was still attached to his leg when he made it to his house. For the record, it wasn't. Unfortunately for Paul, shaking off this told and re-told story—one that clearly still has all of its legs—hasn't been quite so easy over the years.

28 2007: An Unexpected Run

Nobody knew what to expect from the Utah Jazz heading into the 2006–07 season. They had talent with Deron Williams, Carlos Boozer, Andrei Kirilenko, Mehmet Okur, Matt Harpring, and Derek Fisher. Nobody doubted that. But they also had consistency and injury issues, which led to a 41–41 record the previous season.

They'd missed the playoffs three years in a row, which was new territory for Jerry Sloan. Those concerns led six of 10 ESPN basketball experts to predict a fourth straight spring without a postseason appearance. Former NBA player Greg Anthony admitted, "I don't see this being a playoff team."

It didn't even take a full month for naysayers to be quieted. The Jazz reeled off wins in 12 of 13 games for the best start in franchise history—and November Coach of the Month honors for Sloan—to set the stage for a 51-win season. Boozer (20.9 points per game, 11.7 rebounds per game) and Okur (17.6 points per game, 129 three-pointers) were named All-Stars, and Williams gave the franchise hope it had finally found the next John Stockton by averaging 16.2 points and 9.3 assists while showing a fiery, competitive spirit and explosiveness.

Back in the playoffs, the Jazz met up with an old postseason rival—the #%&@ Houston Rockets—in the first round. Utah hadn't won a playoff series since the Big Three advanced to the second round in their last playoff push together in 2000. It didn't appear this would be when that six-year drought would end.

Yao Ming scored 28 and Tracy McGrady exploded for 22 second-half points—after scoring only one in the first half—to lead the No. 4 seed Rockets to an 84–75 Game 1 win in Houston. The biggest news after that game was Kirilenko's teary-eyed meltdown at practice because of his diminished role. Boozer's 41 points in Game 2 weren't enough to overcome another big outing by McGrady (31) and Ming (27) in a 98–90 Rockets victory, giving Houston a 2–0 lead heading to Utah. But the Jazz had played hard in the losses, so they were confident. "If we can get one," Williams said, "then we can build on that." McGrady, who hadn't gotten past the first round in five tries, wasn't making second-round plans yet: "This team is not going to let us relax."

True words by both players. The Jazz defense stymied Houston in Game 3, winning 81–67, and D-Will scored 11 of his 25 in the decisive third quarter of a 98–85 Game 4 victory. The two teams held serve on their home courts in the next two games, leading to a Game 7 at the Toyota Center. The Jazz defied the home-court odds, recovering after blowing a 16-point lead to clinch the series 4–3 with a thrilling 103–99 victory. Utah's hustle on the offensive glass led to a critical three by Okur and two free throws for Boozer in the waning moments. AK-47 then caused some tears in Houston by salting the win with clinching free throws in the final seconds.

While Utah advanced past the first round for the first time since eliminating the Seattle SuperSonics 3–2 in 2000, it was the first time the Rockets failed to make the conference semifinals since 1997. McGrady's much-publicized first-round exit streak reached six. "To win Game 7 on the road in a hostile environment, when they came back and grabbed the lead from us—we grew up a lot in this series," Boozer said. "And it's going to help us in the next series."

Fortunately for the Jazz, they faced the eighth-seeded Golden State Warriors (42–40) instead of the top-seeded Dallas Mavericks (67–15) after the Warriors pulled off the greatest playoff upset in NBA history, stunning the Mavericks 4–2.

Utah accepted the gift and took the conference semifinal series in five games, but the outcome was overshadowed by two events. The Warriors faithful will never forget 6'3" Baron Davis soaring over the 6'9" Kirilenko for a massive posterization dunk in Golden State's only win. And though Jazz fans soured on him that summer, Derek Fisher entering the arena to a hero's welcome in the third quarter—after making a cross-country trip following his baby daughter's eye-cancer surgery in New York earlier in the day—and then hitting a key three-pointer in a Game 2 overtime win remains an all-time great sports moment.

The next series against the San Antonio Spurs was miserable for the Jazz, who'd been a spur in San Antonio's heel in the 1990s-era playoffs with three series wins. "We had a pretty successful run in the playoffs," Williams said. "It got cut short by a better team."

29 Matt Harpring

Basketball fans who hear Matt Harpring's keen insight and strong opinions on televised Utah Jazz games need to know one important thing. This NBA color commentator isn't just a well-dressed tall man with a strong knowledge of hoops, a guy with firsthand experience with professional basketball organizations, and someone who can break down the pick-and-roll and transition defense. That's all factual, but there's one more critical tidbit that shouldn't be overlooked.

Matt Harpring used to play football. That, by the way, isn't a metaphor for how he played basketball, even though it works. But before he enrolled at Georgia Tech to play basketball for Bobby Cremins—whose expressed hope was: "Give me a team full of Matt Harprings"—the coach-pleasing forward was a highly touted 6'7" quarterback for Atlanta's Marist High School.

Broadcasters mentioned Harpring's football playing days so often it became a running joke amongst Jazz fans. The sport is in his blood. His grandfather Norb (Army), dad Jack (Michigan), uncle Chip (Notre Dame), and brothers John and Brian (Akron and Northwestern) were collegiate football players.

Harpring, the family rebel, does have football to credit for his basketball career. Leaning toward playing football in the Big Ten—likely at Wisconsin or Northwestern—Harpring was on a recruiting trip in Chicago when an important mind shift happened. Sitting in the stands watching Northwestern play basketball, a thought popped in his head, Harpring recalled for a Georgia Tech Hall of Fame article on the school's website. *You know what? I can play against these guys*, he told himself. "It changed my perception. I liked football, but I love basketball."

Cremins initially told Harpring he wasn't good enough to play hoops for Georgia Tech and suggested he play for coaching friends at smaller Division I schools, Davidson or Furman. The Rambling Wreck coach, though, had a change of heart after Georgia and Wake Forest, among others, pursued Harpring the basketball player. Originally offered a walk-on opportunity, Harpring convinced Cremins to give him a fair shot to compete for a spot.

Harpring quickly won Cremins over. After a couple of practices, the coach pleaded for his team to follow the ex-football player's gritty, hard-working example, grumbling, "Hey, why don't you guys play like Harpring? He's kicking everyone's [butt]."

Harpring's No. 15 jersey has since been retired by Georgia Tech.

Those who saw Harpring play in the NBA weren't surprised to learn of his gridiron background. He was a good shooter, averaging 11.9 points on 49 percent shooting in seven seasons with Utah. But it was his hard work, tough attitude, bone-crushing picks, and pesky physical tendencies that made him an asset on the court. Like a football player. Like a Jerry Sloan kind of player. Teammates called him "Little Jerry." Owner Larry H. Miller also loved him, even telling Harpring he was "untouchable" in trade talks. In the inspirational book *Behind the Drive*, Harpring shared a conversation he had with the hospitalized team owner the last time they saw each other before Miller's death in February 2009. "I just want to let you know: you've meant so much to this franchise," Miller lovingly told Harpring. "You're one of my favorite players."

After his All-American career at Georgia Tech, Harpring was drafted 15th overall by the Orlando Magic in 1998. He had short stints with the Cleveland Cavaliers and Philadelphia 76ers but spent the majority of his NBA career in Utah—busting his tail and annoying opponents from the end of the Stockton and Malone era until he was traded to the Oklahoma City Thunder on December 22, 2009. Ankle and knee injuries—not to mention a 12-year career full of sacrificing his body on the court and getting it surgically repaired off the court—sidelined him for good. "When the body goes, the body goes—and my body went," Harpring said. "I would love to play until I'm 50, but it doesn't happen."

It didn't take long for the next chapter of his story to unfold. Harpring did some studio analyst work for Atlanta-based TNT and was hired as Jazz play-by-play announcer Craig Bolerjack's wise and witty sidekick in 2010. "I love doing the color…You're involved in the game," Harpring said. "You feel like you're a part of it. You get the emotions, you get the ups and downs, the adrenaline. It's the next best thing to playing without playing."

The best part? He doesn't have to ice his joints or be examined by the team's medical staff after the final buzzer.

Though he maintained a no-nonsense, straight-laced demeanor as a player, a personality that didn't seem like it would translate to colorful commentary on the TV, Harpring's interest was piqued by Hot Rod Hundley. While injured during his career, Harpring joined the late Hundley for a guest spot. The legendary play-by-play voice told him, "You've got to do this. You're a natural at this."

Harpring kept that in mind over the final few years of his career. He studied broadcasters from all sports—yes, including football—and decided to seize the opportunity with the Jazz. This gig allows him to bounce back and forth from Utah and his home in Georgia where the Harprings built a three-story dream home that has an elevator "just in case" his hammered body can't handle climbing stairs in years to come. His wife, Mandy, a Duke medical school graduate, practices medicine in Atlanta after completing a residency at St. Mark's Hospital in Salt Lake City during his basketball career, something that makes Dr. Harpring's husband proud. "She's not Matt's wife or the NBA wife," he said. "Over there, she's regarded as Dr. Harpring. It's a great situation for her."

The Harprings have five children. Though he's considered coaching, his broadcasting job allows him to be an involved dad in their lives. When he played for the Jazz, his wife lauded him for helping with child-care duties when he could. He even had a "man bag" to carry diapers.

"When someone asks how my nanny is working out, I say, 'When I married him, he was great. And now he's even better,'" Dr. Harpring told the *Deseret News*. "Matt is a better father than I ever imagined. He wants to be a part of everything."

30 Banner Careers

The Utah Jazz have yet to raise a banner for an elusive NBA championship, but the franchise has retired jersey numbers, among other things, of these 11 cherished members of its past who helped shape the organization since its inception in 1974.

No. 1—Frank Layden (December 9, 1988) The New York native, who has a sense of humor and basketball mind that are equally sharp, played an integral role with the franchise in the 20 years after it relocated to Utah from New Orleans. He wore hats as general manager, head coach, and team president between 1979–99, earning NBA Coach and Executive of the Year honors in 1983–84 and then helping usher in the Stockton-Malone-Sloan era.

No. 4—Adrian Dantley (April 11, 2007) Though not as flashy as Pete Maravich, A.D. was one of the most gifted scorers in NBA history. He averaged 29.6 points on 56.2 percent shooting in 461 games in a Jazz uniform in the 1980s and is ranked No. 18 on the all-time scoring list (23,177 points). Dantley was a six-time All-Star with the Jazz and helped the franchise win its first division title and qualify for its first playoffs in 1984.

No. 7—Pete Maravich (December 14, 1985) Perhaps the most entertaining basketball player ever, Pistol Pete stole the show by averaging 25.2 points for the five seasons the team was located in New Orleans. He was the first player in Jazz franchise history and still holds records for scoring average (31.1 points per game in 1976–77) and single-game scoring (68 points vs. New York Knicks in 1977).

No. 9—Larry H. Miller (April 14, 2010) Even before watching a Jazz game in person, Miller told his wife, Gail, that they needed to buy the team to help it remain in Utah. He purchased 50 percent interest in 1985, secured the other half the following year, and then helped the main attraction in town blossom into an NBA power. Emotionally charged and highly driven, Miller was passionate about the Jazz, about giving back to the community through philanthropic efforts, and about building a business empire of auto dealerships, movie theaters, and pro sports teams (the Jazz and the Salt Lake Bees, a Triple-A baseball team). The No. 9 represents the number he wore on his jersey as one of the world's best fast-pitch softball pitchers.

No. 12—John Stockton (November 22, 2004) Still considered by some to be the best pure point guard in NBA history, the Gonzaga product holds two NBA career records—15,806 assists and 3,265 steals—that might never be broken. The two-time Olympic gold medal winner and original Dream Team member remarkably played in 1,504 of a possible 1,526 games and played in all 82 games in 17 of his 19 seasons with the Jazz before retiring at age 41.

No. 14—Jeff Hornacek (November 19, 2002) With his sweet stroke from outside, Horny proved to be a terrific complementary player alongside John Stockton and Karl Malone in the heyday of the franchise in the 1990s. He was one of the top shooting guards in NBA history, hitting 49.6 percent of his shots and 40.3 percent from three-point range.

No. 32—Karl Malone (March 23, 2006) Aptly nicknamed The Mailman, the Louisiana Tech power forward used brute strength to punish opponents down low while also honing a nice touch from outside. Malone was a two-time MVP, the only player in league history to be named All-NBA first team 11 times, and finished as the second all-time leading scorer in NBA history behind Kareem Abdul-Jabbar with 36,928 points. Like Stockton, he was a two-time gold medal winner and Dream Teamer with Team USA.

No. 35—Darrell Griffith (December 4, 1993) The second pick of the 1980 draft out of Louisville, "The Golden Griff," as Hot Rod Hundley called him, was an instant force in the NBA. He was named Rookie of the Year after averaging a Jazz rookie-record 20.6 points. Griffith combined athleticism—he came into the NBA with a Dr. Dunkenstein nickname—with an ability to connect from deep with his high-arching three-point shot.

No. 53—Mark Eaton (March 1, 1996) A 7'4" behemoth, Eaton was an imposing defensive presence who led the NBA in blocked shots four times and set a league record for swats in a season (456 overall and 5.56 blocks per game). Still third on the NBA's all-time blocks list behind Hakeem Olajuwon and Kareem Abdul-Jabbar, Eaton also developed a nice hook shot and proved to be a steal after being drafted in the fourth round.

No. 1,223—Jerry Sloan (January 31, 2014) After taking over when Frank Layden resigned on December 9, 1988, Sloan became a permanent fixture on the Utah sideline until he followed suit and shockingly resigned 23-plus years later during the middle of the 2010–11 season. During that successful tenure as the Jazz's head coach, Sloan won 1,223 regular season and playoff games. He guided Utah to 16 straight winning seasons, 20 trips to the playoffs, and was the longest tenured coach with one franchise in all of the major professional sports when he retired.

Microphone—Hot Rod Hundley (January 29, 2010) The beloved announcer called play-by-play action for the franchise in

3,051 games in New Orleans and Salt Lake City before hanging up the microphone after a 35-year run. A two-time All-American at West Virginia and a former No. 1 overall pick—by the Cincinnati Royals in 1957—Hundley's voice became synonymous with the Jazz. Five words he often uttered best sum up the career of this colorful character: "You gotta love it, baby!"

31 Rudy Gobert

When word spread around a Salt Lake City-area elementary school that "The Stifle Tower" had arrived for an assembly before the 2017–18 season, students began chanting something that sounded like it came from a famous sports movie. "Rudy! Rudy! Rudy!"

Kids then erupted in a loud cheer as Rudy Gobert entered the gymnasium after ducking so his head didn't smash into the doorway that was tall enough for most mortals but not for this French giant. The lanky and patient center spent most of the next hour sitting in a faculty-sized desk chair in front of an exuberant and receptive audience of kids in a dual immersion program. The St. Quentin native—kids learned that's his hometown, not Paris— mostly understood what they asked in French.

Some things the inquisitive Foxboro Elementary youngsters learned:

- His favorite colors: *bleu, noir,* et *rouge* (blue, black, and red).
- His height: *Deux metre et quinze centimetre* ("Seven-one," he said in English).
- Favorite countries: France, the U.S., Spain, Mexico, and Guadalupe.

Rudy Gobert dunks on Andrew Wiggins and the Minnesota Timberwolves during a Jazz victory in 2016. (AP Images)

- Favorite player growing up: "When I was young, I didn't watch basketball, but I watched *Space Jam* with Michael Jordan so he was my favorite player."
- Favorite player now: "Today, it is Rudy Gobert."
- How much does he make per game? (Awkward laughs. Next question. The unspoken answer: $258,838.07, not counting incentives, thanks to a four-year, $102-million contract.)
- When he started playing basketball: age 12.

The NBA has learned a lot about Gobert recently, too. The Jazz were extremely impressed with Gobert after a pre-draft workout in 2013 and deftly worked a lopsided deal in their favor to snag him after the Denver Nuggets picked him 27th overall following his three-year professional career in France. Utah has benefited tremendously from his freakish 7'9" wingspan, 9'9" standing reach, improving offensive game, feisty competitiveness, and gregarious personality.

Gobert doesn't lack for confidence either, even answering an ESPN question about the NBA's best defender, "To be honest, right now, I think it's me."

Not many will argue.

Several years into his career, Gobert, whose father, Rudy Bourgarel, played at Marist College before a pro career, blossomed into the most dominating rim protector in the NBA and was awarded with the 2018 NBA Defensive Player of the Year Award. It's easy to see why, too. In 2017–18 he contested a league-best 15 shots per game, swatted 2.4 shots per game, and made a huge defensive impact (100.5 defensive rating while on the floor, 107.5 when not).

"I think it's an empirical fact—empirical from the standpoint that if you look at every number—he has been dominant," Jazz coach Quin Snyder said when asked about Gobert being the league's best defender. "I'm not pining for him. I will. But I am just stating what is happening with our team, and what Rudy is doing is special right now."

Gobert had felt snubbed—using that as motivation—when he'd been overlooked for the award in previous years. He takes great pride in being a defensive menace. "Defense to me is something that when you watch a game you don't really pay attention to…unless you're a specialist. People watch the points, they watch the highlights," Gobert told media after receiving the DPOY award. "It's very rare a team wins a championship when you're not a very good defensive team. I think when you're a very good defensive team, you give yourself a chance every night, on the road, at home. It's a big factor and something to build on."

Gobert has given the Jazz something big to build around, too. As a bonus he's fallen in love with Salt Lake City and considers it his second home even if it's not the first choice for some NBA players who prefer a more robust nightlife. "I'm really grateful to be there," Gobert told ESPN. "It really fits my personality. I just enjoy it."

Gobert makes that clear in his engaging interactions with fans—like the young ones at the elementary school he visited.

While some students asked fun questions about his favorite foods—American (doughnuts), French (liver pâté), and ice cream (gelato)—others inquired about some more pressing and personal matters during two Q&A assemblies (one in French, the other in English).

"Do you have a girlfriend?" a student asked in French.

"No," Gobert answered *en francais*. "I am single."

"Have you ever been dumped?" an English-speaking student later asked, referring to a girlfriend and not Boston transplant Gordon Hayward, who'd just left the Jazz.

Gobert laughed and said, "Who hasn't?"

32 Karl Malone vs....

Larry H. Miller: This was not an infrequent occurrence. But more often than not, it ended with Karl Malone getting more money and Larry Miller shedding some tears.

Greg Ostertag: Malone infamously blasted some teammates for showing up to training camp "like a bunch of fat asses." Even Ostertag admitted that he knew The Mailman was referring to his extra-wide posterior.

Magic Johnson: The Mailman was outspoken about Johnson returning to play in the NBA in 1992 after the superstar had been tested positive for the HIV virus.

Isiah Thomas: The Detroit Pistons guard was sent to the hospital for stitches after being hit in the head by Malone's elbow, but there might have been some exaggerating about the extent of the injury. Isiah Thomas claimed he received 40 stitches, but the *Deseret News* reported that he received "fewer than 10" for a routine laceration over the eyelid and not a vision-threatening injury as the guard claimed.

John Stockton: Yes, really. It happened—at least once. The pick-and-roll pair got along famously well. Not surprisingly, their relationship included the occasional ribbing—and hot tempers. During one game Malone yelled at Stockton, who, according to *The New York Times*, responded by telling him, "You better talk nice to me."

Greg Miller: Malone set his sights on the son of the late Larry H. Miller, believing that the Jazz organization didn't have Jerry Sloan's back when it came to the dispute with Deron Williams that preceded the Hall of Fame coach's sudden resignation. Malone also claimed he had to buy tickets to a game through a scalper, and Greg

Miller then publicly scolded him for lying about it. They eventually made up.

Dennis Rodman: It's debatable which of their battles were more entertaining—the ones on the hardwood or the one in the wrestling ring.

David Robinson: "The Admiral" was momentarily knocked out after being smacked in the head by a powerful Malone elbow. The NBA suspended Malone for a game.

Kobe Bryant: After accusations arose about Malone allegedly saying inappropriate things to Bryant's wife, The Mailman said he wasn't going to get caught up in this drama. "Misery loves company," he told *USA TODAY*. "This is a Hollywood soap opera, and I'm not going to be the star in another Bryant soap opera."

Tim Duncan: Some claim Duncan is the greatest power forward of all time—over Malone. Others know Duncan was a center, including Gregg Popovich, so it's really a non-issue.

Geography: Malone was one of many to reference "the city of Utah" after being drafted by the Jazz. Years later, he jokingly admitted that he knows Utah is a state.

Tom Chambers: In the 1980s The Mailman and the former University of Utah star had a heated exchange during a summer league game at East High School, which is just down the street from where Chambers played college ball, and Chambers reportedly took a swing at Malone before others intervened. Despite that altercation Chambers later played for the Jazz and told the *Deseret News* he loved playing with Malone and Stockton, so all's well that ends well.

33 Greg Ostertag

One of the best stories in Utah Jazz history involves Greg Ostertag.

In 1997 Karl Malone said some teammates came into camp "like a bunch of fat asses," and everybody, even Ostertag himself, knew he was referring to the guy whose jersey number expanded from 00 to OO in the offseason. Ostertag's false front teeth once fell on the court, and a Houston Rockets trainer had to put on gloves and retrieve the bridge. Another time, when the two big dudes passed by each other between the teams' shootaround sessions, Shaquille O'Neal smacked some sense into—or out of—Ostertag and sent him and a dislodged contact lens to the floor with an open-palmed slap. The 7'2", 300-pounder took up ice hockey—The Big Zamboni would've been a great NBA nickname—as a hobby after he retired from basketball for good. He got a tattoo of Fred Flintstone with a basketball inked into his calf, putting his goofy sense of humor on display and openly admitting he just didn't care what anybody thinks of him. Ostertag lovingly donated one of his kidneys to save his sister's life in 2002, becoming the first player in history to play in the NBA after donating an organ.

These are all great stories about the center, who played 10 years for the Jazz from the time he was drafted 28th overall in 1995 to become the BMOC (Big Man On Court) after Mark Eaton until he finished a short second stint in Utah in 2006. But there is still one that tops them all.

The Jazz were in the locker room at halftime of a game when Jerry Sloan said something that ticked off Ostertag. What Big O did next fell somewhere between being daring and a death wish. "Ostertag threw a bag of ice at Jerry's head," the late owner Larry H. Miller later explained his autobiography, *Driven*. You might imagine that Sloan ripped out the rest of Ostertag's teeth or left a tattoo of his foot on the center's backside. Neither happened. In fact, only a quick reaction by Sloan ensued. "Jerry simply moved his head to one side to dodge the ice," Miller explained, "and then kept talking as if nothing happened."

Sloan dodged an ice bag. Ostertag dodged a bullet.

Sloan admitted he was getting on Ostertag in an interview with Jazz radio station 1280 The Zone, but that was nothing out of the ordinary. "I had to send him to the locker room a couple of times. I hated to do it, but you got 11 other people to be concerned about…I knew Greg. I knew him better than he knew himself. But he was good. He's a really good guy."

Ostertag was one big enigma during his NBA career. The big Texan was easy to love with his big personality, big goofy grin, and big heart, but he had a way of easily lighting fuses, too. Everybody, including him, knew he was capable of giving more than he did, and that often caused a rift between him and his coach that occasionally spilled outside of the locker room and into the public. In a radio interview a decade after his retirement, Ostertag said John Stockton, Malone, and Sloan's first wife, Bobbye, would remind him, "If Jerry wasn't yelling at you, he didn't care about you." Ostertag can laugh about it now. "At times," he said, "I thought he cared a little too much." But he knows Sloan only had his best interests—and the best interests of the team—in mind when he'd ride him.

Ostertag's inconsistency—and inability to force himself to work as hard as he could have—was especially infuriating after the Jazz signed him to a six-year, $39 million contract extension after he'd been a steady force against Shaq and the Los Angeles Lakers in Utah's 4–1 second-round series win and was solid in the Western Conference Finals victory in 1997. "He doesn't know how good he can become," Malone once said. That same night in the 1997 preseason, Ostertag admitted, "If I knew, I'd already be doing it."

While paying his final respects at Miller's funeral, the affable big man fondly admitted the late Jazz owner set his sights on him every once in a while, too. "I had to be here. I played for him for 10 years. I knew him well enough, and he yelled at me enough... so it was important to me."

Ostertag's best season statistically came before he signed the big contract. He averaged 7.3 points, 7.3 rebounds, and two blocks in 1996–97 and never came close to being the dominant Eaton-esque defender the team hoped he'd become. He regrets that. "Looking back on it now with what I know now, I would change a lot of things. I would do a lot of things differently," Ostertag told the *Deseret News* in January 2012 while he attempted to play his way back into the NBA with the Texas Legends of the D-League. "I would have worked harder and been a better player, the player that I know I could be instead of just taking it for granted."

Donating a kidney to his younger sister, Amy Hall, was certainly the most worthwhile thing he did during his NBA career. His sister, a Type 1 diabetic since age seven, started experiencing kidney problems in 1999 and three years later needed a new organ. Ostertag offered to donate a kidney after he was deemed to be a perfect donor. "I'm not trying to be a hero," he said at the time. "I'm trying to be a brother." The transplant went well, and the 29-year-old Ostertag was healed and ready to play by the time the Jazz started up again that fall. His sister was doing well, too, he told the *Deseret News*. "All her levels are up, the kidney is working really good, she's back to working eight hours a day."

On second thought, that's the best Ostertag story of them all.

34 Legacy Trust

Gail and Larry Miller were driving down a freeway in Salt Lake City on a spring day in 1985 when the silence in the vehicle was interrupted. "Larry had been quiet for a quite a while," Gail Miller recalled, "and all of a sudden, he blurted out, 'Gail! The Jazz can't leave Utah! We have to do everything we can to keep them here.'"

At that point the Millers had never even actually watched the financially struggling franchise play a game of basketball.

Three decades after the young couple scraped up enough money to buy the team, Gail honored her late husband's desire to keep the Jazz in Utah for a long, long time. In January of 2017 with four generations represented on the dais, she announced that she had transferred ownership of the Utah Jazz and Vivint Smart Home Arena to a legacy trust that will be overseen by her family and posterity in perpetuity.

The trust will help the next generation of Millers avoid paying estate taxes when Gail passes away, but more importantly it will ensure that the NBA team, the majority of the family's car dealerships, and company headquarters remain in Utah. "Our devotion to the Utah Jazz is stronger than ever," she said. "The legacy trust will ensure that the team remains in and benefits Utah. Our goal is and always has been to win an NBA championship. Utah would not be the same without the Utah Jazz."

And thus ended all smart-aleck jokes—or legitimate concerns—about the franchise becoming the Las Vegas or Seattle Jazz. The Millers assuaged fans' apprehension about the family possibly cashing in on their billion-dollar asset through this unprecedented move. It's the first trust of its kind in the NBA. "We knew this would finally put to rest the questions and speculation about the team being sold that have existed for a very long time," son Steve Miller said. "The Jazz are not our family's team. They are a community asset. They are the Utah Jazz."

Greg Miller, who used to be the Jazz CEO and who continues to serve as the team's representative on the influential NBA Board of Governors, pointed out that this move essentially guarantees "perpetual ownership." That is a rarity in the sports world. "It's a privilege to be stewards of such a remarkable community resource," he said.

Gail said it was the latest in a series of moves the organization made to do things "the right way" in terms of assisting the business and community. The Jazz restructured their organization to get more professional input from outside sources in 2015 and ponied up $125 million to renovate, modernize, and secure the 26-year-old arena. "We've had many opportunities to sell the franchise for a huge profit. When you buy it for $22 million and it goes up in price as it has, it could be tempting," Gail said. "But we've been clear from the beginning that our mission is to ensure that the Utah Jazz stay in Utah."

Now maybe people will believe her when she says it. Gail continues to be the trustee of the ownership trust, and a board of managers will take over when she passes away. That board will include Miller family members, including children Greg, Steve, Brian, and Karen, and oldest grandson Zane.

Family members who work for the organization will draw salaries from the trust funds, but the trust will not provide any monetary benefit to the family. The funds are earmarked for the upkeep of the NBA team. Miller believes her late husband, a forward-thinking entrepreneur, would approve of the arrangement. The trust takes a weight off of her shoulders, too. "It gives me a peace of mind," she said, "knowing that it's something that can perpetuate and be cared for, and that the money will be there to make it happen that now we can concentrate on winning that championship and not worry about having to answer, 'Are they going to stay or are they going to go?'"

During the press conference, Gail showcased an autographed basketball that her family was given at a Jazz game in 1985 when it was announced that the Millers had purchased half of the franchise to help ensure that the team would stay in Utah. "It symbolizes hope, sacrifice, commitment, the American dream, and most notably our love for the greatest community," Miller said of the basketball. "We view the legacy trust literally and figuratively as

Family Ties

If you don't think nepotism exists in the NBA, you haven't heard Frank Layden explain why he hired his son to be an assistant coach back in the 1980s. "All I know is I married Scott's mother," he joked.

And that was that.

The younger Layden has long since proven that he belongs in the NBA, having been a successful assistant coach and general manager with the Utah Jazz, New York Knicks, and Minnesota Timberwolves. Though nepotism wasn't the case, the Jazz have had a handful of other interesting family ties.

- **John and David Stockton**—Fifteen years after the Hall of Fame point guard retired from the Jazz, his old team signed his son, David, to finish off the 2018 season. The oldest Stockton son, Michael, previously played for the Jazz's Summer League team before pursuing a pro career in Europe.
- **Corey and Jae Crowder**—Not too long after the Jazz public relations department found one of Corey Crowder's old Jazz shoes and presented it to his son Jae, who was with the Boston Celtics at the time, the son ended up being traded to Utah to play for his old man's team.
- **Paul and Elijah Millsap**—Older brother Paul was a mainstay in the Jazz lineup from 2006–13, but the family tradition carried on from 2014–16 when the younger Millsap was on the roster.
- **Brad Jones**—The former assistant coach was the nephew of Jerry Sloan's late wife, Bobbye Sloan.

passing the ball and all it stands for to future family members, fans, employees, and community, many of whom we will never meet."

The announcement was greeted with widespread approval from Jazz fans. "Larry was once asked how he wanted to be remembered after he was gone. He said, as he choked up, 'I want to be remembered as a man who loved Utah,'" Gail said. "I believe this sentiment runs through our entire family. It's my hope that when the community thinks of our family today, tomorrow, and many years from now, they will think of us as a family who loves Utah."

35 AK-47

Andrei Kirilenko was attending a summer basketball camp in 1999 with the Russian Youth National Team when he got good news: the 18-year-old had been selected in the NBA draft by the Utah Jazz. He was the first from his country to go in the first round. "I was like, 'Wow! This is the Jazz who played just in the Finals against the Chicago Bulls," Kirilenko said. "Karl Malone. John Stockton."

A comrade jokingly gave him a new nickname: *Pochtal'on*— or The Mailman for the non-Russian speakers in the audience. Kirilenko already owned one of the best nicknames in sports: AK-47, which was a clever combo of his initials and jersey number. (Fun fact: Kirilenko was born in the Soviet Union city of Izhevsk, where the assault rifle—not named after him, by the way—was first made.)

Kirilenko remained in Russia for two years, playing for European powerhouse CSKA Moscow and for the national team. In 2000 the versatile forward was named MVP of the Russian League and made his Olympics debut in Sydney, Australia. The following year Kirilenko nervously decided to go play with the other Mailman in Utah. He was apprehensive coming to play in the best league in basketball. The NBA was a mystery to him. He compared it to heaven. He'd heard about it before but didn't know what it was really like. His fears quickly subsided once he arrived in Salt Lake City. "Instantly, from my first year, from summer league, I start feeling like I'm local," Kirilenko said. "The people around the community kind of make everything possible that I feel great and I feel like I'm at home."

That pleasant transition happened despite the fact that he spoke very little English. Kirilenko's decade with Utah—from 2001–11—had some ups (2004 All-Star, NBA All-Defense three times, crazy stat lines) and some downs (injuries, big contract pressures, the 2007 playoffs crying incident). While with the Jazz, though, Kirilenko finished in the top seven of eight different all-time franchise statistical categories—second in blocks (1,380), fourth in seasons played (10) and steals (960), fifth in assists (1,919) and minutes (20,989), sixth in points (8,411), and seventh in rebounds (3,836) and games played (681).

Kirilenko made the All-Rookie first team in 2001–02 and then really exploded onto the scene in 2003–04, the year after Stockton and Malone left. AK-47 led the team in scoring (16.5 points per game), rebounding (8.1 per game), blocks (2.8 per game), steals (1.9 per game), and minutes played (2,895). He helped the Jazz finish a surprisingly good 42–40, which was short of the playoffs for the first time after a two-decade run but far exceeded projections. That led the Jazz to sign him to a massive $86 million deal as they believed he was the one who'd take the franchise-player torch from the departed Stockton and Malone.

That never quite materialized.

Kirilenko's scoring role diminished as Deron Williams and Carlos Boozer entered the fray. In 2007 he scored only 8.3 points and played almost 900 fewer minutes than his best year, but he did contribute in the Western Conference Finals run. That year's playoffs got off to a rocky start for him, though, as a frustrated Kirilenko was spotted crying after a practice following Game 1 against the Houston Rockets in the first round. The 26-year-old was upset about a diminishing role, and there was speculation that Jerry Sloan was being extra hard on him. Then in his 19th season as Utah's head coach, Sloan refuted that he was responsible for his small forward's meltdown. "I'm not one to hurt anybody feelings in all this, but it's come out like I wanted to bury this guy. And that's not the case at all," Sloan said. "I know I may be intimidating, as an individual, but I don't mean to be."

Kirilenko's wife, Russian pop singer Masha Lopatova, suggested that the Jazz should hire a Russian translator for Kirilenko. She pointed out that the Rockets got a Chinese translator for Yao Ming, and it helped. Either way, she hoped it would work out. She'd never seen her husband like that. "With the coach and Andrei, that's certainly a language barrier," Masha told the *Deseret News*, "and it looks like there could be a misunderstanding with both guys."

By the end of the ensuing offseason, the relationship looked to be damaged beyond repair. Kirilenko asked to be traded, writing in a Russian blog, "I want to leave the Jazz…Coach Sloan is one of the reasons." Kirilenko even told Russian paper *Sports Express* he was contemplating leaving the NBA and his $63 million contract.

Kirilenko returned and played the final four seasons of his contract in Utah but was hampered by nagging injuries. He went to Russia during the 2011 lockout and wrapped up his NBA career with the Minnesota Timberwolves and Brooklyn Nets in 2013–14. "They would remember me as AK-47, which is all-around balanced kind of weapon on the floor," Kirilenko said of Utah fans. "That's all I've been doing. I've been trying to go on the floor and give my best, just hustle."

The 6'9" player's size and athleticism resulted in some impressive stat lines, including the rare 5 x 5, which required at least five points, rebounds, assists, blocks, and steals in an outing. Kirilenko did that three times and is one of 12 players to ever achieve that balanced performance in NBA history. He and Hakeem Olajuwon are the only ones who did it more than once. "I was trying to win the games, and that was the bottom line," Kirilenko said. "I had great teammates along the way. Every time I'm thinking, *We need to get a W. We need to get a W.* Night after night. I hope fans can say that, 'I don't know how good he was, but he was hustling. He was trying. Every night.'"

Kirilenko will also be remembered for a few non-basketball-related things like reading Russian novels in front of his locker before every game, getting an enormous World of Warcraft tattoo on his back, and for the well-publicized annual get-out-of-marital-monogamy pass he received from his wife (that he says he never cashed in on).

He'll remember evolving into a man while in Utah. "I look at the time with the Utah Jazz, not only from a basketball standpoint, but from a growing standpoint, and I'm so grateful to the city of Salt Lake City and all the fans. They set such great examples of decorum for myself," the father of three sons said. "It set the standard of how to treat my family, how to be around people, how to be in a community."

The Jazz welcomed him back to Utah in 2016 to honor his career—though not retire his jersey. That happened to be the final game in the Beehive State for Kobe Bryant, whom AK-47 had had some good battles with over the years (including blocking the Black Mamba three times in one quarter). "Thank you very much for all of the memories," Kirilenko told the Jazz crowd, which gave him a loud standing ovation during the 123–75 blowout win against the Los Angeles Lakers. "I will remember them all of my life."

In an entertaining Twitter takeover during his return visit that day, Kirilenko gave fans on @UtahJazz's account these updates: He's now the Russian Basketball Federation president; he'd rather join a team consisting of Malone, Stockton, and Hornacek—"Jazz man forever"—over one with LeBron James, Carmelo Anthony, Dwyane Wade, and Chris Paul; 2004 was his most memorable season because of his All-Star selection and the Jazz exceeding expectations; he'd enjoyed watching Gordon Hayward grow up in Utah; of his 1,380 career blocks, swatting big guys like Shaq and Yao was "always desirable;" it was "easy" to play with Stockton because the ball was in your hands as soon as you were open; and he confidently stated, "I look way better than Kyle Korver. Everybody knows that."

Kirilenko's final tweet on the Jazz account was a hopeful one: "I want to wish Jazz that one day Larry O'Brien trophy will come to this city."

36 Hayward's Fourth of July Fireworks

Most Utah Jazz fans won't look back at July 4, 2017 with fond memories. They'll definitely remember this particular holiday, though. Gordon Hayward instantly became a hero in Boston on that day, but the small forward devolved into Public Enemy No. 1 in Utah and spoiled the Fourth of July festivities for Jazz fans after he officially made his free-agency intentions clear on a blog painfully titled, "Thank you, Utah." "After seven years in Utah, I have decided to join the Boston Celtics," Hayward declared in his post on The Players' Tribune website.

That news on its own was as bad as a patriotic parade being rained on. The way it was handled throughout the day, however, made it worse. Thanks to a clumsy execution of the announcement on the part of Hayward's side, Utah faithful felt like they'd been dumped twice.

The Jazz believed and hoped they'd done everything they could to convince Hayward to remain in Utah, where he'd played hoops since leaving Butler after becoming the poster boy of the NCAA Tournament in 2010. Hayward had been impressed by recruiting pitches in Miami and Boston the previous week, but the Jazz got the last word in at his summer home in San Diego. In a meeting attended by key front-office personnel and a handful of teammates, the Jazz tried to convince the 27-year-old to create a lasting legacy in Utah a la Hall of Famer John Stockton. With Hayward and French big man Rudy Gobert in place, along with some other talented pieces, Utah management tried to entice him with a vision of winning championships, becoming a legend, and creating history in Utah. "The Jazz made a compelling case for Gordon to stay and managed the process well," team president Steve Starks said. "A foundation for success has been established here, and we remain steadfast in our commitment to bring a championship to Utah."

Hayward had strong feelings for Jazz fans and for Utah—and he was particularly close with assistant Johnnie Bryant, teammate Joe Ingles, and detail-oriented head coach Quin Snyder—so the decision was tough. He'd also been wowed by the Miami Heat in the free-agency process, for what it's worth. Hayward's agent, Mark Bartelstein, said his client wanted to "take a deep breath" before announcing his decision after those visits between July 1–3.

That paved the way for a bizarre July 4.

An ESPN report at 12:17 PM Utah time about Hayward picking Boston caused the Internet to explode with sports activity hours before the country's sky lit up with traditional fireworks. National media members from *USA TODAY* and ESPN and local reporters from *The Boston Globe*, *Deseret News*, and *The Salt Lake Tribune* confirmed NBA writer Chris Haynes' tweet about Hayward reaching an agreement with the Celtics.

Understandably, Jazz fans began the mourning process after learning that the guy, who'd won over their hearts and whom they had supported in tougher times, had picked someone else.

Hold the phone! The Jazz received a glimmer of hope when ESPN's Adrian Wojnarowski reported that Hayward hadn't informed the Jazz of his decision. Hayward's agent and people within his inner circle claimed he still hadn't made up his mind. "Gordon hasn't made a decision yet," Bartelstein claimed. "We are still working through it."

People close to Hayward said he was telling them the same thing. He had gone to bed late after speaking to his dad about what to do and was leaning heavily toward Boston but adamantly claimed to have not made up his mind when ESPN broke the news. Some media members, however, stuck with their sources' intel about him being Boston-bound. "People can say now that that report was right. It was not," Bartelstein later told the *Deseret News*. "Anyone that says they knew Gordon knew what he was doing didn't know. How could they know? Because he didn't know."

Over the next five and a half hours, confusion, drama, rumors, and social media silliness spread like ants on a mission at a picnic. "The Indecision," as some called it, took on a life of its own. Memes were created starring Steve Harvey, who became infamously known for naming the wrong beauty pageant winner. People joked about Hayward and his endorsement deal with Bailey's Moving & Storage. Old tweets he'd written about being indecisive over humorous things were retweeted, including a 2011 post that read, "I can't tell which fabreeze I should go with. #help."

The pause gave the Jazz renewed hope. "We trust Gordon and his agent that no decision has been made," Starks wrote on Twitter that afternoon. "Good communication all day and a great relationship."

Meanwhile, Hayward was upset about the development, and Bartelstein was in all-out damage control/clarification/spin mode, depending who you believe. The agent had spent a lot of Monday night, late into the wee hours of Tuesday morning, chatting with Hayward and his inner circle about what to do. At this point, it was down to Boston and Utah. They decided to get some rest and revisit the decision Tuesday morning after spending a great, thought-provoking Monday afternoon with the Jazz at his San Diego home.

About five hours later, the confusion was sorta, kinda clarified when Hayward tweeted out the link to his carefully worded post. In a long, well-written essay, Hayward left no doubt that his heart was set on Boston. He tried to say the right things in his blog. He thanked Jazz fans, writing, "I really want you all to know that you mean the world to me and my family." He called Salt Lake City a "special place" where he grew into a man with his own family. He thanked several members of the Jazz organization and the "first-class" Miller family. Interestingly, he only mentioned one Jazz teammate—Jeremy Evans. "I was literally the last Jazz player left who played under Coach Sloan—and I always took that as a lot more than just some piece of trivia," Hayward wrote. "That was something that truly made me feel like a part of the fabric of this franchise. And that fabric is something that has meant a lot to me, ever since."

All the kind words didn't provide much comfort to Jazz fans whose hearts—not to mention an important part of the franchise's current fabric—were ripped apart for a second time in one day. "Unfortunately for the Jazz, it didn't mean enough for him to continue what he started," the *Deseret News* wrote. "Hayward chose an easier path to becoming an All-Star and to making it further in the playoffs in a lesser Eastern Conference. He chose a storied sports tradition that included the likes of Larry Bird, Bill Russell, Paul Pierce, the Patriots, Bruins, and Red Sox over Stockton and Malone. He chose the possibilities with All-Stars Isaiah Thomas and Al Horford over guys he's fought with in the past like Rudy Gobert and Joe Ingles. But the biggest reason by far? Hayward's relationship with [Brad] Stevens."

Seven years after Utah picked him ninth overall and helped transform him into an All-Star, Hayward turned to the trusted mentor, who'd been a valuable resource in his decision to go pro, to guide him through another tough decision. Fortunately for Boston, Hayward's trusted mentor worked for the Celtics and not the Jazz. "And I guess it's pretty crazy," Hayward wrote. "Because seven years later, I had to make an even tougher decision—and again, Coach Stevens and I found ourselves at a crossroads together. And again, he was the person I knew I could count on the most."

That was a gut punch for the Jazz and their fans. Some people burned No. 20 jerseys and posted videos on social media. Some vented at BBQs, on Facebook and Twitter, and to anyone who'd listen. Some suggested changing the hopeful phrasing of a #stayward billboard campaign to #betrayward. There were some positive reaction, too, as some Jazz fans publicly thanked Hayward for his seven years and for the considerate blog post.

Only time will tell if the grass indeed is greener, a Celtics shade of green, on the other side for Hayward. "We are proud of the player that Gordon developed into with the Jazz and wish him and his family the best of luck," general manager Dennis Lindsey said. "Despite his departure we still have a tremendous coaching staff and very good young core of players in place as we move forward."

37 Visit the Statues

If anybody is unsure how much John Stockton and Karl Malone mean to Utah, they only need to visit the plaza at the intersection of John Stockton Drive and Karl Malone Drive where they'll see larger-than-life bronze statues of John Stockton and Karl Malone.

Stockton is the eight-foot-tall, 800-plus-pound point guard, who's making a one-handed pass similar to the move he made while dishing out an NBA record 15,806 assists. Malone is the imposing and chiseled power forward, who's soaring nearly 18 feet above the ground on his way to the hoop just as he did so many times while becoming the league's second all-time leading scorer with 36,928 points.

Thanks to an investment of about $600,000 by late Jazz owner Larry H. Miller, the contributions of Utah's most legendary duo will always be memorialized on the southeast corner of the arena that used to be home for Stockton and Malone—or the "Statues," as some now fondly call the Hall of Fame players.

Both statues were created by Utah sculptor Brian Challis, who used to be the Millers' neighbor. Stockton's statue was unveiled at a ceremony in March 2005. A year later, Malone's artwork was erected on the same day The Mailman's No. 32 jersey was raised to the Delta Center rafters next to Stockton's No. 12. "This isn't about John or Karl," Stockton said at his statue unveiling. "It's a representation of a time in this franchise's history and the NBA's history. It's really about everybody that came through in those times and the type of effort that was put forth. We had a great run here, led by Jerry [Sloan]."

Challis spent countless hours going through photos of Stockton and Malone and measuring them to find the perfect pose and to obtain precise details—like their posture while passing and shooting, their uniforms creases, their activated muscle structure—to represent their Hall of Fame careers. Both players were deeply touched by the Jazz's gesture and the work done by the sculptor—well, except for a couple of minor details. Stockton joked about his statue, "I think you got the biceps a little too small...they cut me a little short, but that's about all."

The statues are placed within a bronze-and-cement Chinese yin-yang symbol, which Miller described to the *Deseret News* as symbolizing "peace and unity and stuff like that." They went to the NBA Finals with the mountain logo, but both statues bear their likenesses in traditional J-Note jerseys.

Malone loves the fact that people can observe the statues even if they don't have enough money to pay for a game. "The jersey is awesome, the retirement is awesome, but to me, my kids' kids' kids can walk by and say, 'That was my great-great-grandfather right there. That was my great-great-grandpa. That was my grandpa. Or that's my dad,'" Malone said on his special day in March 2006. "And, hell, I can say, 'That's me.'"

Though there were temporary squabbles, Miller wanted Malone to know that his strong feelings for Malone were interminable. "Just so there's no guessing where I'm at," Miller told him at the ceremony, "I love you."

Don't be surprised if a Sloan statue eventually joins Stockton and Malone. "Do you know what these things cost?" Stockton quipped when asked about Sloan getting his own statute. But before he passed away, Miller said he "absolutely" hoped that would happen. The organization just needs Sloan to sign off on the ultimate honor. "It's something that, just as John did at first, Jerry would resist, as far as nature and personality, but he's been pretty special, too," Miller said at Stockton's statue unveiling in March 2005. "[We] might even want to put him on his tractor."

Though Stockton joked about the cost—reportedly between $175,000-$200,000 per statue—he definitely believes Sloan is worth it. "Jerry's been a huge part," Stockton said. "Speaking for myself, none of this happens for me without him. Perfect coach at the perfect time and a great friend, so I think it would be money well spent."

Challis did his own symbolic sculpting while crafting the statues. As chronicled by *The Salt Lake Tribune*, the Murray resident took clay molding he cut from the ball used in Stockton's statue and glued it to Malone's hand. He said, "The way I see it, it's one last Stockton to Malone."

38 The Beginnings in New Orleans

The year 1974 was a big one for Utah basketball fans but not for the reason people at the time thought it would be. During the same year in which the Utah Stars of the American Basketball Association made news by signing the promising and talented Moses Malone out of high school, the NBA awarded an expansion team to the city of New Orleans.

It didn't take too long for these circumstances to intertwine. As it turned out, neither the Utah Stars nor the New Orleans Jazz lasted very long. The plug was pulled on the Stars midway through the 1975–76 season because of financial struggles, and the Jazz left Louisiana after their fifth season in existence several years later for similar reasons.

The future looked bright in NOLA when Fred Rosenfeld and Sam Battistone led a group of nine investors in shelling out $6.15 million to purchase an expansion franchise—the 18th NBA team—on March 7, 1974. The new team hadn't even settled on a nickname before ownership acquired its first player through a trade with the Atlanta Hawks. That player, eventual Hall of Famer Pete Maravich, was a perfect fit for multiple reasons. Not only had he become an adopted son of the Bayou State from his dazzling days at Louisiana State University, but Pistol Pete also played with pizzazz and brought instant credibility and star power to the fledgling franchise.

The team name that was eventually chosen from more than 6,500 submissions—Dukes, Crescents, Pilots, Cajuns, Blues, Deltas, and Knights were among the semifinalists—was also a match made in sports heaven: the New Orleans Jazz. "Jazz is one of those things for which New Orleans is nationally famous and

131

locally proud," Rosenfeld said at the time. "It is a great art form which belongs to New Orleans and its rich history."

This NBA team's management hoped its style of play would reflect the literal definition of jazz, a style of music that's often described as "collective improvisation." The organization also picked colors—even before selecting a name—with a local Mardi Gras flair. When he announced the color scheme, Rosenfeld explained that the choices were symbolic: purple for justice, green for faith, and gold for power. In addition, the team adopted a now iconic logo highlighted by an eighth note and a basketball formed inside the letter J.

Scotty Robertson was hired to be the new franchise's first head coach after he'd coached the Louisiana Tech Bulldogs to a 161–86 record, three Gulf States Conference championships, and two NCAA Tournament showings between 1964–74. The team lost its NBA debut 89–74 at the New York Knicks on October 17, 1974 and didn't put a notch in the win column until edging the Portland Trail Blazers 102–101 in the 12th game of the season on November 10. That rough start doomed Robertson's time with the Jazz. Though a popular Louisiana sports figure, he was fired after New Orleans struggled to a 1–14 start.

Elgin Baylor, who'd had a terrific playing career with the Los Angeles Lakers, coached one game for the Jazz—November 17, 1974—before the franchise chose Butch van Breda Kolff to be their next head coach. Van Breda Kolff had been a longtime coach in the NBA and the ABA, including a stint in which he coached Wilt Chamberlain, Jerry West, and Baylor with the Lakers. Though his Lakers teams went to the NBA Finals in both of his years as their coach—losing to the Boston Celtics each time—he was fired after not putting Chamberlain back into Game 7 after the legendary center checked himself out because of an injury.

The Jazz went 22–44 under van Breda Kolff's direction that first season, ending their inaugural campaign with a 23–59 record. It wasn't until Maravich scored a season-high 47 points on February 8, 1975, that the Jazz won their first road game 106–102, and that win in Atlanta came after starting 0–28 away from the Crescent City. This passage from the February 17, 1975 *Sports Illustrated*, a year and a half into the Jazz's existence, encapsulates what the franchise's rough beginning involved: "So far, the team has had 26 players, two coaches, two arenas, two assistant coaches (Sam Jones and Elgin Baylor, who remain), two presidents, and a partridge in a pear tree."

Unfortunately, the partridge played better defense than most of the Jazz players.

The next season was mostly notable for three things: New Orleans drafted young ABA star Malone, a former Utah Stars player who never actually donned a Jazz uniform because he was traded; the team improved on its previous win total by 15 games, going 38–44; and Maravich continued to shine, averaging 25.9 points, 5.4 assists, and 4.8 rebounds, scoring his 10,000th career point, and earning All-NBA first-team recognition.

The franchise made a seemingly nice acquisition before the 1976–77 season, signing five-time All-Star guard Gail Goodrich to team up with Maravich in the backcourt. That later proved to be a spectacularly bad move when Goodrich's former team, the Lakers, drafted Magic Johnson with the pick they received from New Orleans as compensation for losing a veteran free agent, per NBA rules at the time. The transaction also fizzled that season after Goodrich suffered a torn Achilles tendon injury early on.

A dispute between management and van Breda Kolff led to his dismissal after only 26 games, and Baylor was hired for good this time. The team won Baylor's first game as bench boss—after losing when he was the interim two years earlier—but the Jazz ended up struggling through a 35–47 season after a promising 15–12 start.

Jazz fans, who'd often yell "Showtime!" to encourage Pistol Pete, couldn't get enough of the wildly entertaining Maravich, who set a franchise scoring record that still stands four decades later with 68 points in a 124–107 win at the Superdome against the Knicks. Maravich was the highlight, earning All-Star and All-NBA first-team honors and winning the league's scoring title with an average of 31.1 points.

A knee injury to Maravich proved to be costly to the Jazz in the 1977–78 season. He'd earned another spot on the All-Star team but only played three games after tweaking his knee on January 31, 1978. The Jazz were in the midst of a 10-game winning streak when that injury occurred.

Though Maravich averaged 27 points, his 50 games weren't enough to qualify for another scoring title. Truck Robinson did haul an average of 15.7 boards, including two games with 27 rebounds, to finish as the NBA's top glass crasher. One game above .500 when Maravich was hurt, the Jazz finished 39–43 and missed the playoffs by four games.

The next season was nothing but a sad ending for the Jazz in New Orleans. Maravich again earned All-Star honors, but he never fully recovered from offseason surgery and sat out the final 21 games to rehab the knee. The franchise traded Robinson to the Phoenix Suns after he'd averaged 24.2 points and 13.4 rebounds. And then after going an NBA-worst 26–56, owners Sam Battistone and Larry Hatfield stunned almost everyone by announcing on April 10 that the franchise was relocating to Salt Lake City for the 1979–80 season.

Residents of The Big Easy were especially baffled because the franchise had set numerous attendance records in the enormous Superdome. Even so, Jazz ownership convinced fellow NBA owners to approve the move for financial survival. Scheduling issues with the dome—a popular spot for large conventions—proved to be burdensome, and an 11 percent amusement tax cut into profits. "Being candid, I have to say I would have been very happy to see the franchise remain in New Orleans," then-NBA commissioner

Lawrence O'Brien said at the time. "But because of the league's responsibility to its fans and the parties involved, the NBA decided it would be in the best interest to move the team to Salt Lake City."

New Orleans was included in a pool of cities for future expansion franchises, but the city didn't return to the league until 2002 when the Charlotte Hornets relocated there 13 years after the Jazz left the town on a sour note.

39 Nicknames

When Karl Malone was in college, a Louisiana sportswriter gave him one of the greatest nicknames in the history of basketball: The Mailman. Even at a young age, this power forward delivered—through snow, rain, heat, sleet, and opposing defenses.

Sure, some will sarcastically point out that The Mailman never delivered a championship to his team during his 19-year NBA career. Scottie Pippen playfully—and masterfully—managed to make Malone's popular nickname work against him in the 1997 NBA Finals. With Game 1 tied at 82 and 9.2 seconds remaining, Pippen walked over to Malone at the free-throw line and uttered a now infamous phrase before the Jazz star shot the first of two foul shots. "Just remember," Pippen said. "The Mailman doesn't deliver on Sundays."

The creative trash talking worked. The metaphorical mail was not delivered. Malone missed both tries. Seconds later, Michael Jordan gave the Chicago Bulls a 1–0 series lead by draining a game-winning jumper.

For the vast majority of his career, however, Malone lived up to his nickname—even occasionally on Sundays. This muscular and talented court courier had a penchant for delivering when the Jazz needed him most. It's why he was a first-ballot Hall of Famer.

While The Mailman arguably has the most recognizable nickname in Utah Jazz history, he certainly wasn't the only one who got called something other than his given name. The Jazz have a legacy of players with colorful nicknames.

The Mailman: Frank Layden once joked that Karl Malone needed a new nickname after the first of his 14 All-Star seasons in the NBA. "Karl went from being The Mailman to the Postmaster General," Layden told *The New York Times* in 1988. Like an old stamp, that tongue-in-cheek alternate nickname didn't stick. The original was too good.

Pistol Pete: It's unclear when Pete Maravich was given his nickname and exactly why. "It was either given to him at age 12 by a reporter or when he was in college at LSU," *Sports Illustrated* wrote. "It was either because of his shooting motion (from the hip, like unholstering a pistol) or because of his dead-eye accuracy. But, like all good legends, it makes no difference, as Maravich will always be the supreme talent and showman know simply as Pistol." Decades after his death, the legend lives on. Hip-hop artist Boldly James even included an homage to the Hall of Famer, rapping, "Shooting from the hip—click—quicker than Pistol Pete Maravich."

AK-47: Andrei Kirilenko's rifle-inspired moniker certainly clicks on multiple levels. For one thing, the Russian was born in a city, Izhevsk, in the former Soviet Union where the Kalashnikov assault rifles were created. His initials, his jersey number, his nationality, and the intimidating sound of AK-47 combined to make it a snappy nickname.

The Stifle Tower: He's from France. He towers over the competition. Stifle rhymes with Eiffel. Calling Rudy Gobert "The Stifle Tower" works like crepes with Nutella spread, snails and garlic butter, or baguettes and stinky cheese. Incidentally, Gobert didn't exactly love the nickname that yours truly thought up during his

NBA debut at the 2013 Orlando Pro Summer League. He'd called himself "Gobzilla." That's even what he has on his personalized Utah license plates. (Gobzilla is a fun nickname, but it looks better than it sounds considering Gobert is pronounced with a long "o" like go and not like "aw" in Godzilla.) Others call him The French Rejection, The Gobert Report, or Mont Bloc. Gobert admitted he started liking The Stifle Tower after the Frenchman learned the meaning of the English word stifle: (sti·fle, *verb* 1. make [someone] unable to breathe properly; suffocate; prevent or constrain an activity or idea). The Stifle Tower has been called "the best nickname in

There is no better nickname than AK-47 for Andrei Kirilenko, who scores on a reverse layup against the Memphis Grizzlies in 2002.
(AP Images)

137

the NBA" on ESPN's *SportsCenter*. Bill Simmons proclaimed that Gobert was "Winner of The Best Nickname of the Decade."

Dr. Dunkenstein: Darrell Griffith was a teenager in Louisville, Kentucky, when George Clinton and his funky Parliament band released a single in 1976 that led to a clever nickname for this young high-flying dunker. "George Clinton had a character called Dr. Funkenstein, and it kind of came from that," Griffith told ESPN. "My brother and the homeboys in the neighborhood sort of tagged me with the nickname." Early in his NBA career, Griffith was featured in a classic Dr. Dunkenstein Nike poster wearing a white lab coat and a doctor's head mirror. He was also admiringly called "Golden Griff" by Jazz broadcaster Hot Rod Hundley.

Dinner Bell Mel/The Mealman: Both of these nicknames playfully mocked the weight issues Mel Turpin dealt with during his NBA career. But, sadly, his life ended tragically, when he committed suicide at age 49.

The Trash Man: Adam Keefe wasn't a big stat producer, but the backup big man hustled, did the dirty work not many else wanted to, and helped clean up others' messes—hence his nickname and the reason why he worked his way into Jerry Sloan's rotation on the Jazz's best teams. Keefe didn't mind the moniker. "I have a knack for picking up loose balls," he told the *Los Angeles Times*.

The Fastest of Them All: This might not have been a nickname in the true sense of the word, but Jazz broadcaster Hot Rod Hundley seemed to spout this phrase about the speedy and diminutive Rickey Green every time he said the point guard's name in the 1980s.

The Human Pogo Stick: Jeremy Evans didn't get a lot of court time, and his NBA career didn't last long, but the 6'9" athlete from Western Kentucky had some serious hops. While training at the P3 Sports Science Institute in Santa Barbara, California, in 2014, the forward broke his own record by touching 12'9" in an approach vertical leap drill. That equates to an insane vertical of 44.5". The man, who occasionally got called "Elevator Evans," used his high-soaring abilities to help him win the 2012 Slam Dunk Contest.

Horny: While this nickname for Jeff Hornacek can make one giggle like a teenager, the New York tabloids really had fun with it when the former Jazz player was hired as the head coach of the Knicks in 2015. "Jax [Phil Jackson] gets hot and heavy with HORNACEK," the *Daily News* wrote for its back page subhead. The main headline read: "DO I MAKE YOU HORNY, BABY?" The *New York Post* couldn't resist a sophomoric joke either with "Knicks stunner: Jax zeroes in on ex-Suns coach…PHIL FEELING HORNY."

The Whopper: Billy Paultz will forever remain in Jazz lore because of two things: his awesome nickname and getting punched in the face by Hakeem Olajuwon. Paultz wasn't too fond of his nickname—or, for that matter, getting cold-cocked in a game. Although the moniker seemed fitting due to his massive size— 6'11" and 265 pounds—the enormous Paultz didn't necessarily love being associated with a Burger King menu item.

"I don't know about the [nickname]," Paultz told the *San Antonio Express-News.* "But the way I look at it, if it takes two hands to handle a Whopper, maybe it was all right. I liked the sandwich. There probably was a time or two I ate more than one at a single sitting."

The Milkman: Ty Corbin was teasingly given that humorous Karl Malone-inspired nickname after appearing in a milk mustache commercial while being The Mailman's teammate from 1991 to 1994.

Chocolate Thunder: Darryl Dawkins only had a one-month stint with the Jazz in 1987, but that was long enough to merit a spot on this list because of his unique nickname.

The Big Dawg: Antoine Carr's bark was a big as his bite. And, yes, he'd occasionally do a loud "WOOF!"

Money/Memo: Jazz TV play-by-play broadcaster Craig Bolerjack was fond of exclaiming "Money!" when Mehmet Okur (aka Memo) would hit a three-point shot.

Truck: His given name was Leonard Robinson, but if you got run over by his solid 6'7", 225-pound frame, you'd quickly understand why the former Jazz forward from 1977–79 was called "Truck."

Gentle Ben: Ben Poquette played for the Jazz from 1979 to 1983. He was called "Gentle Ben" by Hot Rod Hundley. Interestingly, hearing that nickname sparked a desire to become a broadcaster in Hundley's eventual replacement, David Locke. "I remember driving home from Jazz games listening to Hot Rod talking about Gentle Ben Poquette and 'The Franchise' Jeff Wilkins and saying to my dad at a very young age that that's what I want to do."

Rodney Hood, Prince of Threes: Jazz shooting guard Rodney Hood can light it up from outside, and this fun nickname—a play on the 1991 movie *Robin Hood: Prince of Thieves*—is reflective of his outside range.

Junkyard Dog: Although DeMarre Carroll isn't the first athlete to go by the Junkyard Dog (see: former NBA forward Jerome Williams or late pro wrestler Sylvester Ritter), he plays with a rough-and-tumble attitude that is worthy of the name. Why does he call himself the Junkyard Dog? "You don't think of no pretty, nice tame dog," Carroll once said. "You think of him being in the junkyard with dirt. You should always play like you have a chip on your shoulder."

Jingles: If this nickname for Joe Ingles doesn't make you smile, it should. Some call him Slow-Mo Joe or Jinglin' Joe, but Jingles is a goofy contraction of the humorous Aussie's name.

Wolfie: Brazilian point guard Raul Neto's first name is pronounced HOW-ool in Portuguese, leading his teammates to give him this funny identity.

Juan Stockton: This wasn't a common household nickname, but it's a fun one that started gaining traction in Spanish point guard Ricky Rubio's first season in Utah.

Not all nicknames are well received. While ex-Jazz player Don Watts went by "Slick," Deron Williams was not amused when Hot Rod Hundley started calling him Slick Willy early in his career. Hundley stopped calling him that upon Williams' request.

Other nicknames worth mentioning: Donovan "Spida" Mitchell; Gordon "G-Time" Hayward (in honor of childhood hero Reggie "Miller Time"); Boris "Bobo" Diaw; Mel "Goose" Counts; Theodore "Blue" Edwards; Louie "Sweets" Nelson; Mike "Brown Bear" Brown; and Enes "The UnderKanter" Kanter, whose favorite wrestler was The Undertaker.

40 Phil Johnson

Nine months after shocking the sports world by resigning together during the 2010–11 season, Jerry Sloan and Phil Johnson returned to the arena for the first time to be inducted into the Utah Sports Hall of Fame. Johnson voiced his concern about the arrangement of a photo shoot. The longtime Jazz assistant was on one end, Natalie Williams (basketball) and Annette Ausseresses (softball) were in the middle, and ex-NFL referee Doug Toole was next to the other bookend, Sloan. "I hate to see him stand that close to an official," Johnson joked.

Sloan and Johnson were close, having shared the Jazz bench together from December 11, 1988 through February 10, 2011. Sloan deservedly earned a spot in the Naismith Basketball Hall of Fame for his role as head coach, but Johnson was at his side for almost all of the 1,223 wins he compiled in the regular season and playoffs. Sloan is quick to credit his faithful right-hand man—a guy who used to coach him, by the way—for helping him help the Jazz succeed. "I was just thrilled to death to be able to have him with me all the time that I coached," he said.

Johnson received many coaching awards throughout his career, which included stints as an assistant coach at Utah State and Weber State in college, as an assistant in the NBA with the Chicago Bulls (twice) and Jazz (twice), and as a head coach for Weber State and the Kings (twice). Johnson was named Big Sky Coach of the Year for the three seasons he coached Weber State, where he got his first head coaching job at age 27 in 1968 and compiled a 68–16 record with three NCAA Tournament appearances. After spending two seasons as the assistant to his junior high, high school, and college coach, Dick Motta, with the Bulls—where he first met Sloan—Johnson was hired as head coach of the Kansas City-Omaha Kings at the age of 32 after the team fired coach Bob Cousy. He was named 1975 NBA Coach of the Year the following season after leading the Kings to the playoffs and a 44–38 record. A couple of jobs and many years later, Johnson was voted as the NBA's top assistant coach four different times for the work he did with Sloan and the Jazz.

The humble Johnson was so valuable behind the scenes and on the bench with the Jazz that Karl Malone, John Stockton, and Larry H. Miller pleaded with him to stay in Utah whenever an NBA head coaching opportunity would arise. He was flattered and told them he would stay, something Miller said he'd always remember. Johnson humorously admitted, "I probably wouldn't have gone anyway."

Sloan hired Johnson, who's six months older, as his assistant coach shortly after taking over for Frank Layden in Utah in 1988. When he left the Jazz after his first stint to coach the Kings for a second time, Johnson had actually recommended that the Jazz hire Sloan to replace him. With similar old-school approaches to basketball and small-town farming backgrounds—Johnson is from Grace, Idaho, and Sloan is from McLeansboro, Illinois—the hardworking pair didn't leave each other's sides (during the season, at least) once Sloan asked Johnson to join his staff in Utah until they fittingly called it quits together in 2011.

Sloan was caught off guard when Johnson said he was leaving with him instead of staying around to take a head coaching job with the Jazz that had long been promised would be his when the Hall of Famer left or retired. "I came with you, I'll leave with you," Johnson said at their resignation press conference. "We haven't really talked about it, but I've thought about it a long time."

Sloan remains the third winningest coach in NBA history, but Johnson has often joked that he finished more games because his boss occasionally earned an early shower after using salty words in run-ins with officials. That's a fun memory for Sloan, who readily admits, "He won a lot of games after I was in the locker room."

There was the time Sloan was tossed when the Jazz were trailing the Los Angeles Clippers by 15 points. As he left the court, Sloan looked at Johnson and sarcastically said, "Win this one." The Jazz lost that one. "I didn't give him much of a rope," Sloan joked. "I didn't want him to get too cocky."

41 Retiring No. 1,223

The joke leading up to a January 31, 2014, ceremony commemorating Jerry Sloan's Utah Jazz career was that his banner would include an image of a tractor or a John Deere logo. The organization instead chose to have four numbers embroidered on the white rectangle cloth underneath the legendary coach's name: 1–2–2–3.

That's how many games Sloan's teams won in the regular season and playoffs from the day he took over as head coach for Frank Layden on December 9, 1988, through his even more surprising midseason exit on February 10, 2011. Remarkably, he coached Utah teams in a total of 1,809 games. "This banner," Jazz president Randy Rigby said, "will serve as a symbol of the enduring legacy of Jerry Sloan, one of the greatest coaches in NBA history and forever a member of the Jazz family."

Many Jazz fans hope Sloan will get his own statue eventually, too. Sloan, who could be as witty as he was gruff, jokingly explained his interpretation of the significance of 1,223 during a pregame press conference that night—from a dais, not from the gray garbage can he routinely stood next to and leaned on for years while addressing media. "I thought," he said, "that's how many technical fouls I had."

The man who took the coaching baton from Sloan—and who'd worked under him as a player and as an assistant—was baffled at Sloan's number of wins. Tyrone Corbin had won 102 games as the Jazz's head coach after being named as Sloan's successor at that point. He knew how demanding of a job it was after just two years, let alone 23-plus. "It's a lot of work, man," Corbin said. "It's a great accomplishment for him."

During his coaching career in Utah, Sloan guided the Jazz to the playoffs 19 times, racked up 13 50-win seasons, won seven division titles, and made it to two NBA Finals (1997, 1998). He finished his coaching career with the third most regular-season wins in NBA history, going 1,221–803 with the Jazz (1988–2011) and Chicago Bulls (1979–82).

More than that, Sloan was a father figure to many players. Though he ranted, raved, and cursed at them like a sailor at times, he pushed them to if not past their limits and cared more for the person than the player. That's why guys like John Stockton, Karl Malone, Mark Eaton, John Crotty, Mehmet Okur, Bryon Russell,

A Letter from the President

As part of the celebration for Jerry Sloan's banner-raising ceremony, the world's most powerful Chicago sports fan sent a handwritten letter to "The Original Bull" on stationery from the White House.

```
Dear Coach—
    Congratulations on your long and remarkable
    career with the Jazz. Utah justly honors you
    for the standards of excellence you set with
    The Mailman and Stockton. But, us Bulls fans
    still claim you for your grit and work ethic.

    Best of luck in the future. With great
    admiration,
                                    Barack Obama
```

Howard Eisley, and Thurl Bailey gathered in his honor in their old opponent-stomping grounds. "It's like a father-son relationship. It's like a big brother relationship. It's like a friends relationship," Stockton said. "I don't know if you get to go through life with many of those opportunities to have that and I have it right there with one man."

It took the Jazz organization a while to finally convince Sloan to allow them to honor him. He kept a low profile for a year or two after stepping down in 2011, eventually attending games with his second wife, Tammy, and then accepting a role as a senior adviser. You can take the coach out of the Jazz, but you can't take the Jazz out of the coach. This gathering was a sweet reminder of better days, of challenges endured. "It gives us a chance to get together for one—but also to say some of the things that we feel, the heartfelt things that we feel," Stockton said. "I'm a very fortunate man. Jerry, I can't thank you enough."

Sloan thanked everybody he could think of almost every time he spoke into the microphone, whether on the dais or on the court addressing the appreciative crowd. He thanked his trusty coaching partner Phil Johnson, his former boss Frank Layden (who hired him as a scout in 1983), his old coach and Utah native Dick Motta, his former assistants, his former players, the Miller family, and Jazz fans. Reminiscent of Lou Gehrig, Sloan, whose health was also starting to show slight signs of deterioration, told the sellout crowd, "I think I'm the most blessed coach in basketball."

It was a night filled with smiling at friends and heroes, cheering, booing referees, enjoying exciting moments on the court, and Hall of Fame players. The arena felt like the Delta Center again. Fitting that another name from that era was raised to the rafters to join Stockton, Malone, Eaton, Pete Maravich, Darrell Griffith, Jeff Hornacek, Larry H. Miller, Hot Rod Hundley, and Adrian Dantley, Sloan was touched. "It's a real honor to be just mentioned in the same breath with all of those guys," he said.

Throughout the game against the Golden State Warriors, prerecorded congratulatory wishes were shared from coaches Gregg Popovich, Doc Rivers, Rick Adelman, and Lenny Wilkens and by former (friendly) foes Shaquille O'Neal and Charles Barkley, Sloan's handpicked Hall of Fame presenter. Barkley didn't miss a chance to take a dig at Malone, a good friend, saying to Sloan, "My only regret is: you know how good you would've been if you'd only had a real power forward like me?"

The crowd, including Malone, roared in laughter.

Earlier in the day, The Mailman shared a message about how Sloan was instrumental in keeping his drive alive throughout a 19-year career: "I didn't want to disappoint you. I really didn't." Malone didn't always deliver results, but the effort was always there. Sloan wasn't disappointed. He also loved what Stockton brought to the court every night. "I thought I was a great coach until we lost these guys," Sloan joked. "I had the opportunity to coach two guys that's willing to pay the price of being good every day."

Supporters wore John Deere hats at a private luncheon earlier in the day, a letter from President Obama was shared, and miniature replicas of Sloan's immortalized 1,223 banner were handed out to fans. "Maybe we'll start a new trend," Corbin said, regarding that unique banner number. "Maybe we should go to four-number jerseys now."

42 Triple OT Thriller

Although he was a talented offensive player and averaged 18.5 points over three and a half seasons in Utah, Jeff Malone is probably remembered most for two things. First, he was "The Other Malone" on the team. Second, he was "The Other Player" in the trade that netted "The Other Jeff" (Hornacek) for Utah.

This Malone, though, played a key role in one of the most memorable regular-season victories, which took place in 1992, in franchise history. After receiving an inbound pass with 4.9 seconds remaining, Malone rushed downcourt and tried to shake Michael Jordan. Malone drove to MJ's right and then hurried to release a shot before the buzzer. His Airness reached in and got called for a foul with 0.5 seconds left. Malone was awarded a pair of free throws. The Jazz guard got a third freebie after Jordan was assessed a technical foul and ejected for bumping referee Tommie Wood while disputing the call.

Malone had missed 17 of his 21 shots on the night and whiffed on a six-foot game-winning attempt after Jordan's tying three-pointer at the end of the first overtime, but all was forgiven after hitting those game-winning free throws to prevent a fourth OT. The free throws overcame a 15-foot tying jumper Jordan hit with 5.6 seconds left.

Jordan had beaten the Jazz the year before with a game-winning shot in the Salt Palace during a stretch of good-'til-the-last-horn matchups between these two teams, whose paths would eventually lead to two NBA Finals showdowns. That made this win even sweeter for Utah. "He hit a big shot that beat us last year," Jazz coach Jerry Sloan said, "and it looked like he was going to do it again."

Both teams ended this game without some of their stars. John Stockton and Scottie Pippen fouled out before Jordan was invited to hit the showers early. As described in Jazz beat writer Brad Rock's *Deseret News* article, "After the game, the Bulls left the Delta Center in a world championship pout, refusing to comment to reporters. The loss was their third in the past five games.

Chicago coach Phil Jackson didn't pull the punches on his thoughts about the call on Jordan when Malone got the ball at the top of the key and drove to attempt a runner. Jordan tried to strip the ball, and the ref deemed he made too much contact. "That's a ridiculous call," Jackson said. "On a desperate run like that, you just don't do that."

The Jazz weren't about to complain that a foul went against Jordan. "I felt comfortable," said Malone, who was mystified why his shot was off so bad overall. "Once Michael got the technical, I said, 'Hey, I've got three shots.' I wasn't going to blow all of those."

The Bulls would have needed a miracle shot to force quadruple overtime, but they didn't get a chance because Will Perdue stepped out of bounds as time expired. Jordan scored 34 points but only made 13-of-34 field goals; Pippen (26 points, 13 rebounds) and Horace Grant (20 points, 13 rebounds) each contributed double-doubles. Karl Malone had a big night with 34 points and 21 rebounds, and Stockton amassed 19 points, 12 rebounds, and even blocked one of Jordan's shots. "It was a great ballgame to play in," Karl Malone said.

Jazz center Mark Eaton told reporters he'd never seen anything quite like this slugfest in his 777 previous NBA games. "It was a wild one," Eaton said. "We kept coming back and coming back and coming back, and we finally outlasted 'em."

43 Carlos Boozer

Carlos Boozer's arrival in Utah was clouded with controversy and accusations. Or was that his exit? Both actually. Those associated with Boozer's first NBA team, the Cleveland Cavaliers, believe the young power forward bamboozled the Cavaliers into getting out of his rookie contract after excelling there for two seasons. As the story goes, Boozer, taken in the second round of the 2002 draft, was set to earn $700,000 in 2004–05, which would have been a steal of a deal considering the trajectory of his career after he'd averaged 15.5 points and 11.4 rebounds the previous season. Reports claimed the 22-year-old from Alaska made a gentleman's agreement with Cleveland—even to the point of shaking hands with general manager Jim Paxson. The Cavs would decline their team option, allowing him to become a restricted free agent and then sign the Duke product for $41 million over six years.

Instead, the Jazz offered Boozer $27 million more than the Cavs in a six-year, $68-million contract that Cleveland was unable to match. "In the final analysis, I decided to trust Carlos and show him the respect he asked for," Gordon Gund wrote in a letter on the Cavs' website. "He did not show that trust and respect in return."

Boozer, a 2001 NCAA champion whom the Jazz were interested in but couldn't draft after trading for Stanford seven-footer Curtis Bortchardt, denied those allegations and pointed out that it would have been against NBA rules per the collective bargaining agreement for him to do a hush-hush deal. "There was no commitment, no handshake," Boozer told reporters after signing with the Jazz. "I'm a man of my word, and the only commitment I gave was to Utah and I kept that commitment."

Boozer's six years with the Jazz were a mixed bag. When it was good, it was really good—not quite Karl Malone good, but pretty darn good nonetheless. In 2006–07 Boozer was named to his first All-Star team—he didn't participate because of an injury—and then teamed with Deron Williams and Mehmet Okur to lift the Jazz to 51 wins and a surprising run to the Western Conference Finals. Boozer's Game 7 performance—35 points, 14 rebounds—against the Houston Rockets was one of the best individual outings in Jazz playoff history. The powerful athlete with a keen ability to use both hands around the rim was a threat inside and from mid-range. He averaged 20.9 points and 11.7 rebounds that season.

Boozer was as lethal the following season, leading the Jazz to an even better regular season—54–28 record—and a second-straight Northwest Division title while earning All-Star and third-team All-NBA honors while averaging a career-high 21.1 points and 10.4 rebounds. Though Utah advanced to the second round in 2008, where they fell to the Los Angeles Lakers, Boozer only shot 41 percent and averaged just 16 points in 12 playoff games that spring.

Boozer's defense was always considered a liability, and his commitment was questioned at times when he sat out for extended periods with injuries in three different seasons. Spoiled by Malone's durability, then-owner Larry H. Miller publicly questioned him after the Jazz went 26–56 while he missed the final 31 games of the 2004–05 season with a foot injury. "Carlos has been terrific some nights," Miller said. "Some nights he acted like he didn't care that much, and I like Carlos a lot. He's here because we need a big presence at the power forward, and I just hope he will be playing the way he ought to [for] 82 games."

Boozer also drew the ire of management and fans through statements he made. While injured toward the end of his time in Utah, he told an ESPN reporter who'd questioned him about whether he'd opt in or not, "I'm going to get a raise regardless. I don't see why I wouldn't." He didn't. Boozer did, however, ask to be traded. He wasn't. He also told a Miami radio station in the summer of 2009 that he would not be playing for Utah the following season. That led to an awkward reunion that fall when, sure enough, he was still on the Jazz. "I didn't know I was going to be here throughout the course of the summer," he said. "But I'm excited to be here."

Boozer and the Jazz functioned well together in 2009–10, but he again received heavy criticism when he sat out the final game of the regular season because of an oblique strain. Utah dropped that home game to the Phoenix Suns and lost home-court advantage. Even so, Boozer and the Jazz won the first round series against the Denver Nuggets—despite Mehmet Okur suffering a nasty Achilles injury—but he struggled in a second-round loss to the Lakers. As KSL-TV sportscaster Jeremiah Jensen aptly described it in a recap of Boozer's time in Utah, "The playoffs played out much like his time with the Jazz—up and down."

Boozer did give the Jazz a parting gift the following offseason by allowing the team to do a sign-and-trade with Chicago instead of signing flat-out with the Bulls. Utah, which had Paul Millsap in the wings raring to take Boozer's position, then used the large trade exception it received to sign Al Jefferson.

Boozer was all smiles and compliments the next time he visited Utah, even though by this time many Jazz fans were as upset with him as Cavs fans had been six years earlier. Asked if it would bother him to be booed upon his return to Utah, Boozer chuckled. "It's all booozzz to me." Regardless of what fans rained down on him, Boozer always will be known for yelling "And one!" after shooting—whether fouled or not.

Boozer was on two U.S. Olympics teams while a Jazz player, winning a bronze medal on the underachieving 2004 team and earning gold with Team USA in 2008.

Like his time with the Jazz, Boozer's relationship with the Chicago Bulls also waned. He was released via the amnesty clause with a year left on his contract. The Lakers picked him up for one season, and then he finished off his pro basketball career in China before retiring on December 18, 2017.

44 Mehmet Okur

Mehmet Okur had played six solid seasons for the Utah Jazz and was providing valuable mentoring services while working his way back from an ugly Achilles injury when general manager Kevin O'Connor did what he called "a lousy thing" to the longtime fan favorite. On December 22, 2011, the Jazz traded Okur to the New Jersey Nets for a second-round pick and a trade exception worth the $10.8 million remaining on his contract. This was a Memo many Jazz fans hoped would never be sent off.

Exiled ex-Utah player Deron Williams was thrilled about the reunion. He tweeted, "Glad to be playing with my boy Memo again!" But Okur and everybody associated with the Jazz felt sick about it. "There's a human part to this that doesn't feel very good," O'Connor admitted. "You've got to look at it from what's best for the Jazz."

Okur was popular in Utah—and still is—for a variety of reasons: his exceptional long-distance range for a 6'11" center, affable personality, charming broken English, and friendly smiles. He was Utah's "Money Man," as broadcaster Craig Bolerjack fondly called him. It had been hard on the franchise and fanbase to witness Okur tear his Achilles tendon in the 2010 playoffs against the Denver Nuggets.

Then, before he ever got back to full strength, he was gone. Okur never fully recovered from that injury and admitted to returning too soon the following year, leading to further complications.

Okur was stunned and saddened after receiving a call from then-CEO Greg Miller about being traded. He thought he'd end his career in Utah. But the Jazz opted to make a business move, something they could afford to do with a bundle of bigs, including Al Jefferson, Paul Millsap, Derrick Favors, and Enes Kanter. Miller

Mehmet Okur pumps his fist after nailing a three-pointer against the Phoenix Suns in 2010. (AP Images)

tried to soften the blow by telling the seven-year Jazzman that they "appreciate everything he did" from hitting game-winners and timely three-pointers to mentoring Kanter, a fellow Turkish native, to playing through injuries and giving "everything he had" since signing as a free agent in 2004. The 27-year-old had played a key role in helping the Jazz advance to the Western Conference Finals in 2007—the same year he was named an All-Star reserve—and in returning to relevance in the post-Stockton-to-Malone era. "To be honest, I was in shock," Okur said a couple of weeks later. "I never got traded before in my life, so I didn't know the feeling."

That interview took place a day before Okur and Williams were set to visit Utah for the first time since they were traded to New Jersey 10 months apart. With all sincerity Okur was worried how he'd be treated by Jazz fans in his return. "Hopefully they won't boo me," he said.

Some blamed Williams for Hall of Fame coach Jerry Sloan's sudden resignation from coaching, so the point guard knew he would receive jeers after what had happened the previous season. Not knowing whether the All-Star would re-sign the following year as a free agent, Utah took a pre-emptive gamble and traded him to ensure a return on that investment. But he shook his head when informed of Okur's concern. "Memo won't get booed," Williams said, grinning. "He didn't run the coach out like I did."

Sure enough, Jazz fans treated Williams like a vile intruder the following night, and the Utah faithful greeted Okur with a hero's welcome. "A lot of good memories, seven years," Memo said. "That system and the players and the coaching staff made me All-Star, better player. And the fans, obviously they've always been there for us and for me."

That proved to be the final season in a career that began a decade earlier with the Detroit Pistons, where Okur won an NBA championship in 2004 before moving on to Utah after two seasons. He teamed up nicely with power forward Carlos Boozer, opening up the interior while luring bigger defenders to the perimeter to chase him. He averaged 15.3 points and connected on 517 "Money" shots from three-point range. Boozer benefited, too.

During a Jazz radio interview, Okur told a story about the first time he met Jerry Sloan. His new coach looked at him as they were headed to Boise, Idaho, for the 2004–05 training camp and asked, "Hey, son, are you in shape?" Okur said he thought he was. He had been playing with the Turkish national team that summer. After his first Jazz practice, Okur learned there were different levels of fitness. He told Sloan, "Coach, I'm not in shape." From then on, Okur made certain to come to camp in "Jerry Sloan shape."

In 2014 the Jazz welcomed Okur back into the fold by appointing him a team ambassador. His job was to work with players, sponsors, and fans; help with alumni, community, and fan-relations efforts; assist in business development; and perhaps advise basketball operations. Okur took a step toward a coaching career in 2017, joining the staff of the Phoenix Suns coach and former Jazz teammate Earl Watson before they were let go.

Showing he still has a sense of humor and an affinity for the Jazz, Okur humorously participated in a Twitter poll created in January 2018 for this book project. Jazz fans were asked to name their favorite moments and players—not counting Stockton and Malone—and to list favorite social media interaction by Utah players. Okur's responses: "1. SAS [San Antonio Spurs] Last-second put back (memo); 2. mehmet okur (money man); 3. I didn't have social media at the time."

45 Rickey Green

If you want a surefire way to impress friends at a party, memorizing a few fun facts about Rickey Green will surely do the trick.

- The point guard scored the five millionth point in NBA history. That trivia-worthy basket was worth remembering, too. The three-pointer—from 24 feet out—happened as time expired in the third quarter of game against the Cleveland Cavaliers on January 25, 1988.
- After retiring from the NBA, Green worked as the assistant recreation director of the Cook County Forest Preserve for more than a decade. He also had his own landscaping and snow removal service in Chicago.
- The former University of Michigan star played for the Honolulu/Billings Volcanos in the CBA in 1979–80 while trying to work his way back into the NBA after struggling early in his pro career with the Golden State Warriors, who drafted him 16th overall in 1977, and the Detroit Pistons. His coach for the latter was Dick Vitale, baby!
- The six-foot guard became the first former CBA player to earn NBA All-Star honors (1984).
- "The Fastest of Them All," as Hot Rod Hundley used to call him, started ahead of John Stockton for the first three seasons of the future Hall of Famer's career.
- The Lime Rickey drink was named after him.

Okay, that last tidbit was a made-up fact to make sure you're paying attention. The rest is true. Thank me later for that info after you're heralded for being the life of the next social gathering you attend.

Green was picked up by the Jazz early in the 1980 season, along with center Jeff Wilkins, after his short stint in the CBA. The playmaker with elite quickness, who excelled at Michigan, became an integral part of the franchise's ascension into a perennial playoff team. Green's career really took off after Frank Layden took over for Tom Nissalke, a former NBA and ABA Coach of the Year who was fired early in his third season with the Jazz.

Years later, Green told the *Chicago Tribune* he remembered the exact moment when the Jazz turned the franchise around. The team, floundering in an 18-game losing streak, was getting ready to play the Kansas City Kings when Layden, then the general manager, entered the locker room and shared some news. Nissalke, the Jazz's first coach in Salt Lake City, had been fired. Layden was taking over as head coach while remaining general manager. "The next thing he tells us is that for that particular game we weren't going to run any plays," Green told the *Tribune*, laughing. "The plan was to just go out there and run and gun and have some fun."

Green had been chatting with Darrell Griffith when Layden informed them of the development and his enticing strategic plan. He said, "I looked at 'Griff' and told him this new system sounded good to me."

The good-natured Layden jokingly reminded the Chicago paper that this was the same Green who later questioned if he'd ever coached a game prior to his taking over the team. Jokes—and occasional player questioning—aside, Green, Layden, and the Jazz had a nice run after that.

Green averaged 14.8 points and 7.8 assists in the 1981–82 season, and, though Utah struggled to a 25–57 record, a solid foundation was in place. The Jazz won five more games the following season and then—sparked by Green's point guard play—enjoyed a breakthrough season the following year. In 1983–84—arguably the most important season in the Jazz's Utah history—Green and talented scorer Adrian Dantley both made the All-Star team en route to leading the franchise to a best-ever 45–37 record, a first Midwest Division championship, and its playoff debut (a second-round showing, no less). Layden earned Coach of the Year and Executive of the Year honors to boot.

Layden cherishes the memory of informing Green, whose NBA career got off to a rocky start, that he'd been named an All-Star. He went to Green's hotel room to inform him that he had some news to share. "The first thing he said was, 'Have I been traded?'" Layden said. "When I told him he made the All-Star team, you could see the tears in his eyes."

Green continued to play an important role with the Jazz even after the franchise drafted John Stockton, the guy who would eventually replace him and become a Hall of Famer. "I remember Rickey coming to me one day after practice during Stockton's rookie season and telling me, 'Coach, John Stockton, he's got it. He's going to be a star,'" Layden said. "Rickey was really the first person to pick that up."

Green held onto the starting position for three years after Stockton was drafted out of Gonzaga, giving the Jazz quite the 1–2 punch at point guard until the Charlotte Hornets snagged Green in the 1988 expansion draft. "I know my first years sitting on the bench, largely behind Rickey Green, was a great learning tool for me," Stockton said. "[I] would recommend that for young guards, especially if teams can manage to do it, to sit some of these highly valued guys coming out, give them a chance to see how the team works without being stuck in the fray."

If Layden had his way, Green's No. 14 jersey would have been retired by the Jazz before Jeff Hornacek ever had a chance to wear it. "People don't realize what a great player Rickey really was and the impact he had," Layden said. "I believed in playing with a lot of big guys—players like Mark Eaton, Karl Malone, Rich Kelley, and Billy Paultz. But it's like having a great offensive line in football without a quarterback. Rickey became my quarterback."

46 Sundiata Gaines

Some eyebrows were raised when the Utah Jazz signed Sundiata Gaines to a 10-day contract in January 2010. For the first time in a long time, beloved veteran Matt Harpring was not the Jazz player wearing No. 15. The injured small forward had recently been traded to the Oklahoma City Thunder, and Gaines enthusiastically snatched up his old jersey number when the Jazz gave the 23-year-old a chance out of the D-League.

Gaines, who'd been called up from the Idaho Stampede of the D-League, was happy to simply have a number in the world's best league. "This is a dream come true right here, so I'm excited about it," the University of Georgia product said. "I hope the fans accept me. I'm just going to do whatever it takes and try to win everybody over."

Only a week later, Gaines won Jazz fans over for a lifetime. In one of the most memorable moments in Utah sports history, Gaines stole the spotlight from LeBron James by hitting a game-winning, buzzer-beating, three-point shot while filling in for injured All-Star point guard Deron Williams during a game televised on TNT on January 14, 2010.

With Williams in the locker room and time running out in regulation, Jazz guard Ronnie Price dished a pass to Gaines after the NBA newcomer had subbed into the game. Kyle Korver was double-teamed, and Price was being hounded, so he twisted toward Gaines and threw it to him. The feisty guard, who said he'd envisioned the play moments earlier on the bench, didn't flinch. The 6'1" Gaines, who was simply told to go to the corner as Jerry Sloan drew up the play, calmly lined up the deep shot, let it fly from the right elbow over 6'6" Anthony Parker, and ended up on his backside for the best basketball view of his life.

Buzzer. Swish. Chaos!

Seconds later, the Jazz's secret weapon was celebrating the spine-tingling moment—and his first NBA three-pointer—atop the scorers' table while fans went berserk in celebration. "It was big. It was real big," Price said. "You never know what's going to happen in a basketball game. That's the best thing about sports: you just never know what the outcome's going to be, and that was one of those crazy, crazy endings."

The moment even evoked strong emotions from a grizzled old veteran coach like Sloan. "I haven't been this excited in a long time. I was so excited I found myself trying to jump," Sloan said. A few days later, the Hall of Fame coach added, "I was thrilled to death. That's a once-in-a-lifetime thing for just about anybody."

The Jazz needed all the help they could get in that 97–96 win at EnergySolutions Arena after Williams re-injured his wrist early in the fourth quarter. Enter Gaines, who capped a 15–0 run with a three-point play earlier in the second half as Utah rallied back into contention.

The Cleveland Cavaliers kept the Jazz's hopes alive by missing three of six free throws in the final 22.2 seconds. Gaines, who went undrafted out of Georgia in 2008 and began his pro career in Italy with NGC Cantu, made the Cavs pay. "That [shot] was unbelievable, man. We tried to have a play that went to the hole, and they did a great job of cutting everything off," Jazz power forward Carlos Boozer said. "Yada got the ball in a tough position…and he made a hell of a shot. This place is pandemonium right now. Unbelievable, unbelievable game."

It was especially crazy, considering Gaines had been toiling away in the D-League a week and a half before making a name for himself on national TV. A week earlier, he had the pleasure of telling his parents that he'd gotten a short-term NBA deal, an announcement that he said brought his mom "almost down into tears." Imagine her emotions after watching—and undoubtedly re-watching—his game-winner against LeBron & Co. "Nothing's going to compare to this—beating the Cavs, especially LeBron," the spunky Gaines said. "I liked seeing his face. I didn't like the face he made after he hit that [go-ahead] three."

After averaging 4.2 points, 1.4 assists, and 0.2 game-winning shots in five games, Gaines was given a second 10-day contract. *Of course he was.* "We were laughing and joking, that's how you get a second 10-day," Jazz guard Ronnie Brewer said. "That's how you stay on the team. Man, he played really big for us."

Gaines finished the season with Utah, but he was waived before the beginning of the 2010–11 campaign. After signing 10-day contracts with the Minnesota Timberwolves, Toronto Raptors, and New Jersey Nets, Gaines finally landed a multi-year deal with the Nets on March 20, 2011. Alas, he suffered a season-ending hip fracture three days later. He played for the Nets again the following season but has bounced around across seas and in the D-League since then.

Gaines was signed by the Jazz again in 2016, but this time it was to play for their new D-League affiliate, the SLC Stars. The 30-year-old spurned bigger financial offers to play elsewhere to return to the state where he'd once pulled the throne out from under a king.

When asked the attraction for returning to Salt Lake City, Gaines told *The Salt Lake Tribune*, "Just being in Utah…That's where my heart is at and what my gut is telling me to do, so I'm here."

The connection with Jazz fans remains strong. They'll always remember that magical moment. "I hear about it all the time," Gaines told *The Tribune*.

47 Griffith Goes Wild

There are incredible comebacks, and then there are ones that defy logic and hyperbolic descriptions. What the Utah Jazz accomplished against the Dallas Mavericks on November 12, 1986, falls into the latter category. When Dallas took a 101–94 lead with 28 seconds on a Rolando Blackman bucket, it appeared as if the proverbial refrigerator door was about to close on this game, as Hot Rod Hundley used to say.

The rally began with a Karl Malone dunk with 20 seconds left, and then Darrell Griffith cut the gap to two with a three-pointer with seven seconds remaining. Blackman appeared to ice the win for Dallas, though, when he sank two free throws for a 103–99 lead. Even after Bobby Hansen quickly scored for Utah, things still looked bleak for the Jazz with three seconds left and the Mavs up by two. This never-say-die group, however, had one final surprise. Rickey Green leaped up to steal a long inbound pass at midcourt with his left hand and in one motion brought the ball to his chest, switched hands, and tossed the ball to Griffith while falling out of bounds.

The Golden Griff, who was the league's all-time leading three-point shooter at the time, caught the pass from Green, squared up to the basket, and unleashed a long shot from the left elbow. The high-arching bomb from 33 feet out—and seemingly that high up in the air—splashed through the nets at the buzzer. Final score: Utah Jazz 104, Dallas Mavericks 103.

Jazz teammates excitedly catapulted off the bench and raced on the court and fans jumped up and down in the Salt Palace stands as Hundley celebrated on air with those who hadn't tuned out when the game seemed out of reach for the home team. "He got it! He got it! Incredible! The Jazz win the game! I can't believe it!" Hundley joyfully exclaimed on the broadcast. "The Jazz win the game! I can't believe it! Unbelievable! The most fantastic finish I have ever seen in my life!"

Jazz coach Frank Layden couldn't believe that his team outscored Dallas 10–2 in the final 20 seconds to win this thriller. "This was the greatest comeback victory I've ever been associated with," Layden said. "We may have come back from a bigger deficit to win but not this kind of a comeback in such a short time."

More than three decades later, the comeback still stands the test of time. But one Utah native was not amused by seeing the Mavericks' seemingly safe lead devolve into a loss in less than 30 seconds. Dallas coach Dick Motta, who was born in Midvale, Utah, and who attended Utah State, was disgusted by his players' performance down the stretch of what should have been a nice road win. "I've seen a lot of dumb things in my life but none this dumb," Motta said. "We had control of the game and we let it get away. I coached hard those last 24 seconds, but sometimes people don't listen."

Coincidentally, there happened to be another huge comeback in the NBA that same night. The Philadelphia 76ers trailed the Seattle SuperSonics 87–60 with 7:07 remaining in the third quarter, but the visiting Sixers ended up winning 121–114 after impressively erasing that 27-point deficit.

48 Gather at the J-Note

Of all the things the Utah Jazz freshened up or installed during their $125 million arena renovation in 2016 and '17, one addition in front of the beautiful new main entrance of Vivint Smart Home Arena definitely gets passersby to pay attention—or take note.

Before opening the doors of the refurbished building to the public on September 26, 2017, Jazz owner Gail Miller and other team dignitaries unveiled the project's most notable *piece de resistance*—a 14-foot-high and 21-foot-wide J-Note statue, a popular logo design that merges a basketball and a musical note. Banners on each side of the spacious arena entryway between the navy blue, green, and gold hoops edifice and the 12,000-square foot atrium spell out T-A-K-E N-O-T-E. This clever play on words has become a popular mantra, and the organization encourages fans to use the #takenote hashtag on social media when posting about the Jazz.

Similar to the John Stockton and Karl Malone statues on the corner of the city streets named after them—the intersection of 100 South and 300 West—the J-Note is the focal point of the plaza's northeastern corner. It sits a couple hundred yards to the north of the statues on the corner of South Temple and 300 West near the TRAX train stop. On the day of the unveiling, Jazz president Steve Starks said, "This new J-Note will become one of the iconic photo opportunities along the Wasatch Front."

Sure enough, as soon as the black cloth was pulled off during an afternoon ceremony for the arena's grand opening, the J-Note instantly became a spot for fans to gather and—as we do in this day and age—take selfies. The Jazz even had employees stationed by the photo-op spot to help take pictures before games.

Although eye-catching during the day, the structure really shines at night. The 20-inch thick J-Note, mounted on a round 15-inch tall white concrete base, is illuminated with LED lighting that beams from white lines on the ball and note. Flashy video boards on the arena add extra visual appeal in the background, creating a stunning scene to welcome and beckon fans to enter and enjoy the excitement inside.

The J-Note was an integral part of the team's logo from the inception of the franchise in 1974 until the Jazz changed the font and added mountains to more accurately reflect the organization's current location in 1996. As NBA teams paid homage to their roots and retro looks became popular in the early 2000s, fans became more vocal about bringing back the J-Note. That officially happened during the 2010 offseason when the Jazz unveiled an updated version of their classic look—and subbed navy for purple—as a secondary logo. "The music note is great. It unites our past and future," Deron Williams said at the time. "We have a lot of history here and bringing back the Jazz note unites us even more."

49 Cruise Down John Stockton and Karl Malone Drive

During the retirement ceremony that he only agreed to attend after being double-teamed by his wife Nada and Utah Jazz owner Larry H. Miller, John Stockton was informed that a stretch of the road in front of the Delta Center was going to be named after him. Then-Salt Lake County mayor Nancy Workman presented the Hall of Fame point guard with a replica of the street sign: John Stockton Drive.

Three years later, a street that crossed Stockton Drive on the southeast corner of the arena also took on a new name. As *Deseret News* reporter Kersten Swinyard cleverly wrote in 2006, "Turning from 300 West onto 100 South will soon become the greatest of Utah's sports catchphrases—Stockton to Malone."

Ever since the Salt Lake City Council officially approved the honorary name change, the section of 100 South between 300 West and 400 West has been called Karl Malone Drive. The Jazz had to pay the city about $700 for the street-sign application and switch.

Miller pushed for the city to approve a street named after Malone, whom the organization forgave after The Mailman re-routed his career to Los Angeles traffic as a Laker for the final season of his career in 2003–04. "This is a small token of our appreciation," Salt Lake City councilman Carlton Christensen said during the council meeting. "He had not heard anything about this, so he was quite taken," said Malone's agent, Dwight Manley. "It's a great surprise."

50 Quin Snyder

Quin Snyder was doing a pregame interview at Staples Center before his first game at the helm of the Utah Jazz in 2014 when a Los Angeles broadcaster spoke to the new NBA head coach about his time with the Los Angeles Clippers while Larry Brown was the Clippers coach. He hired Snyder, who was briefly married to his daughter, out of Duke after the point guard had experienced three Final Fours with the Blue Devils. More than two decades later, Snyder laughed at the phrase used by the TV personality to describe the basketball journey he'd been on since his NBA coaching debut in 1992–93. "'Covered a lot of ground,'" Snyder said, chuckling while repeating the phrase. "I like that."

If anything, it was an understatement.

Between his first stint as an assistant in the early 1990s in L.A. and his first game as a head coach in the league with Utah, Snyder's coaching adventure included stops in North Carolina to be Mike Krzyzewski's assistant at Duke; Missouri for an NCAA head coaching gig with the Tigers at the age of 32; Austin, Texas, to coach the San Antonio Spurs' D-League team; Philadelphia as the 76ers' player development coach; Los Angeles to be an assistant for the Lakers; Russia as a CSKA Moscow assistant; and Atlanta, where he was Mike Budenholzer's lead assistant with the Hawks.

Snyder, a Mercer Island native who became the first Washington state player to become a McDonald's All-American, definitely covered a lot of ground while climbing up the coaching ladder before convincing Jazz ownership in an interview at then-CEO Greg Miller's kitchen table in Salt Lake City that he was the right man to replace Tyrone Corbin and become the franchise's eighth head coach.

Snyder was ready to establish some roots after bouncing around since 2007, when he decided to continue pursuing his coaching aspirations after a rough ending to his Missouri tenure that included an early Elite Eight appearance. In a seven-year stretch, Snyder lived in Europe and in all four time zones in the continental United States. He moved every offseason for five straight years from 2010 to 2014 to get different experiences with the aforementioned teams. Although that required a lot of packing—not to mention patience from his wife, Amy—it also gave him myriad learning opportunities with a group of coaches he referred to as "some of the best minds in basketball." The list was impressive: Coach K, Gregg Popovich, Larry Brown, Doug Collins, Ettore Messina, Mike Brown, and Mike Budenholzer. His new job in Utah offered him the opportunity to work with another hoops legend: Jerry Sloan, who became an adviser in retirement.

An avid learner with a curious mind—traits that came in handy while graduating with a double major as an undergrad and then earning MBA and Juris Doctorate degrees at Duke—Snyder soaked in all of the different philosophies and patterns from his successful mentors. "I persevered through some things and just tried to work hard and have been fortunate to have support from a lot of good people," Snyder said at his introductory press conference in Utah. "Hopefully, this is the result from a lot of that hard work."

Snyder reunited with an old friend from the Spurs organization, Dennis Lindsey, who left San Antonio to become the Jazz general manager. They shared impressive characteristics: a desire to

Following a circuitous route back to the NBA, the always immaculately dressed and always passionate Quin Snyder has become one of the better head coaches in the NBA. (AP Images)

build a championship-caliber foundation based on detail-oriented hard work; a creative up-tempo offense; a stingy, relentless, and energetic defense; and a competitive moxie. As Snyder put it after joining Lindsey in Utah, "The fit for me in this job is terrific."

The then-47-year-old was undaunted at the task of rebuilding a team that had struggled to a 25–57 season the previous year after management opted to let its top veteran players, Al Jefferson and Paul Millsap, go elsewhere and begin to rebuild. Snyder's new players bought in immediately, including the team's most-promising young player, fifth-year wing Gordon Hayward. "Coach is our leader. We're definitely behind him 100 percent," Hayward said before the 2014–15 season tipped off. "That's what we're most excited about—him and what he brings to us as a team…We're excited to follow his lead."

Snyder, who developed a strong bond with Hayward, learned the NBA game from his coaching mentors, from veteran players like Mark Jackson and Ron Harper with the Clippers, from Kobe Bryant with the Lakers, from ex-Jazzman Millsap in Atlanta, and from learning the Spurs way in Austin and game-flow concepts and out-of-the-box thinking while coaching in Russia for a year. "Our focus, I think, has got to be process-oriented, where we have those small successes, whether it's in practice, it's individual, it's in a game," Snyder said. "Sometimes it may not equate to the result we want, but it will equate to a growth process that will ultimately give us that result."

Things got off to a rough start under Snyder in Utah. The Jazz began his first season 5–16 and lost nine in a row in his second month. His team even had an identical 19–33 mark as Corbin's squad had the previous year at that juncture of the season. Same old Jazz, right? Not at all. The Jazz just had to adjust to the coach's perfectionist and engaged ways. They had to learn to fight through adversity, how to overcome injuries, how to play his way, and, mostly, how to win. "At the beginning of the year, it was a learning experience for everybody," Derrick Favors said. "We learned a lot from it."

It showed.

One of the worst defensive teams in the first half of the season, the Jazz transformed into one of the most-stifling Ds after the All-Star break. They passed better. They played more efficiently. And they started winning, closing 19–10 to go 38–44 on the season. That was a 13-game improvement, including wins over LeBron James' Cleveland Cavaliers, the Golden State Warriors, and the Spurs. "The group," Lindsey said, "is moving in the right direction."

The Jazz GM liked to point out the fact that Utah's players succeeded, even though they had a younger starting unit than the starters at nearby Brigham Young University. The progress continued the next season as Snyder guided the Jazz to a 40–42 mark and had the team within two games of extending their season.

The elusive playoffs happened at the end of the 2016–17 campaign. Continuing to build on the youth movement with Hayward and Favors, Jazz management gave Snyder more depth and experience, as he'd hoped, by adding veterans Joe Johnson, Boris Diaw, and George Hill to the roster. The combination resulted in a stellar 51–31 record and a spot in the postseason for the first time since 2012. The Jazz even shocked the favored Clippers in the first round—clinching a thrilling seven-game series with a Game 7 road blowout win—before getting swept out of the second round by the eventual NBA champion Warriors. "I don't know that I've been part of a year that's been like this. It's been unusual in many respects," Snyder said. "We won 51 games. We won a first-round playoff series. It wasn't just our challenges with our health, but that was certainly a component that brought a lot of other things to life. You found results because you had adversity. The way our team responded to that was good to see."

Like their coach, this playoff team was competitive and resilient, and the Jazz needed to be after they lost 160-plus games because of injuries while being forced to use 23 different starting lineups. Sparked by an All-Star year from Hayward and an All-NBA first-team season by Rudy Gobert, that season's success improved Snyder's record at Utah to 129–117 through his first three seasons. This Jazz team was one of only a handful of NBA teams to go from winning totals in the 20s to the 30s, 40s, and 50s in four successive years.

Snyder had traveled too far in his career, figuratively and literally, to settle for anything less. The coach's next season was perhaps an even better coaching job as the Hayward-less Jazz bounced back from a 19–28 start to win 48 games and advance to the second round yet again while being led by rookie Donovan Mitchell and Rudy Gobert. "I believe…that he was destined to be a pro coach," Coach K said. "He has his PhD now in basketball."

Another of Snyder's former mentors was asked to describe his former pupil during Utah's run to the playoffs. Popovich smirked. "Eh, he's done a decent job," he said, "not that great, could've done a lot better." As reporters laughed, Pop wiped the grin off his face and shared his real thoughts. "Quin is a wonderful, wonderful person," he said, "and a wonderful, wonderful coach."

51 Short Shorts

In honor of John Stockton's trunks, this chapter will be short.
The End.

* * *

Okay, not *that* short.

Though the Hall of Famer's career, his list of accomplishments, and his most famous shot were all long, it's the size of his shorts that some NBA fans remember most. Even as players like Michael Jordan, Michigan's Fab Five, Greg Ostertag, and pretty much everyone else shunned the form-fitting, undercarriage-tugging fashion of the 1980s in favor of baggy apparel that could double as parachutes, Stockton continued to wear the NBA version of Daisy Dukes until he retired in 2003. "To be honest, for the first 15 years, I didn't know we had a say in it," Stockton said at his retirement ceremony. "I figured shorts are shorts."

Stockton never had a say in what size of bottoms he wore as a kid either. He pretty much just felt lucky he wasn't stuck with hand-me-downs from his older brother Steve. Aside from not being picky, he liked the length of shorts he wore anyway, so why change just because everybody else around looked like kids sporting their dads' uniforms? Playful mocking couldn't sway him either. "It came as a surprise when people were making fun of me. *I can change them?*" Stockton said, recalling when he apparently discovered that extra shorts material did, in fact, exist. "And I didn't want to at that point…Styles are going to come and go. I think it's easier to stay with what you're comfortable with."

In other words, Stockton proudly owned his trademark wardrobe like the singers who sang "We wear short shorts" in the Royal Teens' famous 1950s hit song, "Short Shorts." Stockton joked about his mid-thigh shorts, too. During his retirement ceremony, he mentioned how his first NBA coach, Frank Layden, advised him to not change who he was from when he entered the league out of Gonzaga in 1984. "I haven't changed a thing," Stockton said. "I haven't even changed the length of my shorts."

Shaquille O'Neal was among nine players the NBA fined $5,000 in 2001 for wearing shorts too low. (For the record, Stockton was not one of them.) As a gag before a game, Shaq joked that he didn't want to wear "John Stockton shorts" and then tried to squeeze into a pair of the small guard's shorts he received from a member of Utah's staff. O'Neal then mockingly asked, "Are these better, Stern?" in reference to then-NBA commissioner David Stern. O'Neal tried them on again in 1996 when he and Stockton were Dream Team II teammates. They didn't fit any better.

Stockton's shorts became a hot topic two decades after his retirement when a player with an all-time great Jazz-related name burst onto the Utah high school basketball scene in 2014–15.

Long story short, so to speak, Rylan and Kelly Shorts attended a Team USA exhibition basketball game in Phoenix in 1996 when a van drove up next to them. The driver asked Rylan where he got his Utah Jazz hat. Next thing the Shorts know, Stockton, Jerry Sloan, and Karl Malone—all members of the Atlanta-bound Dream Team II—hopped out and started chatting with them. Those three briefly visited with the Shorts, signed autographs, and went on their way. Rylan had already vowed to name his first child Stockton, and his wife was on board after that chance encounter.

In 1998 the couple welcomed a baby boy to their family: Stockton Malone Shorts.

Stockton Shorts, the player, blossomed into a basketball star for Copper Hills High in West Jordan and was named Utah Player of the Year for the 2016–17 season by *The Salt Lake Tribune*. The 6'5" guard/forward began his collegiate career at Snow College in Ephraim, Utah, the following year.

For the record, yes, this Stockton wears No. 12, but, no, Shorts does not wear shorts befitting his name. "I could never wear shorts up that high," he told *The Spokesman-Review*. "It would be weird."

Shaq would agree; the other Stockton wouldn't. He also wouldn't be surprised if his style returns to popularity. "Oh, they'll come back around," the Hall of Famer said at his statue unveiling ceremony. "Everything comes back."

52 All-Star Game

Remember that time John Stockton and Karl Malone dominated at the Delta Center, hoisted up a trophy in a fun on-court celebration, and overshadowed Michael Jordan and his team? Forget what happened a couple of times later in the decade. Utah Jazz fans will always have that special moment when the dream All-Star Game scenario played out in 1993.

After helping the West outlast the East 135–132 in an overtime thriller—certainly one of the all-time great All-Star contests—Malone and Stockton were named co-MVPs in front of a packed house of enthralled fans. They each received four of the 11 votes. Malone led a victorious West team, which also included Charles Barkley, Clyde Drexler, David Robinson, and Hakeem Olajuwon, with 28 points and 10 rebounds. Stockton shined with 15 assists, nine points, and six boards. "The real winner was the host city, keen to show it deserves its place in basketball's big time," wrote the *Los Angeles Times'* award-winning writer Mark Heisler. "Things fell into place nicely. The surrounding mountains were loaded with snow. So was the city itself Saturday when a surprise blizzard dropped an inch of snow in 10 minutes. Undeterred, hardy local fans stayed in line on the street outside the Salt Palace, waiting to get into the Jam Session, a merchandise fair, and three-on-three basketball tournament. So gracious were the fans…they didn't even boo Jordan, who had said that what he liked best was the fact their home was 'a skip and hop from Vegas' and then proceeded to prove it."

After miffing Utahns leading up to All-Star Weekend, suggesting that the NBA should avoid winter wonderlands, Jordan finished with 30 points. He chartered a private jet so he could golf

All-Star Return?

The Jazz are hoping to give NBA owner Michael Jordan an opportunity to return to Salt Lake City for All-Star Weekend in 2022 or '23. Having transformed the old Delta Center into a dazzling arena through a $125 million renovation, Jazz officials submitted a proposal to host the league's midseason funfest three decades after the first one. "We feel like we're in a great position to be able to be awarded that All-Star Game," Jazz president Steve Starks said in 2018. "There's a story to tell about Salt Lake and the Jazz and what we have to offer that we think will be unique."

Utah's capital city has the infrastructure, including hotel rooms and convention center space, and proved again at the 2002 Winter Olympics that it's capable of hosting big parties. Then there's always that other unique bonus about Salt Lake City—it's only a hop and a skip away from Sin City.

in Las Vegas and returned to the festivities on Saturday during the wintery storm. "Why not keep it in a warm place?" Jordan infamously said. "Let us play golf for a couple of days, let us relax. They don't play the Super Bowl in cold weather places. The best thing about Utah is it's a hop and skip from Las Vegas."

That proximity, of course, is the exact reason why Brigham Young settled the Mormons' roots in the Salt Lake Valley. Locals humorously pointed out the flaw in MJ's argument. Not exactly a tropical paradise in July let alone February, Minnesota hosted the previous year's Super Bowl and was on board for the next NBA All-Star Game. Unlike some Utahns, the Jazz didn't freak out. "This event and this league is bigger than one player, including Michael Jordan," Jazz general manager Tim Howells told the *Deseret News*. "It's unfortunate that he'd make a statement like that, but it's really not that big of a deal. I guess Michael ought to tone down his game so he won't have to keep making these trips."

53 The Olympics

Before they teamed up in Utah, put together Hall of Fame careers, won gold medals, and had statues erected in their honor, John Stockton and Karl Malone were cut from the same basketball team. The year was 1984 and the two future Jazzmen were among six dozen amateur players invited to participate in the Olympic Trials at Indiana University for the Summer Games in Los Angeles. "They said they was gettin' the best 72," a young Malone told *Sports Illustrated,* "and they wasn't tellin' no stories."

Stockton was among the final 20 players but was cut along with Charles Barkley, Terry Porter, and Maurice Martin as Bobby Knight trimmed the pool down to 16. Tim McCormick, Lancaster Gordon, Johnny Dawkins, and Chuck Person were the final cuts.

Knight's final USA roster included guards Michael Jordan, Chris Mullin, Steve Alford, Alvin Robertson, Vern Fleming, and Leon Wood; forwards Wayman Tisdale, Sam Perkins, Joe Kleine, and Jeff Turner; and centers Patrick Ewing and Jon Koncak. Even though three future Hall of Famers were cut—Stockton, Malone, and Barkley—the USA cruised to the gold medal in L.A. by walloping eight opponents by an average of 32 points.

Team USA assistant George Raveling, then Iowa's head coach, explained to *The Sporting News* how tough a decision it was to cut Stockton, who was primarily not kept on because he was two inches shorter than the 6'3" Wood: "Coach [Knight] had a talk with John. He told him, 'You probably should have made this team, you're good enough. But I am going to do everything I can to promote you, so that the NBA and all the scouts and teams know what kind of player you are.'"

Jazz Players in the Olympics

1960: Walt Bellamy (USA)

1968: Spencer Haywood (USA)

1976: Adrian Dantley (USA)

1988: Danny Manning (USA), Jose Ortiz (Puerto Rico)

1992: Karl Malone* and John Stockton*(USA), Jose Ortiz (Puerto Rico)

1996: Karl Malone* and John Stockton*(USA), Jose Ortiz (Puerto Rico)

2000: Andrei Kirilenko* (Russia), Raul Lopez (Spain)

2004: Carlos Boozer* (USA), Carlos Arroyo and Jose Ortiz (Puerto Rico)

2008: Carlos Boozer* and Deron Williams* (USA), Raul Lopez (Spain), Andrei Kirilenko (Russia)

2016: Boris Diaw* and Rudy Gobert* (France), Joe Ingles* (Australia), Raul Neto* (Brazil)

* = on Jazz roster at the time

Three other players who eventually wound up in Utah—Tyrone Corbin, Antoine Carr, and Dell Curry—were also chopped. "The guys that played was worthy of going, but I always thought about it," Malone said at his Hall of Fame press conference 25 years later. "And once it came and went, I never thought I would have an opportunity to play."

Only eight years passed, however, before Team USA gave the Jazz legends a second chance after the country decided to allow professionals to play. You might say it played out like a dream for everybody involved in the 1992 Olympics. Considered the best basketball team ever assembled, the Dream Team included Stockton, Malone, Jordan, Barkley, Ewing, Mullin, Magic Johnson, Larry Bird, Scottie Pippen, David Robinson, Clyde Drexler, and Christian Laettner, the sole collegiate player selected. The late Chuck Daly was Team USA's head coach.

Jerry West joked that the Dream Team was more like a "Nightmare Team." The Americans easily marched through their awestruck competition, beating eight opponents [mercifully] by an average of 43.8 points en route to reclaiming gold for a country that had settled for a bronze medal in the previous Olympics. The games were a cakewalk in Barcelona, Spain, but Malone said practices were anything but that. "The most competitive and most challenging thing I ever did was the practices. It was truly off the chart," he said. "Once the game started, we all felt that was fun. We was representing our country."

Stockton's experience was marred a bit after he broke his right leg in a collision with Jordan during an Olympic qualifier in June. Stockton explained in his autobiography *Assisted* that Daly was leaning toward cutting him from the team because of the injury, but teammates rallied behind him and preserved his spot. Stockton finished his extensive six-week rehab in time to play in the final three games. Stockton and Malone then stood side by side on the podium for an emotional gold medal ceremony and national anthem. "I've always had great admiration for our armed forces," Malone said. "The closest to me representing our country was playing on the gold medal team."

Stockton, Malone, and Jazz coach Jerry Sloan, selected as an assistant to Lenny Wilkens, all participated on the Dream Team at the 1996 Summer Games in Atlanta where Team USA again waltzed through the competition for a gold medal. That stellar squad also included Barkley, Pippen, Robinson, Anfernee Hardaway, Grant Hill, Reggie Miller, Hakeem Olajuwon, Shaquille O'Neal, Gary Payton, and Mitch Richmond.

Carlos Boozer is the only other player in Jazz history who participated on two Olympic teams while with Utah. He won a bronze medal on the disappointing 2004 team but teamed with Jazz point guard Deron Williams to bring gold back to the United States from Beijing, China, in 2008. Stockton, Malone, and Thurl Bailey were among the torchbearers leading up to the 2002 Winter Olympics in Salt Lake City. Mark Eaton carried the torch prior to the 1996 Atlanta Games.

54 Eat at Eaton's Restaurant

The first week of March 1996 was a memorable one for Mark Eaton. On March 1—officially proclaimed "Mark Eaton Day" in Utah by governor Mike Leavitt—the former center had his No. 53 jersey retired by the Utah Jazz in a ceremony at the Delta Center. Later in the week, Eaton and a different team began a different kind of legacy; they opened a restaurant called Tuscany.

More than two decades later, the popular fine-dining spot in a scenic, wooded area in the southeastern part of the Salt Lake Valley—17 miles away from the Jazz's arena—continues to provide customers with a "Northern Italian gastronomic extravaganza," as Zagat describes it.

"It's almost impossible to replace the camaraderie and excitement our Jazz teams experienced together on the court," Eaton said when the restaurant celebrated its 20-year anniversary in 2016. "But we've come close here at Tuscany, and I'm very proud of the two successful decades my team has spent together in the very challenging restaurant business."

Tuscany has accumulated dozens of awards over the decades for its delicious cuisine, wine selection, professional service, and elegant atmosphere. The surrounding area is replete with lush natural beauty. And the restaurant has a rustic, authentic look as it was built to resemble a Northern Italian Alps chalet. The restaurant proudly boasts that its mouth-watering signature menu items—the double-cut marinated pork chop and the 7'4" chocolate cake, which is just slightly smaller in real life—are as iconic to Utahns as the teams Eaton played on during his 12-year NBA career. "We all feed off of each other's commitment to making this restaurant special," Tuscany server Sydney Malmrose said. "I'm proud to be a role player on this incredible team at Tuscany."

On January 27, 2016, Malmrose helped deliver a child at the restaurant. Heather and Eric Bailey were at Tuscany for an early Valentine's Day date when their third child decided to join them for dinner. Surprise! Someday that baby boy—named Christopher—will have quite the Mark Eaton story to tell.

Other Jazz Restaurants

Eaton, who has a great name for a person in the food industry, isn't the only former Jazz man to try his hand in the restaurant business. Some others (all closed) include:

- **Hot Rod Hundley's Restaurant**—This restaurant wasn't too far from Tuscany—in location, at least. However, it was on the other end of the spectrum in terms of style (sports memorabilia) and menu (bar food). Owned by the Jazz's popular broadcaster, Hot Rod Hundley's was suited for sports fans with an appetite for choices such as Texas Ranger Rings, Trevino's Treats, Ty Cobb Salad, Mickey Mantle's Melt, a Stockton Burger, and The Mailman's Slam Dunk sandwich.
- **The Brown Bear's Burgers and Dogs**—Mike Brown, a popular role player in the 1990s with the nickname "Brown Bear," operated this fast food joint for three years. "We had a great location. It was in Sugarhouse," Brown said in a "Where Are They Now" feature done by the team. "It was Jazz-oriented, and I had something like 30 jerseys up on the wall with the team's colors: purple, gold, and green. It was a good business, it was profitable, and I enjoyed doing it." This restaurant even lasted for a year after Brown was traded to the Minnesota Timberwolves before it permanently hibernated.
- **Green Street**—Former Jazz coach Tom Nissalke was a part-owner of this popular sports bar in Trolley Square for 20 years.

Heather had been feeling contractions during the first few courses before excusing herself to visit the restroom. Eric became concerned when his wife was gone for a while, so Malmrose agreed to check in on her. Malmrose later told Fox 13 that she joked with Eric, "Hey, you want me to go check on your wife and make sure she's not going into labor in the bathroom?…We rush into the bathroom, and I arrive just in time to basically catch."

That joke became a reality. Other than that once-in-a-lifetime experience, Eaton's high-end restaurant does not deliver.

55 Malone's All-Star Snub

On January 27, 1990, the Salt Palace was evacuated due to steam about an hour after the Utah Jazz blew out the Milwaukee Bucks 144–96 in what was the largest margin of victory in franchise history. Coincidentally, Karl Malone also had steam coming out of his ears and smoke off of his hot-shooting hand that night. Two days earlier, The Mailman learned the shocking news that fans had voted Los Angeles Lakers role player A.C. Green to be an All-Star starter over him (160,788 votes to 159,562), and the upset star had a message to deliver.

Before we get to that, there's an oft-overlooked fact as people recall Malone's famous snub game: it was actually his second game after the All-Star starters were announced. He scored 26 points with five rebounds in a win against the New York Knicks a couple of hours after being informed of the results. Pity the Bucks for being the ones who happened to be scheduled to play the Jazz after Malone had had two days to stew over the All-Star snub.

Sixty-one points later, the point was made. Malone was definitely deserving of being an All-Star starter regardless of what fans had to say about it. Milwaukee coach Del Harris, whose team was playing its fourth game in five nights, jokingly suggested that Malone should boycott that particular game in his pregame comments. "I knew he would come out and make a statement. I didn't realize he would write a whole book in one night," Harris joked after Malone became just the 13th NBA player to surpass the 60-point mark. "That should be a lesson—people in Milwaukee next year should vote for Karl Malone. Stuff the ballot box."

John Stockton, who was voted in as the starting point guard for the Western Conference All-Stars, begged to differ. That isn't surprising, considering a month earlier he spread fake news that Armon Gilliam of the Charlotte Hornets disrespected Malone in a TV interview and then pleasantly watched as the Jazz power forward blew up for 52 points against the Hornets. Regarding the All-Star Snub explosion, Stockton joked, "If he did this because they didn't vote him in, I hope they never vote him in."

They definitely should have, though. Malone was averaging 30.6 points—second highest in the league—was fifth in rebounding with an average of 11.1, and had the fourth highest field-goal percentage at 58.4 percent. Malone also had been named All-Star Game MVP the previous year. And Green? He was only the Lakers' fourth leading scorer with an average of 14.4 points and also pulled down fewer rebounds than The Mailman with 9.6 a night. "I'm surprised to be on the team," Green told the *Los Angeles Times*. "I never knew my position in the balloting, and it's really out of the players' control who the fans vote for. Neither one of us did any campaigning. On paper, you'd think [Malone] would be on the team. I mean, he does it night in, night out. That's what you have to do to be an All-Star."

After hearing the news, Green, a fifth-year veteran and first-time All-Star—his only selection in 16 seasons, by the way—told his mother, "I always knew Jesus loved me and always knew you and Dad loved me, but I guess [the fans] like me, too."

It certainly helped Green's cause that he played for the Showtime Lakers in Los Angeles instead of a small-market team in the Rockies. "That's going to happen," Jazz center Mark Eaton said. "We're not in the media capital of the world."

Malone showed off his full arsenal in his revenge game. He had 30 points and 10 rebounds by halftime. He even scored nine points at the free-throw line, going from 52 points to 61, while Jose Ortiz waited to check in at the scorer's table. "I'll never score 61 again," Malone said after the game. "It's just something that I can't imagine...I always thought that when I had a game like this, I'd retire, but now I'm going to have to stop and think about that for a minute. I'm still young."

Malone also reconsidered his initial reaction to skip the All-Star Game in Miami after the coaches unanimously voted him in as a reserve. "The first couple of days, it hurts," he said, "but after a while you have to take a little time and think about things."

56 Home, Sweet Home

A look at where the New Orleans/Utah Jazz have played over the years:

Delta Center/EnergySolutions Arena/Vivint Smart Home Arena (1991–present)

A few years after Larry H. Miller's death, then-NBA commissioner David Stern spoke of the late Jazz owner's legacy. "Larry decided that this team was going to be a community asset. It was not about the profit," Stern said. "It was about the community, and that was true when he built what was then the Delta Center. He knew he was cementing the bond between the team and community, forgoing enormous profits and large amounts of money if the team had been considered to move anywhere else."

That concrete bond went up in a hurry, too, once plans were approved for a new arena. Construction on the Delta Center, located a half of a mile west of the Salt Palace in Utah's capital city, began on June 11, 1990, and wrapped up only 15 months and 24 days later. That was record time for an arena of its size at the time. Miller and his wife, Gail, financed $66 million and received a $20 million bond to build the sports and entertainment mecca. "One of the most exciting things about this building is it should enhance our sense of community," Miller told the *Deseret News* in 1991. "I'm grateful for the opportunity to give something back."

Since then, the arena has welcomed world-class athletes, entertainers, and events, including the NBA All-Star Game in 1993, the NBA Finals in 1997 and 1998, the 2002 Winter Olympics, Garth Brooks, U2, and the Rolling Stones. Nearly two million people visit the arena annually for games and entertainment.

The arena has experienced drastic changes over the years, including having its naming rights bought by successful companies with strong local ties: Delta, EnergySolutions, and Vivint. An extremely rare tornado in downtown Salt Lake City caused nearly $4 million in damages to the roof in 1999. And most recently, the building underwent a $125 million renovation that gave the arena a sleek, modern look in the interior with cushioned seats, enormous state-of-the-art video scoreboards, solar panels, free public Wi-Fi, enhanced clubs and suites, 400-plus TVs, upgraded dining options, concourse-level porch areas that overlook the arena, a grand 12,000-square-foot atrium, and a large illuminated J-Note statue outside the main entrance on the northeast plaza. "It's the same old building," a teary-eyed Gail Miller said before officially opening the doors and welcoming the world back into the arena, "but it has a new spirit, and it welcomes you."

Miller felt similar emotions for the remodeled grand opening on September 26, 2017, as she did when the building first opened its doors 26 years earlier. "It's just represented such a huge part of my life and my family's life," Miller said of the arena. "You can't invest that kind of commitment without feeling emotional...The Jazz and the building cannot be separated. They're here to stay."

That's great news for Jazz fans but perhaps not such great news for visitors. It's been called the "Decibel Center" by some announcers because of how loud it gets. When things really get rocking, decibel meters have even showed that the arena noise equals that of a jet engine at takeoff. Combine the concrete interior, the loud fans, the 4,300-foot altitude, and a tradition of strong Utah teams, and it's no wonder why the arena is considered one of the toughest plays to play. "That's our sixth man, and we need this place to be hostile, night in and night out. I think our fans do a great job of that," Jazz forward Joe Johnson said after a regular-season game in 2017, "felt like a playoff atmosphere, especially late. When you get the crowd into it like that, that helps out a lot."

Loyola Field House, New Orleans (1974–75)

Before hosting Jazz games, this 6,500-seat arena was previously home of the ABA's New Orleans Buccaneers from 1967 to 1969. The Bucs played their third season in NOLA at Tulane before relocating to Memphis in 1970, opening the door for the Jazz a few years later. Unfortunately for fans who'd like to see where the Jazz played in their early days, the building was demolished in 1986 and replaced by a parking lot and rec center. Pete Maravich called it the Jazz's "snake pit," and the NBA thought it was a hazard and made the team pay $5,000 to install restraining nets so players wouldn't tumble over a court that was raised three feet above floor level. The arena didn't have air conditioning, heat, or parking.

Municipal Auditorium (1974–75)

Like the Loyola Field House, the Jazz played games during their inaugural season in this historic building, which is next to the French Quarter. Unlike Loyola's gym, however, the Municipal Auditorium remains standing. Don't expect to watch an event or take a tour there, though. It's no longer functional and has been vacant since incurring damage from levee failures after Hurricane Katrina in 2005. New Orleans is still negotiating with FEMA for restoration funds, according to *The New Orleans Advocate*. Jazz wasn't the only thing to play in this venue; Elvis and Led Zeppelin were among the popular acts to put on concerts there.

Louisiana Superdome (1975–79)

This massive stadium, which seats more than 70,000, is well known for having hosted the Super Bowl seven times and the Final Four on five occasions, for being home of the New Orleans Saints, and for providing shelter from Hurricane Katrina for thousands of people. It's also where Pete Maravich and the Jazz played for four seasons before relocating to Utah. Though attendance was often low for Jazz games, the franchise set an NBA record when 35,077 witnessed Pistol Pete square off against Julius Erving and the Philadelphia 76ers in 1977.

Salt Palace (1979–91)

The Salt Palace, which was sprayed with salt crystals to reflect sunlight, was listed by the *Deseret News* as the most missed Utah building. Erected nearly six decades after the first one burned down in 1910, the second Salt Palace remains near and dear to many Utahns' hearts. From 1969 through 1993, the cream-colored cylinder (aka "The Drum") was the hot spot in the state for sports, entertainment, and business conferences. Who cares if John Denver once supposedly likened it to a grain silo? This big bin was critical in helping Utah attract professional basketball, minor league hockey, and the Winter Olympics. (Interestingly, Salt Palace II, which has been replaced by the more utilitarian and stylish Salt Palace Convention Center, was constructed in hopes of luring the 1972 Winter Games to Utah.)

After the Salt Palace's completion, the *Deseret News* claimed it was "evidence that Salt Lake City belonged on the list of major cities." Before the Jazz came along in 1979, the Utah Stars had already christened the building with an ABA championship, winning a Game 7 thriller against the Kentucky Colonels on May 18, 1971.

Home of the Salt Lake Golden Eagles, the Salt Palace provided an intimate place to enjoy NBA basketball from 1979 to 1991. Ron Boone played there with the Stars and the Jazz. "It was a fun arena," Boone said. "It was open. Some arenas are dark. That one was bright."

Before the 25-year-old building was demolished on March 19, 1994, Mark Eaton strolled down memory lane. "I have a lot of special memories attached to the sports arena," Eaton told the *Deseret News*. "The first nine years of my career were spent here, and they were the best years of my career."

Frank Layden was also sentimental about his time as a Jazz coach and team president during the Salt Palace era. "There was a closeness there, a rhythm," Layden told the *Deseret News*. "The sound system, the fans, the scoreboard—everything just worked together like a ballet."

Thomas & Mack Center (1983–84)

Despite the Salt Palace's charm, fans didn't exactly flock to the arena after the Jazz uprooted from New Orleans. Only 7,721 fans attended the first NBA game at the Salt Palace—a 131–107 loss to the Milwaukee Buck on October 15, 1979—and it wasn't until March 27, 1980, that the arena had its first sellout (12,015). As the team tried to establish itself on the court and in the community, ownership flirted with finding a new home. During the 1983–84 season, the Jazz actually played 11 home games about 425 miles away at the Thomas & Mack Center in Las Vegas.

Interest skyrocketed in the Jazz in Utah after the team's success that year, and things stabilized thanks to Larry H. Miller becoming the owner, so the Sin City experiment was short-lived. One of the biggest milestones in NBA history, though, happened in Las Vegas that season. On April 5, 1985, Kareem Abdul-Jabbar broke Wilt Chamberlain's all-time scoring mark. The *Las Vegas Sun* listed that famous sky hook as the most memorable moment in T&M's first three decades. "A crowd of 18,389, heavily favoring the Lakers, turned out to give the 37-year-old Abdul-Jabbar a 45-second standing ovation when he was introduced," *Sun* reporter John Katsilometes wrote. "As always, everyone knew what was coming, but no one could stop it: a sky hook, this one from 12 feet, made Abdul-Jabbar the all-time scoring champ. It was indeed a jackpot in Vegas."

Utah played two more games in Las Vegas the following season to honor its two-year commitment, but the Jazz haven't strayed from Salt Lake City since then.

57 Bryon Russell

Of the many influential people Michael Jordan thanked in his Hall of Fame speech for motivating him, one was especially surprising. At the end of his shining enshrinement moment, Air Jordan personally thanked Bryon Russell.

Yes, *that* Bryon Russell.

The Utah Jazz took a flier on Russell, drafting the affable personality and talented wing with the 45th pick in 1993. Russell proved early in his career that he was a second-round steal, as he went on to start 48 games as a rookie and established himself as a reliable rotation player in Jerry Sloan's system. The 6'7" guard/forward was somebody who could defend and slash. He became even more valuable by extending his range and still ranks third overall for career three-pointers in Jazz history.

Despite going late in the draft, Russell received an invitation to participate in the first NBA All-Star Rookie Game midway through a rookie year in which he averaged five points and 2.7 rebounds. Russell became even more valuable to the Jazz's rotation alongside John Stockton, Jeff Hornacek, and Karl Malone over the years. Unfortunately for Jazz fans, Russell apparently did something his rookie season that helped M.J., too.

Jordan was out of basketball and playing minor league baseball when he met the charmingly confident Long Beach State player during that 1993–94 season. During Utah's visit to Chicago that year, Jordan attended and greeted his Olympic buddies, Stockton and Malone, when the fateful encounter with B-Russ happened. Russell introduced himself and, perhaps thinking M.J.'s hoops career was over for good, told Jordan, "Why'd you quit? You know I could guard you. If I ever see you in a pair of shorts…" (Stockton's face and shaking head were priceless additions to this story when a camera pointed at him as Jordan shared the story.)

Turns out, Jordan wasn't finished with basketball—or Russell—after all. After his short baseball career, Jordan returned to hoops a year later. He made it a point to give Russell a message at the mid-court jump circle before a Bulls–Jazz game in 1996. Jordan asked the Utah guard if he remembered the trash he talked in 1994 about being able to guard him and shut him down. He then added, "Well, now you get your chance."

Russell admitted to ESPN that the story Jordan told was true. "It happened just like he said it. Karl, Stockton were there. We was at the gym working out," Russell said. "I was a big fan, obviously, and I walked over there and spoke those words to him. He laughed. Stockton laughed. Karl laughed. That's what got the ball rolling and got him back into basketball."

The rest is history. A few years later, Jordan hit his most famous and final championship shot over a sprawling Russell in the 1998 NBA Finals. It was the second year in a row the Bulls beat the Jazz. Jordan has relished that ever since.

Russell will forever be linked with Jordan because of that controversial and historical moment at the end of Game 6 in the 1998 NBA Finals. The Jazz guard teetered a bit to the left of the top of the key as Jordan made a move, and then His Airness pushed off to gain more separation. As Russell regained his balance and lunged at Jordan, it was too late. The iconic shot had been released. Swish. History made. Nobody but Jordan knew it at the time—maybe Russell remembered—but he'd gotten revenge on a fun-loving rookie who'd said the wrong thing to the wrong person.

Even though he apparently doomed them from the get-go, Russell was one of the reasons the Jazz had their best ever regular season—a 64–18 record—and finally made it out of the West to the NBA Finals in 1996–97. He was a fourth scoring option behind the Big Three and set a single-season franchise record for three-pointers made with 108. That was quite remarkable, considering he only made 2-of-22 as a rookie when his mouth wasn't the only thing that misfired. "I was just happy to be a part of it, happy to be around a bunch of great guys and a hell of a coach," Russell said. "That was more exciting to me than anything. I was going to play hard no matter what."

To Russell's credit, he had better statistics during nine postseasons with the Jazz than in the the regular seasons. He averaged 13.3 points and 4.6 rebounds in 96 playoff games from 1994 to

Bryon Russell dunks over Houston Rockets center Hakeem Olajuwon during the 1997 Western Conference Finals. (AP Images)

2002 compared to 9.2 points and 3.8 boards in 628 regular season games.

Fans will always remember him for his huge smile, amicable persona, and old-school high socks. Stockton still credits his inbound pass in Game 6 of the 1997 Western Conference Finals for being a vital part of The Shot that sent the Jazz to the championship round for the first time. "Going to the Finals back to back, that was incredible. One year was good, and the next year was great," Russell recalled in 2017 as that first NBA Finals team gathered for a 20-year reunion. "The only thing that was disappointing was that we didn't win a ring."

In the aftermath of Jordan's Hall of Fame call-out—"keeping me relevant," Russell joked—he also hoped he'd get a chance to take Jordan on. Utah Flash owner Brandt Andersen even staged a hoax one-on-one event at halftime of a D-League home game in 2009, a move that infuriated fans who showed up thinking the two retired NBA players were going to play at Utah Valley University for a $100,000 prize for the charity of their choice—only to realize they'd been fooled when a Jordan impostor showed up. Russell really wanted it to happen, though. "When [Jordan] said my name in his Hall of Fame speech, my thought was, *Oh yeah. We've got to bring back '98*," he told ESPN. "It's just going to be a one-on-one. I know I can whup his ass now. He doesn't have no referees, or Scottie, Kukoc, or Dennis Rodman...it'll just be me and him."

Nearly a decade later, Russell is still waiting for his turn for revenge.

58 The Greatest Comeback

Dick Motta's Dallas Mavericks suffered a rough loss to the Utah Jazz after surrendering a seven-point lead with 28 seconds remaining in 1986, prompting a brutally honest quote from the legendary coach. "I've seen a lot of dumb things in my life," he said, "but none this dumb."

Motta spoke a decade too soon.

A night after the Midvale, Utah, native took over the Denver Nuggets head coaching position from Bernie Bickerstaff, Motta was once again flabbergasted in the aftermath of a Jazz comeback. This time, though, it was the biggest comeback in NBA history. "When you are 34 points ahead," a dismayed Motta said, "you're basically obligated to go on and win."

And that was just the halftime deficit the Jazz overcame in front of a raucous Delta Center crowd. Late in the second quarter in what turned out to be one of the most memorable moments of a very memorable 1996–97 season, Utah trailed 70–34.

More than two decades later, that 36-point comeback in Utah's improbable 107–103 win remains the largest turnaround win in NBA history. It wasn't nearly as significant as a rally the Jazz made in Game 6 of the Western Conference Finals later that season at the Houston Rockets to put Utah in the championship series for the first time, but it still goes down in franchise lore. John Stockton even brought it up on his own while speaking with media at a 20-year reunion of the organization's first NBA Finals appearance.

The first half was flat-out miserable for the Jazz, who entered this game on an eight-game winning streak. Denver shot 73 percent from the field, including hitting 14 of its first 15 shots, and took a 70–36 halftime lead. "We were shell-shocked," Jazz shooting guard

Jeff Hornacek said. "If they went through a shooting drill with nobody on them, that's about what they would probably shoot."

But Denver, showing why it went 21–61, was colder than a January day on a Rocky Mountain ski slope the second half. The Nuggets only made six field goals the entire second half.

Utah, meanwhile, heated up to outscore Denver 71–33 in the final two quarters. "We looked like deer in headlights," Motta said.

Karl Malone sensed that, and he and his teammates took advantage. The Mailman finished with 31 points, 17 rebounds, and six assists. Hornacek tossed in 29 points in a victory that kept alive what eventually became a 15-game winning streak. "I started believing it when we cut it from 36 down to like 18. You could start seeing the look in their face. They didn't want to take those shots," Malone said. "Then all of a sudden, we get it down 13, then we cut down to nine, then we cut it down to eight, then four."

Malone's top-of-the-key pass to Bryon Russell resulted in a hammer dunk and Hot Rod Hundley's "Unbelievable!" call on the radio (no TV for this one) to all but clinch the victory with 14.4 seconds left. Utah got contributions from a variety of players in the comeback, including Stockton, Chris Morris, and Shandon Anderson. "That was one of the most fun games I've ever been a part of," Stockton said. "You don't experience those many times in a lifetime."

Nuggets guard Bryant Stith drained four three-pointers in the fourth quarter to keep Denver in it, but his teammates only combined for six points in the final 12 minutes as Utah made history. "There is no excuse for us losing this game. We expected them to make a run and to have a comeback in the second half but not 36 points," Stith said. "This is a disappointing loss and a bad way to go into Thanksgiving."

59 Tyrone Corbin

If things had gone as planned, the Utah Jazz wouldn't be introducing a new head coach to replace a 71-year-old Tyrone Corbin for quite some time. That, at least, is how general manager Kevin O'Connor envisioned it happening when he hired Corbin as a successor to Jerry Sloan after the Hall of Fame coach's nearly 23-year run. "Ty, if you do about the same as Jerry does, [in] 2034 we'll have another one of these [introductory] conferences," O'Connor said during an unexpected media session to announce the end of Sloan's era and the beginning of Corbin's on February 10, 2011. "We hope it happens again, and it will happen again because Ty will do a terrific job."

The Jazz were so confident in the 48-year-old Corbin succeeding they didn't hold a job search after Sloan and his would-be successor Phil Johnson both stepped down. It was similar to how the Jazz handed the reins over to Sloan when Frank Layden surprisingly stepped down in December 1988.

Corbin had worked under Sloan as a coach and a player for 10 years. The 48-year-old was a well-respected assistant, knew the Jazz system, had the trust of players, was liked by fans, earned Sloan's endorsement, and gave the change-resistant organization the continuity it desired. "My time is up, and it's time for me to move on," Sloan said. "My energy level has dropped off a little bit, and I think it's time that somebody else gets a chance. Ty's a wonderful guy and will do a great job coaching."

Corbin grew up in South Carolina but chose to play college ball at DePaul in Chicago, where he averaged 11.5 points and increased his scoring output in each of his four years. He'd made a big enough name for himself to receive an invitation to the 1984 Olympic

Trials with future teammates John Stockton and Karl Malone. A year after Sloan was hired as Layden's assistant, Corbin, a computer science major, was taken 35th overall by the San Antonio Spurs in the 1985 NBA Draft. Over the course of his 16-year NBA career, the 6'6" journeyman played with the Spurs, Cleveland Cavaliers, Minnesota Timberwolves, Jazz, Atlanta Hawks, Sacramento Kings, Miami Heat, and Hawks and Kings again before calling it a career with the Toronto Raptors in 2001.

While with Utah from 1991–94, the versatile wing played in 233 games, averaging 9.6 points, 5.6 rebounds, and 28.2 minutes. He was a regular rotation player on two Western Conference Finals teams with Utah before being traded to Atlanta for Adam Keefe before the start of the 1994–95 season. "I was shocked," Corbin admitted to the *Deseret News*. It wouldn't be the last time he left the organization on a down note.

After his NBA playing career ended, Corbin was a player/ mentor for the Charleston Lowgators in the D-League for two years and got his first NBA coaching opportunity as manager of player development with the New York Knicks in 2003–04. The Jazz were fond of the well-liked Corbin, who was jokingly called The Milkman after doing milk commercials while on the same team as The Mailman, from his playing days. "We had tremendous respect for him as a player," Sloan said. "He is an upbeat guy and an exciting individual."

Corbin had a smile that could light up a gym, and his affable personality allowed him to connect with players. He was proficient in helping big men improve and proved to be a valuable part of Sloan's staff as the team rebuilt its roster in the post-Stockton-to-Malone era. With a decade of Sloan mentorship under his belt, Corbin was in the running for multiple head coaching jobs, which is pretty rare for a second assistant. That's why the Jazz felt so comfortable and confident in hiring him without an interim tag attached to his title. "He's ready to be a head coach," O'Connor said. "He'll do it differently. He might even smile."

Corbin took over at an interesting juncture. Less than two weeks into a new position he felt "bittersweet" to take because of his relationship with Sloan, Utah management pulled the rug out from under him by trading away his best player, All-Star point guard Deron Williams. The shell-shocked Jazz plummeted in the standings, falling out of the playoff picture while going 8–20 after Sloan's resignation. Corbin's son, Tyrell Corbin, had a much better spring, earning Utah's Mr. Basketball honors after wrapping up a prep career that included a state championship in 2009 and a scoring average of 24.8 points as a senior at Salt Lake City's West High School.

Corbin led the Jazz back into the postseason in the lockout-shortened 2012 season, but Utah just missed out on the playoffs the following year after going a respectable 43–39. Now under the direction of new general manager Dennis Lindsey, the Jazz again challenged Corbin by allowing his two best players, Al Jefferson and Paul Millsap, to leave in free agency. It was time to rebuild with a young core featuring Gordon Hayward, Derrick Favors, Enes Kanter, and Alec Burks.

The head coach was in a difficult position heading into the final year of his contract. He had to balance trying to win—something more likely to happen by playing his few veterans—with developing the team's youth. The season turned out to be a disaster—unless you were rooting for a higher draft pick than usual or for a new coach (and there wasn't a shortage of fans hoping for both). The Jazz only won 25 games and finished with the league's worst defense. In addition, Corbin had to have set NBA records for using variations of the phrase "It is what it is" and for sweat produced on the sidelines. Hired as his full-time assistant, Jeff Hornacek was familiar with that trait of his old teammate. "Before Friday night's game, I looked over at him on the bench, and sweat was coming off his head," Hornacek told *The Salt Lake Tribune* columnist Gordon Monson after Corbin's first game as head coach. "I thought, *Uh-oh*, and handed him a towel."

Five days after the 2013–14 season ended, Corbin was informed that his contract would not be renewed after he coached the team to a 112–146 record with mix-and-match rosters and in some less-than-ideal circumstances. He later landed jobs in Sacramento as an assistant and interim head coach and as an assistant with the Phoenix Suns—first with former Jazz player Earl Watson and then under Jay Triano after Watson was fired. "He's a good man. He's a good coach…As you guys know, our team stayed together under three-plus years of volatile change. Frankly, Ty gets credit for that." Lindsey said. "He's Jazz fiber through and through. Just what you would think, he's a gentleman in every way."

60 Jazz Villains

There's a truth that exists in sports that few are willing to acknowledge. There are no good guys. There are no bad guys. There are just guys who wear your team's uniforms or don't. John Stockton and Karl Malone are a perfect example of that. Fans and opponents from 29 NBA teams not located between Logan and St. George called them dirty. Fans and teammates from Utah called them crafty, physical, and lauded the tricks (or sharp, powerful elbows) they had up their sleeves.

There are some other exceptions to the good guy/bad guy rule of thumb—some dark-hearted, Lex Luther-level troubled souls who were so evil and so intent on destroying everything good in the world that even their own mothers wouldn't claim them. These are those wretched villains for Jazz fans.

Gordon Hayward: This is a recent, sad development. For seven years Hayward was adored as he grew up from being a baby-faced kid out of Butler and transformed into a versatile All-Star. That all changed when he bolted for the Boston Celtics while stringing along the Jazz and fans on July 4, 2017. A #stayward billboard campaign financed by fans turned into feelings of #betrayward in the community he left behind.

Carlos Boozer: There was a short period when Jazz fans thought Booz was The Next Karl Malone. Between injuries and defensive deficiencies, he became a target for scorn as a Utah player. That only amplified after he left for the Chicago Bulls.

Derek Fisher: Before he weaseled—okay, worked—his way out of his Jazz contract, Fisher was momentarily beloved in Utah. He was a terrific mentor for Deron Williams. He was charismatic. He had that amazing playoff game, in which he returned from being with his ailing daughter to make a huge shot. All of that goodwill went down the drain when he talked Larry H. Miller into letting him out of his contract so he could move to a city that had better medical care for his daughter and her rare eye disorder. Or so he claimed that was the reason. Shortly after talking his way out of Utah, Fisher quickly re-signed with the Los Angeles Lakers and ended up helping them win another championship. Jazz fans still vehemently believe Fisher lied to Miller.

Larry Bird: Although amazingly talented, Bird was among the love-to-hate legends for Jazz fans and seemingly for all non-Celtics fans around the NBA. Might as well throw fellow Boston Celtics Danny Ainge and Kevin McHale in there, too. They were fun to cheer against.

Dennis Rodman: The Worm had a way of infuriating Jazz fans, whether it was tripping (accidentally on purpose) a driving John Stockton while with the San Antonio Spurs or getting all tangled up with Karl Malone during his run with the Chicago Bulls or for any and many of his bizarre antics. It didn't help his cause in Utah that his teams often got the upper hand and he didn't back down.

Hakeem Olajuwon: Jazz fans had ample reasons to dislike The Dream. For one thing, he won two championships during Michael Jordan's first retirement when many thought Utah had its best chance to claim a crown. Utah fans also got on him for his liberal use of the pivot foot. Olajuwon had already become an enemy for Jazz fans, however, when he smacked Billy Paultz in the face in a 1985 playoff game.

Kobe Bryant: Jazz fans thought Kobe was a prima donna from about the time word came out that he refused to play for anybody but the hated Los Angeles Lakers. Many Utah faithful still fondly recall the time Bryant shot four airballs during a playoff game in his rookie season. They're not quite so fond of all of the Lakers fans who wore No. 8 and No. 24 jerseys in Utah or of the fact that he ended his career with a 60-point explosion against the Jazz.

LeBron James: The Decision didn't sit well with Jazz fans—in part because it made some feel like everything is stacked against small-market teams. LeBron has often been complimentary of Utah's fans and legacy, but Jazz faithful still relish their seven-game home winning streak over LBJ's teams from 2010 to 2018.

Rony Seikaly: The Jazz thought they had the scoring center they'd desired when they pulled off a deal sending Greg Foster, Chris Morris, and a first-round draft pick to the Orlando Magic for Seikaly before the trade deadline in February 1998. As Loren Jorgensen of the *Deseret News* wrote, "Two days after completing a trade that seemed too good to be true, the Utah Jazz found out that it was." Seikaly was booked on at least five flights to Utah, but he didn't show up for any of them, so the Jazz voided the deal. Jazz general manager Scott Layden claimed money was at the root of Seikaly's no-show, but the center later said Utah nixed the trade because of an injured foot and that he wanted to compete for a title with the Jazz. Utah management—and Jazz fans—blamed him. "If someone doesn't want to be here," Layden said, "then maybe we're better off."

Derek Harper: In 1997 the then-Dallas Mavericks guard said something that will forever be part of Jazz lore. During an ESPN interview, Harper was asked about a potential trade that would have sent him to Utah instead of his preferred destination with the Houston Rockets. His response: "There was a Utah deal, but you go live in Utah. Nothing against Utah or their team, but I don't want to live there." Like Jazz fans, Karl Malone was not impressed after he heard it live on TV. "That kind of makes me [upset]," Malone said. "I'll say this, I've got teammates here I respect, and that's all I'm going to say about it."

Deron Williams: There is a segment of Jazz Nation who will always blame the former All-Star point guard for Jerry Sloan shockingly deciding to call it quits in the middle of the 2009–10 season. Sloan denies that, and so does Williams. "He just said it was his time. That was his decision. He felt it was time," Williams said in his first interview after Sloan's abrupt resignation. "Maybe arguing was the last straw. So, there, I am guilty of that. But I think anybody who believes that I could force Coach Sloan to resign is crazy. He's stronger than that."

Less than two weeks later, however, the Jazz traded their franchise player to the New Jersey Nets and began a rebuilding process. Management said it was because it didn't know if he'd re-sign when he became a free agent in 2011. Either way, D-Will heard boobirds every time his name was announced or when he touched the ball in ensuing trips to Utah. Even so, Williams still has a home and lives in the Beehive State for part of the year.

Dick Bavetta: Conspiracy theorists are convinced that the NBA's most well-known referee purposely swallowed his whistle when Michael Jordan pushed Bryon Russell off him before his most iconic shot, which essentially won the 1998 NBA Finals for the Chicago Bulls. An even more egregious error happened earlier in Game 6, though, when Bavetta waved off a Howard Eisley three-pointer because he said the shot clock had expired. Replays, not part of the NBA at the time, showed Eisley had clearly gotten the shot off in time.

Enes Kanter: Like others before him, the Turkish center was loved by Jazz fans before he was loathed. That all changed when he told reporters that he wanted to be traded before the 2015 All-Star break and then when he dissed Jazz management, teammates, fans, and Salt Lake City after settling in Oklahoma City with the Thunder. Kanter did graciously admit to liking Utah's mountains, though. He later tried to make peace with Utah, but the damage had been done.

Dirk Nowitzki: The Dallas Mavericks superstar laughs about it now, but he definitely got off to bad start with Jazz fans when he said the infamous words, "Utah is a bad city." He's never heard the end of it from Utah faithful since then. ESPN even wrote about the rivalry, which included several run-ins with Matt Harpring and Andrei Kirilenko—not to mention hitting a lot of clutch shots. "Nowitzki might be hated more in Utah than any other NBA outpost, but he finds humor in the whole situation," ESPN's Tim McMahon wrote in an article in which Nowitzki admitted he actually likes the city.

Carmelo Anthony: Fuel was poured on the fire of this rivalry during the 2010 playoffs when Nike made a "Melo's people of Utah" commercial that went over like a Baby Ruth bar in a swimming pool in Jazzland. The commercial featured dramatic music and the Salt Lake City skyline and mountain backdrop while a narrator dramatically and sarcastically made Melo sound like the greatest player ever: "Every millennia or so a person comes along with the power to unite the world. This year that person is

Carmelo Anthony. His dominant game this season is a testament to human potential, but while he's gotten himself here, he can't do it alone, but he'll also have us, Melo's people of Utah. We're proud to support this soon-to-be champion, Carmelo Anthony, the common denominator of our hearts." At the end there was a cutout of Melo's head with a big, cheesy smile elevated above the mountains like the rising sun as the music crescendoed. It was funny, making a local villain pretend to be the hero.

Anthony told *The Denver Post* that the ad was supposed to make it sound like all of Utah was in his corner. "It's just stirring some stuff up. If we had played Phoenix, it would be the same thing," he said. His anticipated reaction for Game 3: "Of course, they'll boo me. It's the playoffs." He was right. Jazz fans haven't stopped booing him since regardless of where he's played.

Delonte West: While with the Dallas Mavericks, the guard strangely decided to poke his index finger into a young Gordon Hayward's ear during a game. Call it a West Willy. Call it weird. Whatever you call it, West instantly received the derision of Jazz fans.

Tim Duncan: Maybe it's the fact that he wore a look of bewilderment on his face seemingly every time a referee called him for a foul. Maybe it was because he won championships with the San Antonio Spurs, and Utah's stars weren't able to deliver that. Or maybe it's because many people consider him to be the best power forward of all time much to the chagrin of Jazz fans who love Karl Malone and who insist (correctly) that Duncan played center more often than power forward. It all adds up to one thing: The Big Fundamental isn't liked much in these parts.

Michael Jordan: Some Jazz fans still have nightmares thinking of the most iconic shot in MJ's history—and one of the most famous shots in NBA history—when he hit that soft mid-range jumper near the end of Game 6 to win the 1998 NBA Finals for the Chicago Bulls and rip the hearts out of the Jazz for a second straight year. Jordan even called out Bryon Russell during his Hall of Fame speech, remembering something the Jazz guard said as a youngster while conveniently omitting the controversial push-off that led to him getting that wide-open look at the Delta Center. Throw in Jordan's disapproval of Salt Lake City as the host city of the 1993 All-Star Game—he preferred to be golfing in a warmer climate and did fly to Las Vegas—and The Flu Game (or was it food poisoning or a hangover?) and him breaking Utah state code by smoking cigars in the arena locker room, and there just never has been a villain who hurt the Jazz more where it counts than His Airness. There was a mutual respect between Jordan and his Olympic teammates Karl Malone and John Stockton, and there were dozens of entertaining games between the Bulls and Jazz. So the rivalry was fun even if it was extremely painful.

Dishonorable mention: Gary Payton, Shawn Kemp, Derrick Coleman, Kenyon Martin, Jerry Stackhouse, Jimmer Fredette (not counting his BYU loyalists, of course), redshirt rookie Ben Simmons (due to controversy about the Rookie of the Year show-down over true rookie Donovan Mitchell because Simmons had been drafted the previous year), Mark Jackson (rumors of him backstabbing Stockton in the Hall of Famer's last season), and the Celtics' Butler duo, (Brad Stevens and that No. 20 guy).

61 Thurl Bailey

Frank Layden consulted with the late Jimmy Valvano before the 1983 NBA Draft. Coming off of a 30–52 season and desperate to improve sooner than later, the Utah Jazz had the seventh pick. They needed an impact player, another piece to help bring stability to a shaky organization, and the legendary North Carolina State coach was certain he had just the guy.

His name was Thurl Bailey. "Coach, take him," Valvano told Layden, "because he's going to get better and better. He's going to become a better professional than a college player."

That is saying something, considering Bailey was first-team All-ACC and was the leading scorer and rebounder on the 1983 national champion Wolfpack team that pulled off one of the greatest upsets in NCAA men's basketball history. Bailey's "Cardiac Pack," a No. 6 seed, went on a fun Cinderella run in the NCAA Tournament, including a win against Utah, and stunned the heavily favored Phi Slama Jama Houston team that featured Hakeem Olajuwon, Clyde Drexler, and BYU coach Dave Rose. You've undoubtedly seen video of Valvano wildly running around the court looking for someone to hug after Lorenzo Charles made a game-winning put-back dunk at the buzzer in the 54–52 win.

Turns out, Big T also joined the Jazz party just at the right time—and/or the party picked a great time to invite him. His rookie season was a breakthrough year for the franchise, which improved its record by 15 games (45–37), won its first division title (Midwest), and made it to the playoffs for the first time in its 10-year history. "This was groundbreaking. This was trailblazing in a way," Bailey said, echoing his old coach, who claimed that season's success saved the Jazz in Utah. "Maybe if not for that particular year, the importance of that year, who knows how long it would have [kept] going."

Bailey was named to the All-Rookie first team and, as his college coach predicted, he just kept getting better. More than two decades after retiring, Bailey's name is sprinkled throughout the Jazz's all-time career records list as empirical data to attest to his versatility: seasons played (10 in two stints, fourth), minutes (20,523, sixth), games (708, fifth), points (9,897, fifth), field goals made/attempted (3,989/8,420, fifth), free throws made/attempted (1,915/2,357, sixth), rebounds (3,881, sixth), and blocks (879, sixth).

With his size, athleticism, mid-range jumper, and hook shot, Bailey proved to be a valuable offensive weapon and complementary scorer. He averaged in double figures for seven straight seasons. He was the second option behind Karl Malone in his best two years—1987–88 and 1988–89—when he scored 19.6 and 19.5 points a game, respectively, while doing a host of other things to benefit the rising Western Conference power. Bailey was traded to the Minnesota Timberwolves for Tyrone Corbin in 1992 and returned to Utah for his final season in 1998–99 after spending several seasons playing in Europe.

It wasn't just his basketball skills that made Big T a fan favorite. He was heavily involved in community activities, even earning the J. Walter Kennedy Citizenship Award in 1989. Though he had a competitive spirit, he also had a calm demeanor and a thoughtful personality. He served as team captain for several seasons in his 16-year basketball career.

Though retired from basketball, Bailey has shown he's as multi-dimensional off the court as he was on it. He's still affiliated with the Jazz, providing game commentary as a studio analyst, and stays busy as a singer and recording artist—he told *Sports Illustrated* his first album *Faith in Your Heart* featured love songs "kinda like Barry White without all the begging"—a motivational speaker, philanthropist, and an actor. He's even vice president of strategic accounts of Fertile Earth, a Utah-based fertilizer company. "I'm proud of Thurl," Layden told the *Deseret News*. "He's done well, and it's not about making money. He's doing things with his life."

Bailey, a permanent Utah resident, often speaks about his spiritual conversion to the LDS faith, which happened after he met his eventual second wife, Sindi. Talk-show host Nancy Hanson once asked Bailey about his life's purpose in an interview aired on the Mormon Channel. Bailey shared a story from his playing days in Italy. While making frequent trips to Switzerland, he was asked three questions by border patrol agents: Where have you been? Why are you here? Where are you going? During one of his drives along the shores of Italy's Lake Cuomo, he had an epiphany, leading to him being baptized into the LDS faith by his father-in-law in 1995. "I realized that question about purpose really spoke to me," Bailey told Hanson. "*Why am I here? What am I supposed to be doing? Is it basketball that really defines me?* Basketball was the vehicle that I was blessed with. Now I had to work at it, but I was blessed with these tools to be able to find what that purpose is. During that journey I realized that I'm here to take what I have to bless other people."

62 Tough Jerry

During his NBA career, Jerry Sloan had a reputation for being a hard-nosed guy who didn't suffer fools, wouldn't take guff, and wasn't afraid to mix it up with anyone—and that was just as a coach. He was even pricklier as a player. As Frank Layden famously said, as quoted in Michael C. Lewis' *To The Brink* book on the Jazz, "Nobody fights with Jerry because you know the price would be too high. You might come out the winner. At his age, you might even lick him. But you'd lose an eye, an arm, your testicles in the process. Everything would be gone."

As a player, Sloan used his feistiness as a way to get under opponents' skin on defense and to establish dominance. His scrappiness led to him lovingly being called "The Original Bull" and getting his No. 4 jersey retired by the Chicago Bulls. As a coach, Sloan demanded toughness from his players and wasn't afraid to lead by example. He was also as protective of his guys as a mama bear with her cubs.

Though 35 years younger than Sloan, Kenyon Martin, known for being a bruiser in the league during his playing days, found that out when he played for the New Jersey Nets. "I feel bad about it now," Martin wrote of one particular run-in with Sloan in The Players' Tribune, "but you might remember that I once hit Karl Malone upside the head. He went down hard. Given his reputation as a tough guy, I thought he was going to get up, and we were going to get it on. But he didn't do nothing. His coach did, though. Jerry Sloan ran down the sideline, screaming, 'What the hell? I'm going to kick your ass!' I was so surprised. I was like, 'Whoa! Sit your old ass down before I hit you, too!' We got into it, and they had to separate us. That was when I realized that Jerry Sloan was a tough dude."

The tough dude who patrolled Utah's sideline for 23-plus seasons also had some choice words for Jerry Stackhouse when the Dallas Mavericks guard smacked Matt Harpring in the face by swinging his elbows while trying to clear space. The Jazz coach was infuriated. Sloan barked for a moment at the officials and at Stackhouse and then returned to the bench. Stackhouse continued to mouth off and stare at Sloan. He was ejected later on after swiping at Jarron Collins' arms as the Jazz center went up for a shot. "My thing was to try to protect our player," Sloan said. "The officials handled it. I didn't get into it with Stackhouse. I just said I thought it was a flagrant foul. He thought I was going after him."

Stackhouse had a history with the Jazz. Two seasons earlier, the shooting guard got so upset at Jazz rookie Kirk Snyder that he met him outside while Snyder was headed for the team bus. The two then scuffled on the lower level of the American Airlines Center in Dallas. Stackhouse was suspended a game. In 1996 Stackhouse was fined $7,500 after grabbing Jazz guard Jeff Hornacek's throat and

Jerry Sloan was not only tough on referees, but the hard-nosed head coach was also someone you didn't want to meet in a dark alley. (AP Images)

hitting him in the face. That resulted in a two-game suspension. The usually mild-mannered Hornacek was fined $1,000 for throwing a punch. Both were ejected.

Sloan might not have remembered those incidents, but Stackhouse did. "It's personal," he said. "I don't care much for them, and they don't care much for me."

In the 1999 playoffs, Sloan had seen enough of Rasheed Wallace's antics. After the Portland Trail Blazers forward flailed his arm and entangled Thurl Bailey, Sloan jumped off of the bench and lunged toward the player on the court. He stopped as a referee interceded. "Did you see the roundhouse thing that Wallace threw?" Sloan grumbled afterward. That was about the fourth incident he'd seen from Wallace. Sloan complained, saying, "That tells me he's gotten the game out of perspective. I'd just as soon lose as play that way. I've told that to Karl Malone. I've told that to all my players. I don't want to win that bad."

Wallace claimed the Jazz sent Bailey into the game "to get me heated" and ejected, but he wasn't falling for it. "That wasn't no roundhouse," he said. "I'm not stupid enough to sit up here and throw a punch, 'cause that's going to mean what? I miss the next game. I might wrestle with them or whatever, but I'm not going to bite the full apple."

Sloan's most infamous run-in on the court came against a referee. The NBA suspended him for seven games in 2003 after he shoved referee Courtney Kirkland in a blow-up at Sacramento. Sloan became enraged at the officials after he thought Kirkland missed an out-of-bounds call against Kings guard Doug Christie. He jumped to his feet, bickered with Kirkland, and—as assistant Phil Johnson stepped between them, as Johnson was famous for doing—pushed the official in the chest with his left hand. He claimed Kirkland told him, "I'm not going to take that from you tonight." That pushed his buttons.

Jazz management called the suspension "excessive," but Sloan later apologized. "As a coach, obviously I did something wrong," he said. "Pushing an official, that is a no-no in this business."

Sloan had previously been fined $2,000 and suspended one game for bumping official Bob Delany while arguing during a game against the Phoenix Suns in 1993.

Then there was the time Chris Webber set a hard pick with his shoulder, knocking John Stockton to the ground. "And I'm really cool with Stockton, but I was trying to show the rest of the team, like, I'm going to get the technical, you guys. I'll be the bad guy," Webber said in an interview with DanOnTheStreet.com. "Well, Stockton kind of laughed. I laughed. I looked at the bench, and Sloan looked at me. I said, 'You want some?' He was like, 'Damn right, I want some.'"

Webber was stunned as the older coach in a nicely tailored suit started walking toward him. "It's a good thing there was a ref there because, hey, he's one of the toughest guys in the league. I don't want to fight that guy," Webber said. "When your team is led by one of the toughest guys in the league, your team is going to be tough."

ESPN's Dr. Jack Ramsey credited Sloan the player for igniting his first NBA team, Chicago, with his fiery attitude. "Sloan was in the middle of everything they did, and the Bulls adopted his no-holds-barred demeanor," he said. "[Dick] Motta once told me that Sloan and [Norm] Van Lier got into it at practice sometimes in battles that carried off the floor and out into the corridors of the building."

Sloan, who was known to get into screaming matches with some players at practice, was once asked if he'd ever encountered a situation with fans like the Malice at the Palace. "Uh, yeah, I've had a few little incidents like that," he said. "Back then when we played, Van Lier and I...somebody threw an aerosol can in our huddle one time, and we went up there and let the guy know we didn't want him to throw any more of those."

63 Silly Moments

Here are some of the more bizarre and entertaining moments in Jazz history:

- One of the best stories involving Karl Malone happened when he visited Salt Lake City for the first time after being drafted by the Jazz. His visit took place at the same time as the annual Pioneer Day parade, which happened to be on his 22nd birthday—July 24, 1985. Coach Frank Layden asked the rookie from Louisiana Tech to ride on the Jazz team float and participate in the parade that winds its way through the capital on the state holiday. The best part: Layden told Malone that the parade was being held in his honor. The Mailman believed him. "That's no urban legend," he later told *The Salt Lake Tribune*. "That's the truth...I was waving like a pageant queen. If there were cell phones back then, I would have called my mom and said, 'You won't believe it. All of Utah is here for me.'" At the end of the parade, Layden broke the news and told Malone, "I can't believe you fell for that one."

- There's a story involving a player's hair that even trumps the time ex-Jazz big Carlos Boozer sprayed his bald head with fake black hair when he played for the Chicago Bulls. During a game played in Las Vegas in 1984—when the Jazz held some home games in Sin City—backup guard Jerry Eaves left fans wondering what in the heck was on the court. As the story goes, the Utah player was cutting his own hair in his hotel room earlier in the day when his hand slipped. A chunk of his Afro was accidentally chopped off his head. Going bald wasn't popular at that point, so shaving his head wasn't an option.

Instead, Eaves glued the glob of hair back on. The quick fix worked just fine, but then *Deseret News* columnist Brad Rock explained, "he started sweating."

- Karl Malone was getting ready to shoot free throws in a game against the Philadelphia 76ers when a fan tossed a rat onto the hardwood from a portal area at the top of the Delta Center's lower bowl. The rat hit the court face-first and slid across the lane in front of Malone, who didn't flinch but later expressed his condolences for the "poor little fella." Jazz forward Scott Padgett took action. He kicked the rodent to the sideline and another poor little fella, assistant trainer Terry Clark, hauled it off in a bag. "The referees looked kinda scared to go get it," Padgett said, "so I thought I'd try to get on with the game." Though some wondered if it was a fake rat, Clark confirmed that was not the case. "Dadgum, it was real," he told the *Deseret News*. "Real dead." As Jazz beat writer Tim Buckley humorously described the situation, "In basketball parlance, a gym rat is a good thing. A rat in the gym is not." For the record, Malone hit his free throw in the 98–69 blowout win. Arena security officials chased the suspected rodent tosser outside, but that rat escaped on foot.

- In 2004 Jazz owner Larry H. Miller really got into the spirit of a retro night. Donning an old-school warm-up suit with the classic Jazz logo and J-Note, just like the players sported, he joined the team huddle before tip-off. Miller then ripped off the tear-away pants to reveal an actual Utah Jazz uniform, John Stockton-esque short shorts, headband, and high socks. Miller, whose name appeared on the back of the jersey, accompanied an amused Greg Ostertag to center court before settling into his usual courtside seat. Unfortunately, No. 9 didn't see any actual playing time in that game against the Miami Heat. He scored points with players and fans, though. Jazz guard Raja Bell called Miller "a sight to see." In his broken English,

Russian forward Andrei Kirilenko said, "He's hilarious. He should be Man of the Year, Comic Man of the Year. I never seen it before."

- What old-time Jazz fan can forget the time Morganna rushed onto the Salt Palace court and laid a big smooch on Frank Layden's cheek? That wasn't unusual. Morganna, the bleach-blonde-headed, large-bosomed kissing bandit who seemed to be cut from the same mold as Dolly Parton, was well known in the 1970s and '80s for running onto the playing surface to kiss famous sports figures and then bouncing away. She began her kissing career by smooching Pete Rose on a dare during a 1970 game. Her act became so popular she went on tour like the San Diego Chicken. Layden made Morganna's appearance a kiss to remember. She rushed over to the Jazz huddle and pecked his cheek. As she fled off, Layden, ever an entertainer himself, jokingly fell to the court spread-eagle style and hammed it up. Hot Rod Hundley was also the recipient of a Morganna kiss at an Old-Timers' Game. He remained standing.

- Greg Ostertag had his moments where he was a terrific asset on the court, especially defensively with his huge 7'2" frame. He could also be quite goofy, carefree, and childlike, as one might surmise of a grown adult with a colorful Fred Flintstone tattoo inked on his right calf. (It's also rumored that Ostertag had Jerry Sloan's foot tattooed on his behind.) Big O also liked to occasionally take out his fake front teeth during games. He lost his teeth after falling at a Las Vegas water slide while in high school. In 2001 his replacement chompers fell to the court during a game in Houston. A Rockets trainer had to retrieve them with a towel.

- Rodney Hood might not laugh about it, but he gained fans across the country after replays of him smacking a cellphone out of a fan's hand went viral. Hood had been ejected from a game in Washington in 2018 and was heading out of the arena when the 25-year-old guard passed by a middle-aged Wizards fan who appeared to be recording his exit. The NBA fined Hood $35,000 for sending the smartphone soaring. It wasn't reported how the fan's phone fared.

- The most memorable moment from the Jazz's game at the Sacramento Kings in December 2014 cost Enes Kanter $25,000. In the second half, Kanter was frustrated about being called for traveling when he slammed the ball on the court, stormed toward the Jazz bench, and threw his mouthpiece into the stands. A Kings fan about five rows behind the Utah players caught Kanter's airborne mouth guard. The man then humorously held it up like he'd just made a winning touchdown reception. "At least the guy caught it," Kanter said, grinning. "He's not going to sue me, I hope." A Jazz team attendant, wearing gloves, retrieved the mouthpiece from the fan. A group of fans near the Jazz bench chanted "Kanter sucks!" after he fouled out in the fourth quarter. The Turkish center looked over and blew the fans a kiss.

- Ukrainian center Kyrylo Fesenko didn't last long with the Jazz, but he became a fan favorite because of his humorous personality. In 2008 Fez cracked up his teammates, among others, when the showed up to summer league training camp with a bleached blond hairdo. "I was like, 'I guess you're going for the Backstreet Boys look,'" Jazz guard Morris Almond said. "If that's hot in Ukraine, that's hot in Ukraine, but, you know, over here…" Almond jokingly told Fesenko he didn't want to be around when Jazz coach Jerry Sloan saw him. Sloan didn't seem amused. "I'm not worried about his hair. I'm worried about what he does on the floor," he said. Sloan pointed out that he wanted to see Fesenko, notorious for goofing off, take basketball more seriously and improve his skills: "He's got to figure out what he wants to do: play basketball or be a clown."

- Before the playoffs began in 2008, a Salt Lake City boutique store near the arena sold "I [heart] Kyle" and "Mrs. Korver" T-shirts. Located in the Gateway Mall, Masha Kirilenko's Fleur de Lis store also sold "I [heart] A.K. 47" shirts. Korver wasn't thrilled, telling reporters at shootaround before a Houston Rockets playoff game, "I don't know if I want to talk about this right now." Andrei Kirilenko opted for self-deprecation. "I think Kyle is selling way more. Kyle is a little bit more good looking."

On the bright side, Korver did get commission on sales of shirts with his name on it. His jerseys flew off the racks that season. In the four months following his trade from the Philadelphia 76ers, Korver was only behind D-Will in adult

Officer Olden

Olden Polynice ran afoul of the law by pretending to be the law. "It's a joke," Polynice told the *Deseret News* in late October 2000 after being charged in 3rd District Court for impersonating a police officer. "C'mon now."

It was apparently such a funny joke—teammates laughed about it with him—that Polynice repeated the misdemeanor crime in West Valley City a month later. Both incidents happened during confrontations with fellow motorists and included him pulling out a fake badge, an honorary one given to him by the Los Angeles Police Department, and identifying himself as a cop.

Polynice might have gotten away with it if he hadn't been a 6'11", 250-pound behemoth who happened to be on TV every other night during the NBA season. "It's a serious charge," Polynice's attorney Walter F. Bugden told the Utah paper after his client took the law into his own hands a second time. "Olden is taking it seriously and intends to deal with it in a responsible way."

The 36-year-old pleaded guilty, was given 100 hours of community service, and received a one-game suspension from the NBA. He also apologized for disorderly conduct.

Jazz jerseys sold and he led sales of kids' jerseys, often bought by women, *The Salt Lake Tribune* reported. There's one thing Korver probably liked less than the shirts: Ashton Kutcher comparisons.

- Greg Foster infuriated the Los Angeles Lakers—and his own coach wasn't too thrilled either—by doing a throat-slash gesture, moving his index finger across his neck, while passing by the visitors' bench after a dunk late in a 106–91 Jazz win at the Delta Center. Shaquille O'Neal called Foster "a bum." Robert Horry intimated that Foster was immature. And Lakers coach Dell Harris got a technical foul, pleading with the refs to give Foster a technical for taunting. "Greg Foster hasn't earned the right to be anything in this league," Harris said. "He's lucky that he's just been able to stick with a team."

64 Derrick Favors

Upon returning from Team USA's minicamp in Las Vegas in 2013, Derrick Favors bought a house in the mountains above his NBA workplace. The largest purchase of the 22-year-old's life included his only two must-have amenities: a finished basement and a movie theater.

It also has plenty of room for his pit bull, Gotti, to roam free. Buying a home in Utah was a symbolic move at that point, and he continued to remain loyal to his home-away-from-home a half-decade later when he re-signed with the Jazz yet again. "I love Atlanta. It's my home. Atlanta—my mother, my family, my friends, the city—shaped me in so many ways," he told the team's website. "But Utah is my home, too. This is where I grew up."

Not long after he was traded in the Deron Williams deal, Salt Lake City won over this Southerner's heart. It didn't even matter if southern cooking was hard to find. He doesn't eat that greasy comfort food during the season anyway.

Before arriving in Utah, Favors knew approximately two things about the Beehive State (and the state's nickname was not one of them). When he was a 19-year-old Nets rookie, he was somewhat familiar with the Jazz because, well, that comes with the territory of being an NBA player. The second thing Favors understood was that on February 23, 2011, he was following in the footsteps of Karl Malone. "I knew nothing about Utah. Nothing at all," Favors said. "Down South, they don't talk that much about Utah."

Though the 6'10" big man hasn't quite emerged as a statistical powerhouse like Malone, Carlos Boozer, or Paul Millsap, he has been a steady and reliable force for Utah. In 500 games with the Jazz leading up to the 2018–19 season, Favors averaged 12.1 points on 51.8 percent shooting, 7.4 rebounds, 1.3 blocks, and 1.2 assists. He's proven valuable as a physical power forward and as an athletic center.

Best of all, Favors is a consummate professional who complements his teammates. "Last year was a little different for me personally. I had to sacrifice a lot. I had to sacrifice touches. I had to sacrifice shots, minutes, everything really," Favors told utahjazz. com. "But I knew it was best for the team. I had to find a way to just make an impact. It was worth the sacrifice. We won a lot of games, made it to the second round of the playoffs. But now I want more. I want to win a championship." Favors has had that as a goal since arriving in the NBA. "If I don't get nothing else out of my career, I want to win a championship," Favors said. "I've got goals of being an All-Star. At the end of my career, I want to give that speech—that Hall of Fame speech. That's one of my biggest goals. But if I don't get any of those, I at least want to win a championship."

Favors did go to the Naismith Basketball Hall of Fame in Springfield, Massachusetts, with his South Atlanta High School team, the 2009 Georgia Class 3A state champions, but he's never actually heard one of the enshrinement speeches. "I don't want to listen to one," he said. "The first one I listen to, I want it to be mine."

Favors, though, has gotten an earful from someone who has delivered an emotion-filled Hall of Fame speech. During the 2018 offseason, the veteran worked out multiple times with Malone. Favors smiled while admitting he beat Malone in a game of H-O-R-S-E—"He don't want me to tell nobody"—but he admiringly described the 50-something-year-old as a "still strong guy" who "could come out here and still hold his own."

Once Favors arrived in Utah, he quickly discovered that the Jazz had two veteran big men—Millsap and Al Jefferson—who led the team in scoring and minutes played. "It was frustrating at first," he admitted. "Then I had to sit down and just realize that these two guys are good and I've just got to learn as much as I can from them."

In 2011 Favors began the lockout-shortened season as the starting power forward ahead of Millsap. That, however, lasted two games before he returned to a reserve role that continued through the 2012–13 campaign. That meant more waiting for the young man hoping to win a championship and become an All-Star and Hall of Famer. Though he didn't like sitting, it actually helped him while also providing motivation. "I was thankful and blessed to play behind [Millsap and Jefferson] because those two [were] great guys," he said, "and I learned a lot from them."

Favors has become more vocal over the years, which is perhaps the area in which he's improved the most, considering how quiet he was when he arrived. "I'm not scared to talk and say what I need to say," he said. "It's just if I have to, I'll do it."

Favors' little brother, Brandon, can attest. Neither of them have had their dads in their lives, but the maturing Jazz player has taken on a long-distance role as a father figure for Brandon. "I'm real close to him. I'm more of a male role [model] with him—the older, big brother role," he said. "I've got to go there and make sure his head is on straight, make sure he's doing good. I make sure he's doing school. I make sure he keeps his room clean. It's hard right now, but we're working on it."

In a different supervisory role, Favors has also looked after the best interests of his favorite animal—the pit bull he bought in April 2013. He had to set some house rules with his girlfriend when she dressed Gotti up in a fluorescent green shirt. "I was so mad," he said, shaking his head while cracking a smile. He told his thoughtful-but-misguided girlfriend, "Don't buy my pit bull no shirt. Let him be a pit bull."

 **Bear**

Bear debuted as the Jazz's new mascot at the Delta Center on November 4, 1994, doing a stunt the NBA has long since banned. He quickly won over the crowd by rappelling down from a catwalk high above the court. Years later, he still chuckles about his first review, courtesy of *Deseret News* columnist Doug Robinson: "Bear appears to be in dire need of Ritalin. He possesses serious energy. Winnie the Pooh, he's not." Christopher Robin's chubbier friend might struggle to strut on stilts, walk on handrails, do one-paw handstands atop a 21-foot ladder, and bike off a ramp at the bottom of stairs.

Along with 50-some home games, Bear makes about 250 out-of-arena appearances. Ninety-five percent of the visits are for philanthropic purposes—putting smiles on faces of kids at places like Primary Children's Medical Center. He also helps children in need get Christmas presents through his Bear Hugs for Kids program. "The most important part of my job is doing charity work, doing things with children, and trying to be part of the community," he said. "But all of it is fun."

The original Bear, who kept his identity top secret until his name became public knowledge after he was fired by the Jazz prior to the 2018–19 season, became tamer over the years. Ritalin was no longer required for the NBA's longest-tenured mascot (the man behind the mask, that is). Though Jon Absey is no longer the man inside the mascot suit—and good luck recognizing him without the fur—the beloved Bear mascot lives on for the Jazz. But be forewarned: he might douse you in Silly String if you ask for his name.

66 Joe Ingles

After being waived by the Los Angeles Clippers at the end of the 2014 training camp, 27-year-old Joe Ingles figured it might be time to return to Australia and to move on from his lofty career aspirations. "That," he told *The Daily Autograph*, "was probably the first time when I was like, 'Maybe I won't make the NBA.'"

Two days later, Ingles went to lunch with his wife, Ranae. She'd flown from Down Under to be with him as he began his NBA career in L.A. only to arrive in time to hear about her husband's bad news. A phone call during their meal changed everything. Ingles wouldn't be getting his first warm vacation in years in the Down Under summer after all. The Utah Jazz had claimed him off of waivers.

Because of his age, Ingles openly admits this was his probably his last chance at cracking an NBA roster. Though Ingles grew up in Australia and plays for the Boomers in international competitions, Ingles left his homeland to pursue a professional career—and hopefully a path to the NBA. Ingles had played in Spain with CB Granada (2009–10) and FC Barcelona (2010–13) before spending a year in Israel with Maccabi Tel Aviv (2013–14).

That experience paid off. Jazz coach Quin Snyder was very familiar with Ingles' game from his time coaching with CSKA Moscow as he made his own off-the-beaten-path journey to the NBA. Snyder liked what he saw from the left-handed wing player when he saw him during the 2012–13 season.

Utah needed another wing player to bolster the end of their bench, so Jazz management claimed Ingles. After one full practice, the 6'8" guard/forward had already shown enough to make it clear he'd be in the rotation. The Clippers' loss was the Jazz's gain. "There's always guys that you recognize their ability, and circumstances don't allow you to keep them," Snyder said. "But from that standpoint for us, he's a settling influence [with] his ability to pass the ball…He's obviously a good fit for our group."

Ingles became a nice one-two punch on the perimeter with Gordon Hayward, eventually starting at shooting guard, and then when the All-Star small forward bolted for the Boston Celtics, the versatile player moved into Hayward's spot. Ingles was a seamless fit in the locker room. He gelled with teammates, including fellow Aussie Dante Exum, who grew up a fan of his. He developed a strong relationship with Snyder, and the coach's tough-love advice helped transform him into an even better all-around player. With his humorous personality combined with his ability to pass, shoot, and defend (surprisingly well for a guy nicknamed "Slow Mo Joe"), it's no wonder Ingles has been a fan favorite.

The Jazz signed Ingles early in the 2017 free-agency period to a four-year, $52 million contract, which gave him a significant raise from the two-year, $4.5 million deal he'd signed in 2015. Utah loved what he brought to the organization and hoped his re-signing would help influence Hayward, his best friend on the team at the time, to stick around Utah. That didn't work, but he continued to be a strong asset to the Jazz's success even without Hayward.

Ingles was a steal on his previous contract, ranking third in the NBA in three-point field-goal percentage at .441, finishing in the top 20 in the league in defensive rating (104.7), and often playing point guard as well as his other wing positions for the Jazz. He played a pivotal role in Utah's first-round win against his previous NBA team, the Clippers, in the 2017 playoffs.

Ingles was understandably miffed at the Clippers, but he said he had no regrets with how the situation worked out. "I did all I can to make the team and wasn't what they wanted or good enough or whatever it was, so it worked out perfectly," he said. "I'm very happy here. It's been great."

For what it's worth, Doc Rivers, then the Clippers head coach and general manager, has publicly lamented the organization's decision to let Ingles go. Rivers loved the potential he saw in the scrappy Ingles, but following an injury to Jordan Farmar, they decided to keep point guard Jared Cunningham as an emergency backup point guard to Chris Paul instead. Cunningham was waived early that season, while Ingles went on to carve out quite the niche for himself in Utah. "Obviously, if we would have done that back then," Rivers told *The Orange County Register*, "people would have been like, 'You kept Joe Ingles?'"

Judging the impact Ingles had on Utah's team, the skeptics wouldn't have questioned the decision for long even if Ingles doesn't appear to have the athleticism of many NBA wings. "It's like watching film of football and how a player runs a 4.9 [40-yard dash], but then when you watch the game, he's always the first guy there,"

Rivers told *The Register*. "He just moves a little quicker because he's sharper."

Ingles—or "Jingles," as some fans affectionately call him—has a sharp wit, too. He uses that on the court as one of the NBA's best trash talkers and puts it on display for the public's entertainment during a weekly radio show with the Jazz-owned station as well as in interviews and on social media. One of Ingles' best one-liners came after a reporter jokingly asked if the sharpshooter considered himself to be the Steph Curry of Australia. Without missing a beat, Ingles responded: "Steph Curry is the Joe Ingles of America."

Already a fan favorite, the Aussie Steph Curry's legend grew even more on November 12, 2018, when he sported a makeshift headband after he took an elbow above his eye from MarShon Brooks of the Memphis Grizzlies. Ingles left the court with blood running down his face and returned with a humorous, classic new look. After Ingles received four stitches in the training room, team-mates and fans went nuts online about the wrap he wore upon his return to the game. Hamming it up, Ingles even did an Aaron Rodgers-esque championship belt celebration during his team-high 19-point effort in the 96–88 win. His wife joked on social media, "The twins are going to want headbands tomorrow."

67 Jazz vs. LeBron

Before he teamed up with him on the Cleveland Cavaliers, former Jazz sharpshooter Kyle Korver described LeBron James. "He's a freak. He really is. If you're comparing weight, he weighs as much as [Carlos Boozer]. That's amazing, isn't it?" Korver said. "He's as fast as he needs to be. He can jump as high as he needs to. He's amazing."

Having been around the NBA since the mid-1960s, Hall of Fame coach Jerry Sloan said he's never seen an athlete with as complete of a package that James uses to dazzle and destroy. The 6'8", 250-pound "freak" has an unparalleled combination of size, speed, strength, and skills. "He's a wonderful player." Sloan said. "I don't think I've ever seen a guy that big that's got that much talent and can do so many different things and play such an easy game, so to speak."

Keep in mind, James is similar in stature to Karl Malone, another freak of nature athlete who measured 6'9", 250 pounds during his playing days. "You're not going to stop him. He's so big and powerful," Sloan said. "Athletically, he's just loaded with talent and he uses it very well. He passes the ball, he defends, he's a terrific defender. He just plays basketball with all the stuff that he has, and that's really tough to handle for his size."

Best way to defend him? "Hope he misses," Korver said. He was joking—well, kind of. "You've got to really bust your can," Sloan explained, "and hopefully do the best you can to try to keep everybody else from killing ya."

That philosophy has paid off for Utah over the years. Utah has enjoyed more success against James and his teams than most NBA organizations. Even though he's struggled to beat the Jazz, losing seven times in a row in Salt Lake City between 2010–18, James has enjoyed the matchups. He'll undoubtedly never forget a standing ovation he received in Utah. "I was telling a couple of my friends yesterday about some of the times that I've had here, the games I've played here, the buzzer-beater games, so it's always been pretty fun," James said in January 2017 before losing a sixth game in a row at Utah. "These fans, they've seen some great basketball over the years, obviously, from the Malone and Stockton era to the present. I'm happy that I'm in the…building that created a lot of memories."

Here are some of the more memorable memories:

Cavs 102, Jazz 96 (January 17, 2004 at Utah): James gave the Jazz more than they could handle in their first meeting: 29 points, seven rebounds, and a road win. He didn't lead the Cavaliers in scoring, though. Boozer, who would join the Jazz the next season, did with 32 points, helping Cleveland win at the Delta Center for the first time in 13 tries.

Jazz 97, Cavs 88 (March 19, 2004 at Cleveland): Utah returned the favor, picking up the franchise's first win against James. Raja Bell led the way with 23 points and some feisty defense on James, who blamed a bad chest cold for a 14-point effort. "I wasn't able to breathe," he said. "The energy that I usually have in my legs I just couldn't get."

Cavs 108, Jazz 90 (January 21, 2006 at Utah): This was James' version of the MJ flu game. He almost didn't play and even got precautionary X-rays earlier in the day at a local hospital. By the end of the night, the 21-year-old had scored 51 points and left the court to a standing ovation—by a wowed crowd in Utah, mind you. "I just wanted to showcase my talents to the crowd," he said. "It was awesome, having the opposing fans cheer for you. It gets no better than that."

Jazz 103, Cavs 101 (November 7, 2007 at Utah): James' first triple-double—32 points, 15 rebounds, 13 assists—was nice and all. But Deron Williams one-upped his future Team USA teammate by making a clutch drive with 1.3 seconds left in the ESPN-televised thriller.

Cavs 105, Jazz 93 (November 15, 2008 at Cleveland): Sloan lauded James after the star scored 16 of his 38 points in the fourth quarter, calling him "a terrific player." But Sloan also said his players were too awed: "If you say, 'I'm not going to touch him,' you'll be standing there 20 years from now. You might as well just come get an autograph and go home."

Jazz 97, Cavs 96 (January 14, 2010 at Utah): James went off for 18 of his 36 points in the final quarter, helping give Cleveland a lead after trailing by double digits. That, however, only set the table for a different hero. This was the night when Sundiata Gaines, a D-League player on a 10-day contract with Utah, introduced himself to the sports world. Filling in for an injured Williams, Gaines somehow ended up with the ball as time was running out, and the Jazz were trailing by two. The rest is history: Gaines sank a deep three-pointer and ended up celebrating with Jazz fans on top of the scorer's table at EnergySolutions Arena. Wisely, the Jazz signed him to a second 10-day contract the next day.

Jazz 116, Heat 114 OT (November 9, 2010 at Miami): James racked up his second triple-double against the Jazz, but nobody will remember that thanks to what Paul Millsap did. Utah's power forward went bonkers, scoring 46 points, including three three-pointers and an off-balanced buzzer-beater in the final 28.7 seconds of regulation. James, perhaps stunned like his South Beach supporters clearly were, didn't score in overtime.

Jazz 99, Heat 98 (March 2, 2012 at Utah): Though he scored 35, including 17 in the fourth, and added 10 rebounds and six assists, James took heat because he passed instead of taking the game-winning shot. Miami center Udonis Haslem then missed a long jumper before the buzzer. "I just try to make the right plays and do what it takes to win basketball games," James said. "At the end of the day, games are not lost on one shot at the end or me not taking a shot. But I know the chatter will begin. I wanted that game as bad as anyone else on that floor." Devin Harris was the Jazz hero, converting a three-point play with 4.5 seconds left.

Jazz 94, Heat 89 (February 8, 2014 at Utah): This was James' worst game against Utah, but the Jazz still needed late back-to-back three-pointers from Marvin Williams to secure the win. The King only scored 13 points—the same as Utah rookie Trey Burke—snapping a streak of six straight games with 30-plus in SLC.

Jazz 102, Cavs 100 (November 5, 2014 at Utah): James had another big game with 31 points, but Gordon Hayward overshadowed him with a game-winning step-back jumper at the horn. "To win the game after being in control the whole game and then see it slipping away," Hayward said, "was pretty special."

Jazz 100, Cavs 92 (January 10, 2017 at Utah): This game didn't have any last-second heroics, but it included an incredible mano-a-mano duel between James and Hayward in the second half. During one stretch Hayward scored 11 of his 28 points in a 16–0 Jazz run after halftime. Cleveland had just gone on a 17–0 spurt and James had 13 points in the third quarter. It was one of those games that showed how Hayward had arrived as an All-Star player.

Jazz 104, Cavs 101 (December 30, 2017 at Utah): James and the Jazz celebrated on this day as the superstar turned 33, and Utah beat his team for the seventh time in a row at home. James didn't score in the pivotal third quarter when the Jazz used a 23–3 surge to turn things around, but he finished with a team-high 29 points. The more impressive 29-point game came from Utah rookie sensation Donovan Mitchell, who also contributed six assists, four rebounds, and three steals. A sweet drive by Mitchell gave the Jazz a three-point cushion in the late going. "He's a player," James said. "Kid's got a lot of game…He's not afraid of the moment. He just goes out and plays ball. They put him in situations where he can succeed, and he just shot and took advantage of it."

68 Ron Boone

If it tells you anything about what Ron Boone values from his professional basketball career, his Twitter handle is @1041straight. That's a well-earned moniker for the talented man who's now known more for providing color commentary for Jazz broadcasts than for his splendid accomplishments as a player. During his ABA and NBA playing career, however, Boone played in 1,041 straight games despite suffering a broken nose, dislocated shoulders, and a slew of other injuries and illnesses over 13 years.

Boone's amazing longevity streak, the longest in professional basketball at the time, was finally snapped in Utah when the Jazz needed to open up roster space for Rickey Green in 1981. "It was a horrible moment for me because Ron is such a class guy," then-Jazz coach Tom Nissalke told the *Deseret News*.

General manager Frank Layden took the blame, opting to not use the flexible injury list to keep Boone on the roster because it would have been bending the rules. It was one of the toughest decisions he'd ever had to make, he told sports journalist Dave Blackwell.

Remarkably, Boone—or "Booner," "Ironman," "The Legend," or "Chief," as he's been called over the years—had played at least 20 minutes in every game with the Dallas/Texas Chaparrals, the Utah Stars, the Spirits of St. Louis, the Kansas City Kings, the Los Angeles Lakers, and the Jazz up to that point. Boone, the third highest scorer in ABA history (12,153 points), helped the Stars win a championship in Utah in 1971. That was the first of four years he was named an ABA All-Star.

It also gave him an introduction to the unlikely place that the Nebraska native would call home. Seven years after his NBA career ended with the Jazz, Boone returned to the organization in 1988 as a commentator to help Hot Rod Hundley fill the airwaves with basketball knowledge. He's been the broadcast partner of the late Hundley, Craig Bolerjack, and radio play-by-play announcer David Locke ever since and is a beloved part of Jazz lore. "Coming here to play with the Stars was really the start of something very special for me," Boone told the *Deseret News*. "I knew absolutely nothing about Utah when I arrived here, but…I have learned to love this area."

69 "How 'Bout This Jazz?"

Many Utah Jazz fans would not recognize Dan Roberts if they saw him in public—until he started talking. Once Roberts began to bellow out things like "How 'bout this Jazz?" and "Jazz fans, bring the noise!" with his rich, baritone voice, he'd lose his anonymity.

While Hot Rod Hundley, Craig Bolerjack, and David Locke have acted as the voices of the Jazz over the airwaves for years, it's Roberts' powerful pipes that fans have heard inside the arena since he introduced the relocated franchise's first starting lineup nearly four decades ago. "I go back to the opening tip-off," Roberts said. "It was a slow start obviously, but we just kept going and going and going, and I've become acceptable background ambience now."

Roberts has been a fixture of the franchise ever since he first introduced the likes of Ron Boone, Allan Bristow, and Adrian Dantley to new NBA fans for the first time on October 15, 1979. He's called out announcements, team intros, names of players, promo blurbs, and exuberantly egged on the crowd for nearly

2,000 Jazz home games at the old Salt Palace and in their current arena. "Anybody that's ever played in Salt Lake has come across my tongue," Roberts proudly said.

Roberts has a remarkable attendance record, too. He's only missed about 10 games in 39 years as the Jazz's public-address announcer. The job, he boasts, comes with a sweet perk. "I get paid to sit at midcourt," he said.

Plus, Roberts gets to eat catered pregame dinners; meet basketball celebrities such as Bill Russell, Bob Cousy, Wilt Chamberlain, and Michael Jordan; and watch a lot of basketball on the clock. He describes Magic Johnson as being "very, very cordial." Larry Bird? "Basically okay." And Roberts laughs about how Dennis Rodman pointed at his microphone one time and told him, "You do a pretty good job with that thing." Over the years, Roberts has been there at courtside for the beginning of a community's love affair with its pro team, for the entire Stockton-to-Malone Hall of Fame era, for an All-Star Game (1993), for two NBA Finals (1997 and 1998), for Sundiata Gaines' magical make against LeBron James, and so on.

Jazz fans, how 'bout this job?

When he's not up front and center for Jazz home games, Roberts makes a living as a full-time kitchen and bath designer. His voice and enthusiasm at Jazz home games is what he's best known for, of course. Roberts has earned money with his voice since he dabbled with a radio career at KALL in the early 1970s. He was the arena announcer for the Utah Stars from 1971 to 1975, announced games for the Utah Prospectors of the Western Basketball Association, and did voice work for University of Utah games upon then-Ute-coach Jerry Pimm's recommendation. Though he had a volunteer post for the Utes, it paid off nicely. He got to call arguably the most famous basketball game in history: Magic vs. Bird (the NCAA Championship Game featuring Michigan State and Indiana State at the Special Events Center).

Roberts didn't have to donate his time for long. His voice struck a chord with Jazz brass when the franchise relocated from New Orleans in 1979. "And," he laughed, "here I am."

Roberts doesn't have plans on hanging up his mic anytime soon. Not only does the gig give him some spending money—helping him put a daughter through college—but "the possibility of winning it all" keeps him going. "I want to be part of that," Roberts said. "And as far as I'm concerned, I'm going to hang on until I can't get over the table anymore. And if I'm 85 years old when that's the case, so be it."

Roberts admits the job has made him a seat snob. He once took a grandson to a Harlem Globetrotters game, but his seat in the middle of the lower bowl felt like it was in the nosebleed section. "I was only 10 rows up from the court," he said, laughing, "and I'm going, 'I hate this seat.'"

Roberts said there isn't a hard part to his job. He follows the ball and the officials so he can make the right call. And he admits that he occasionally has to "manufacture exuberance."

The biggest challenge? Pronouncing names. He took to Google to find the proper way to say Giannis Antetokounmpo and can now roll The Greek Freak's name off of his tongue like he's saying John Smith. John Stockton did once chide him for pronouncing Gonzaga incorrectly.

"It's Gon-ZAG-a," Stockton told Roberts. "Not Gon-zahg-a."

Roberts introduced his signature call—"How 'bout this Jazz?"—five or six years after the Jazz arrived. Roberts laughs (now at least) that he was once called a "flippant truck-pull announcer" by a Portland writer and a "hip, flip disc-jockey type" by an Oakland columnist.

Roberts credits Jazz fans for providing the deafening decibels that make the arena one of the loudest in the NBA. "I don't create it. I take advantage of it," he said. "I milk it. I nurse it. I bring it along and keep it moving."

Roberts loves Jazz fans because they've been through thick and thin over the decades but keep bringing the noise. "I've been with them as children, I've been with them as parents, and I've been with them as grandparents," he said. "The evolution of that has been kind of cool to be a part of, and I've enjoyed that immensely."

70 Thirty Pieces of Silver

The Utah Jazz have had some interesting punishments over the years. Jerry Sloan was suspended seven games for shoving a ref. Enes Kanter was fined $25,000 for tossing his mouthpiece into the Sacramento crowd. Rodney Hood forked over $35,000 for smacking a cellphone out of fan's hand after being ejected at Washington. Aussie Joe Ingles had to pay $15,000 for hitting Kiwi Steve Adams below the belt. Karl Malone was fined $10,000 for getting in a strange argument with Dallas Mavericks coach Don Nelson, and $10,000 for popping Isiah Thomas in the eye, and another $10,000 for elbowing Brian Grant, and…

But none compare to the fine Frank Layden gave Adrian Dantley and Malone in 1986, which a *Los Angeles Times* reporter described as "a new level of pettiness." The Jazz were playing against the Suns in Phoenix on March 7, 1986, when The Mailman missed three of four free throws in the final seconds in the 105–103 win. Layden, the coach and GM, got mad. Malone got mad. And everyone within the Greater Phoenix Metro Area heard the two bicker in public there on the court. The confrontation escalated in the locker room when Dantley stood up for Malone. That infuriated Layden. He sent A.D. back to Utah while the Jazz traveled to play the Portland Trail Blazers—a game Utah lost 104–90—for what he called a "disciplinary matter." That set Dantley off. He thought his reputation had been tarnished.

Layden felt betrayed and decided to give out two unique and symbolic fines. Punishment No. 1: The Mailman was forced to pay two pennies "for getting his two cents worth" in the verbal altercation. Malone yelled that he was "not a mule or a dog" and told his coach he could speak to him "like a human," the UPI reported. Punishment No. 2: Dantley's fine was stranger and a higher level of pettiness or hilariousness, depending on your point of view. The 10-year NBA veteran had to pay 30 pieces of silver. Dantley attended a Catholic high school (DeMatha Catholic High) and college (Notre Dame) so it didn't take a priest to explain the fine was a biblical reference to the amount Judas Iscariot was paid to betray Jesus Christ. Yes, those were actual team-issued fines. "It's 30 dimes," Layden said. "It's 30 pieces of silver."

Malone got over it. (That was evident when the jovial Layden abruptly stepped down as coach in December 1988. Malone paid his respect by scribbling the name "Frank" on his basketball shoes and dedicated the rest of his career to his first NBA coach.) But the rift between Layden and Dantley only got worse. Their relationship suffered a huge blow when Dantley was a temporary holdout in 1984, even though the two sides were only about $100,000 apart in contract negotiations. After he sat out the preseason, practices, and the first six games of the 1984–85 regular season, Dantley's fines were substantially bigger than Layden's handful of symbolic change. He racked up $44,000 in fines—$6,000 for each regular-season game missed, $500 for each skipped exhibition contest, and $150 for being a practice no-show.

Layden openly expressed his frustrations with Dantley and agent David Falk. "I don't like being held hostage," Layden told the *Los Angeles Times*. "What Dantley doesn't realize is that if I was President Carter, I would have bombed Iran to get the hostages out."

Things smoothed over for a while. In 1985 Dantley even gave Layden a Christmas gift—a pipe. Thomas Bonk of the *L.A. Times* surmised the present symbolized a peace pipe to show that their up-and-down, six-year relationship was on better terms. Dantley humorously stashed the pipe inside of a lunch pail. That was an inside joke, referring to Layden's answer to a Boston reporter who asked if the coach felt sorry for the 6'5" Dantley being forced to guard bigger guys like 6'10" Kevin McHale and 6'11" Bill Walton. "Hell, don't feel sorry for Dantley," Layden said. "Feel sorry for the guy who carries a lunch pail."

The peace didn't last long. The Phoenix incident happened two and a half months later. Dantley was then traded to the Detroit

Adrian Dantley, who drives on New York Knicks forward Campy Russell, starred for the Jazz in the early 1980s before receiving a unique punishment from Frank Layden. (AP Images)

Pistons five months after the 30-dime fine, which Layden later admitted to regretting, along with playing hardball in contract negotiations.

Some might chuckle, looking back on the strangeness of the incident as one of the sillier moments in Jazz history, but Dantley still doesn't find any humor in it. "It's not funny to me," he told the *Deseret News* 20 years later.

When it happened, Dantley demanded that the Jazz distribute a press release apologizing for making him look bad. He held his own press conference to defend himself, a move that also irked Layden and other members of the Jazz's front office. The ongoing fiasco led to resentment on both sides. "The biggest benefit to us in the Adrian Dantley trade was addition by subtraction," then-Jazz president Dave Checketts said later in the 1986–87 season. "We knew we had to get rid of him and we were never so happy to get rid of a guy in the history of the franchise."

Things were hairy for a while until Utah delivered its own peace offering and retired Dantley's No. 4 jersey in 2007. Three-plus decades later, Layden doesn't feel bad about this particular fine. "I never regret when I'm right," he said.

71 Derek Fisher

Even though he provided one of the greatest single moments in Jazz history and only played in Utah for one season, it's safe to say that Derek Fisher is one of the least popular former players to have come and gone. To put it into context: he got booed nearly as loudly as his friend, Kobe Bryant, in Utah after his short time in a Jazz uniform ended.

Before becoming a villain in Jazzland, Fisher played an integral part in helping the team return to the Western Conference Finals for the first time since the Stockton-to-Malone era a decade earlier. A 6'1" point guard and three-time champion from his first stint with the Los Angeles Lakers, Fisher brilliantly filled the role as a steady veteran in the backcourt and as a valuable veteran mentor to Utah's rising star, Deron Williams. "When I played with him, he was like a coach out there on the floor," Williams told *Newsday* years later. "I always thought that Fish would make a great coach if he ever decided to go that route."

Fisher ended an eight-year run with the Lakers—culminating in the famous shot he made after catching and releasing the ball with only 0.4 seconds on the clock in the conference finals against the San Antonio Spurs en route to the 2004 championship—and signed a six-year, $37-million contract with the Golden State Warriors. Two years into his disappointing run with the Warriors, Fisher was traded to Utah on July 12, 2006, in exchange for Keith McLeod, Andre Owens, and Devin Brown. The 32-year-old proved to be a reliable asset for Jerry Sloan, averaging 10 points, 3.3 assists, and one steal mostly as an undersized shooting guard on a 51–31 team.

Days before the Jazz were to face Fisher's old team, the Warriors, in the second round of the Western Conference playoffs, his 10-month-old daughter, Tatum, was diagnosed with a rare form of eye cancer. Fisher was granted permission to leave the team and attend to his twin baby's health as she was treated for retinoblastoma, a cancerous tumor in her left eye, at New York Presbyterian Hospital. The condition often results in patients losing an eye and can be fatal, so the Jazz certainly understood his desire to be with family during the urgent surgery. "The uncertainty…was tough," Fisher told *The Salt Lake Tribune*.

Fisher missed Game 1 of the series, a 116–112 Jazz victory, and then headed back to Salt Lake City on a charter flight with his wife and daughter after the successful surgery ended at 2:15 PM MT on May 9. His hope was to make it to Utah in time for the 7:00 PM playoff tip-off. Upon his arrival, Fisher received a police escort for the two-mile drive from the Salt Lake International Airport to EnergySolutions Arena. The game was in progress. As his family went home, he quickly changed into his uniform, stretched, and entered the arena to thunderous applause late in the third quarter.

Williams had just been called for his fourth foul, and Utah's other backup point guard, rookie Dee Brown, was at the hospital getting his injured neck examined after colliding with Mehmet Okur earlier in the game. Fisher's arrival was well-timed. He immediately entered the game—didn't even sit on the bench— with 3:18 remaining in the quarter. "I asked him if he was all right, and he said he was," Sloan said. "He's gone through a lot the last few days, and basketball was probably a good opportunity for him."

Even with Fisher in the lineup, the Warriors seized a five-point lead with 52.9 seconds remaining after going on a 12–1 run. With the Jazz still trailing by three points, Fisher forced Baron Davis into a turnover to give Utah the ball with 27.4 seconds left. Okur missed a game-tying three-pointer, but the Jazz were kept alive after the Warriors' Mickael Pietrus missed two free throws and Davis split a pair at the charity stripe. Williams forced overtime by sinking an open mid-range jumper in the final seconds.

Fisher then all but clinched the victory in overtime by draining a three-pointer from the corner to put Utah up by six with 1:06 to go. It was his only shot of the game and the first shot he'd taken anywhere in three days. "There's not enough that could be said about him, what he did tonight," Williams said.

Fisher wore sunglasses to and from practices and shoot-arounds after finding out about his daughter's condition a week earlier. It was a heart-wrenching trial. "We have been on an emotional roller coaster and we will probably be on it for years to come because it is a cancer," Fisher said. "But we're going to help her beat it and help other kids beat this as well."

Two months later, Fisher called for a meeting with team owner Larry H. Miller and Jazz executives. He asked for and was granted a release from the three remaining years on his contract because he said he wanted to live in one of the six or seven cities around the nation that could provide the best care for his young daughter. Fisher was hopeful of continuing his NBA career elsewhere, but he spoke of being willing to retire if it was in his family's best interest.

"He's focused on the most important thing," a teary-eyed Miller said in a press conference to announce Fisher's early departure from Utah.

"Life for me outweighs the game of basketball," Fisher said. "When it comes to decisions related to [my family], I do what's best."

Some in Utah, however, became skeptical of Fisher's intentions when he re-signed with the Lakers less than two weeks later. Many fans—and some Jazz personnel behind the scenes—thought he'd taken advantage of the kind-hearted Miller to get out of that contract so he could rejoin his old team. Fisher helped the Lakers win two more titles before ending his 18-year career with the Dallas Mavericks and Oklahoma City Thunder.

Fans still feel Fisher did the franchise wrong, but the late Miller tried to think the best of a player who gave his team a lot in his one season. "It did look funny when we just released Derek outright...and like three weeks later he signed with the Lakers," Miller told *The Salt Lake Tribune* three months after the fact. "And I've been asked a lot since then, 'Did Derek put you guys together?' You know what? There's no real way to know that. What I've chosen to do is to say, 'I don't think so,' partly because

I don't want to believe it. But also because I think he's a man of integrity...The request when it came to us seemed perfectly legitimate and actually irrefutable. I mean, how are you going to tell a guy, 'No, you can't take care of your family, your child?'"

Two years later, Fisher said he had fond feelings for his time in Utah even if he'd plunged from his fan favorite status. "It was a good experience," he said. "There was definitely a reason we were here when we found out about Tatum's diagnosis. I don't think I could have been in a better situation in terms of teammates and in their ability to support me in that situation. The coaching staff was very supportive and in Kevin [O'Connor] and Larry, from a management and ownership standpoint, they let me determine what was important."

And Tatum? "We're thankful," he said, "that things have continued to get better."

72 Front-Office Personnel

In recent decades the Utah Jazz have been heralded for their stability and steady leadership at the top of the organization—a situation that tended to trickle downward and has led to success. It wasn't always that way.

The franchise's first head coach, in fact, only lasted a month before getting fired. Scotty Robertson did guide the Jazz to their first ever win—a 102–101 victory against the Portland Trail Blazers on November 10, 1974—after 11 straight losses to begin the season. But Robertson lasted 1,794 fewer games with the Jazz than Jerry Sloan. Here's a look at the key front-office players over the course of the first 45 years of the franchise.

Head Coaches

Scotty Robertson (May 28, 1974–November 17, 1974): His stint was short with the Jazz—just 15 games—but the popular New Orleans figure and former Louisiana Tech head coach went on to coach the Chicago Bulls and Detroit Pistons in a long NBA career.

Bill "Butch" van Breda Kolff (November 18, 1974–December 14, 1976): Technically the third coach in Jazz history—Elgin Baylor acted as interim head coach for one game after Robertson was fired—van Breda Kolff joined the Jazz after coaching the Los Angeles Lakers, Detroit Pistons, Phoenix Suns, and Memphis Tams (ABA). New Orleans went 74–100 under his guidance before he was fired early in the 1976–77 season after a dispute with ownership.

Elgin Baylor (November 17, 1974, December 16, 1976–April 12, 1979): The former Lakers standout player, who later settled in for a long career as the Los Angeles Clippers general manager, lost his first game at the helm in 1974. He got a chance to coach the team for real when van Breda Kolff was let go a couple of years later. Led by Pete Maravich, Baylor's 1977–78 team flirted with the playoffs before finishing four games out at 39–43. Management opted to part ways with Baylor (86–135 with the Jazz) when the team moved to Utah in 1979.

Tom Nissalke (June 18, 1979–December 10, 1981): Beehive State basketball fans were familiar with Nissalke, who was the head coach of the Utah Stars when the franchise folded early in the 1976 season. He returned to Salt Lake City as the Utah Jazz's first bench boss with the distinction of earning Coach of the Year honors in the ABA (1972 Dallas Chaparrals) and NBA (1977 Houston Rockets). Nissalke's tenure in Utah—at least as head coach—didn't last long. His teams struggled to gain traction and fans, going 60–124 before Frank Layden fired him and hired himself. Nissalke eventually shared his expert insight on Jazz radio and TV.

Frank Layden (December 10, 1981–December 9, 1988): Layden's first season as head coach of the Jazz ended as poorly as it began under Nissalke. Utah went 25–57 on the year, including a 17–45 mark under Layden. A season-ending injury to Adrian Dantley, who missed 60 games, derailed his first full season, but Utah improved nonetheless to 30–52. And then it all changed in 1983–84 when the Jazz proved they had heart to match their rising talent. Layden was named NBA Coach of the Year after the Jazz shockingly went 45–37, won the Midwest Division, and made it to the second round of the playoffs. Layden's teams were playoff regulars after that, but the job wore him down, and he stepped aside early in the 1988–89 season after compiling a 277–294 record in Utah in eight seasons.

Jerry Sloan (December 9, 1988–February 10, 2011): Layden's second hire was even better than his first. Sloan's leadership combined with the stellar play of John Stockton and Karl Malone led the franchise to an elite status in the NBA. Sloan coached for 23 seasons, racking up an incredible 1,223 wins in the regular season and playoffs to become the first coach in NBA history to win 1,000 games with one team. Like his old boss, Sloan eventually felt drained and called it quits midseason, shocking the sports world on February 10, 2011. His remains the longest tenure in NBA history. His final Jazz record was 1,127–682.

Tyrone Corbin (February 10, 2011–April 21, 2014): Management wanted as smooth of a transition as possible—and because longtime lead assistant Phil Johnson opted to resign with Sloan—the Jazz hired Corbin, an assistant coach and former Utah player. He was dealt a tough hand after franchise player Deron Williams was traded less than two weeks into his tenure. Corbin led the Jazz back to the playoffs the following year with Al Jefferson and Paul Millsap, but the front office again put him in a tough spot by allowing those two to sign elsewhere after the team fell just shy of the playoffs following a 43–39 season in 2012–13. Corbin's contract was not renewed after the young, rebuilding Jazz went 25–57 in 2013–14. His final record was 112–146.

Quin Snyder (June 6, 2014—present): The Jazz opted to take the franchise in a different direction, and the man they hired made perfect sense, considering the 47-year-old Snyder's connection with GM Dennis Lindsey and his coaching resume. A former Duke point guard and three-time Final Four participant, Snyder had garnered coaching experience with Duke, Missouri, Los Angeles (Clippers and Lakers), the Philadelphia 76ers, Russia (CSKA Moscow), the Atlanta Hawks, and in the Spurs organization (D-League Austin Toros) while preparing for a head coaching opportunity at this level. The young Jazz responded, going 38–44 in his first year, 40–42 in Year Two, and then making the big leap to a 51–31 season and a second-round playoff push in his third year. Snyder picked up his 150th Jazz win during the 2017–18 season.

General Managers

Bill Bertka (May 8, 1974–October 5, 1976): The organization's first GM has Hot Rod Hundley to thank. According to the *Los Angeles Times*, Hundley recommended that the Los Angeles Lakers hire him as a scout, which they did in 1968. He left the Jazz in 1981 and returned to L.A. to become a Lakers assistant and stayed on the Lakers bench longer than anyone while working with Bill Sharman, Pat Riley, and Phil Jackson.

Barry Mendelson (October 5, 1976–March 23, 1977): Mendelson had various roles with the Jazz organization from the get-go and moved on to a career in sports, media, and entertainment before being hired as a Madison Square Garden executive.

Lewis Schaffel (April 16, 1977–September 22, 1978): Owner Sam Battistone hired the 34-year-old Schaffel to try to keep Pete Maravich in New Orleans. Pistol Pete demanded that the team get another first-rate frontcourt man, according to *Sports Illustrated*, leading the franchise to sign Truck Robinson.

Tom Willingham (September 22, 1978–May 9, 1979): The Jazz experienced rough times under Willingham's direction with Robinson demanding and receiving a trade, a season-ending injury to Maravich, and the end of the Crescent City era.

Frank Layden (May 9, 1979–June 15, 1987): The gregarious personality joined the team for its relocation after a three-year run as an assistant with the Atlanta Hawks from 1976 to 1979. The former Niagara University player and coach quickly pulled off a

Ownership Timeline

March 7, 1974: Part of a nine-man group, Fred Rosenfeld and Sam Battistone paid $6.15 million to buy the expansion franchise in New Orleans, the NBA's 18th team.

April 10, 1979: Co-owners Sam Battistone and Larry Hatfield—Rosenfeld had been bought out—announced the franchise was relocating from New Orleans to Salt Lake City, Utah.

February 27, 1982: Sam Battistone bought out Larry Hatfield to become club's sole owner.

May 25, 1983: Purchase of 50 percent of the Jazz by Dr. Gerald Bagley and his son, Thomas, was approved by the NBA Board of Governors.

April 11, 1985: Local automobile dealer Larry H. Miller bought 50 percent share from Bagley and his son, making him an equal co-owner with Sam Battistone.

June 24, 1986: Offers to relocate the franchise were spurned after Larry H. Miller bought the Jazz outright.

February 20, 2009: Larry H. Miller died at the age of 64 as result of complications from type 2 diabetes. Ownership stayed in the family with Gail Miller, his widow, and his children.

January 23, 2017: The Millers announced that ownership of the Utah Jazz and Vivint Smart Home Arena were transferred to a legacy trust, guaranteeing the franchise will remain in Utah for generations. The trust will be maintained by current and future members of the Miller family.

trade with the Lakers to acquire a star scorer in Adrian Dantley, took over as head coach in 1981, garnered league honors (Coach and Executive of the Year) for the breakout season of 1983–84, and set the team up for the future by drafting John Stockton and Karl Malone.

Dave Checketts (June 15, 1987–June 1, 1989): Before taking one of the elite jobs in sports—president and CEO of Madison Square Garden—a 28-year-old Checketts was hired as the youngest GM in NBA history. Layden kept his duties as head coach until calling quits on Checketts' watch in 1988.

Scott Layden (June 1, 1989–August 10, 1999): The younger Layden had been a scout and an assistant coach for his dad's team, and some credit him for convincing management to draft an unheralded point guard out of Gonzaga in 1984. His biggest move as GM was to trade for Jeff Hornacek, who gave the team a third strong option behind Stockton and Malone. He left for the New York Knicks in 1999 after the Jazz's two NBA Finals appearances.

Kevin O'Connor (August 26, 1999–August 7, 2012): The Bronx native helped navigate the franchise through the end of its most successful period with Hall of Famers Stockton and Malone and built a team that returned to the Western Conference Finals with Deron Williams, Carlos Boozer, and Mehmet Okur in 2007 before stepping down in 2012 after beginning a rebuilding project.

Dennis Lindsey (August 7, 2012–present): Having been groomed in the successful Houston and San Antonio franchises, Lindsey took the baton from O'Connor and eventually constructed a roster that returned to the playoffs in 2017 for the first time in five years before one of its top two players, Gordon Hayward, left for the Boston Celtics and threw a wrench in the franchise's plans for the future. His two early successes included pulling off draft-day trades for potential cornerstones Rudy Gobert and Donovan Mitchell.

73 Watch Summer League Games

In 1984 then-Utah Jazz general manager Dave Checketts hatched a plan to give professional players and amateurs some much-needed playing opportunities in the summer. He offered two members of the team's public relations staff, Kim Turner and Dave Allred, a $1,000 bonus if the pro-am event drew a big enough crowd to make a profit, according to *The Salt Lake Tribune*.

The Jazz weren't certain who would show up and only pulled out two sets of bleachers at Westminster College for a game that featured former BYU players Danny Ainge pitted against a team led by ex-Utah star Tom Chambers. But the idea was a slam dunk. Fans packed the high-school-sized gym, and Salt Lake City had a new summertime tradition: the Rocky Mountain Revue.

Not only did the basketball league have a catchy name and offer offseason basketball action to temporarily quench die-hard fans' thirst, but other NBA franchises loved the concept of sending teams of newly drafted players, hopefuls, and prospects for a couple of weeks of practices, games, and camaraderie building.

Other than two NBA lockouts (1995 and 1998) and a break in 1988—which led to a revival and a restructured Revue—the summer showcase had a strong 25-year run before the fledgling Vegas Summer League surged in popularity and gave the Jazz no option but to pull the plug in 2009. For a few years, the Jazz were able to convince some teams to participate in both the Revue and in the NBA-backed Las Vegas league, but budgets were tight in a struggling economy, and Utah could only garner commitments from five other teams that year before shutting it down. "We're really going to miss it," Kevin O'Connor, the Jazz's GM at the time, told the *Deseret News*. "We're annoyed. We put on a terrific show for basketball and are disappointed we're not going to be able to put it on again this year, disappointed for our fans, too."

The Revue had several locations over the years as it evolved into what was considered the best run summer league. After its surprising reception at Westminster, a private school in the city's eclectic Sugar House neighborhood, where the Jazz used to practice, the summer league bounced from nearby East High School (long before Zac Efron helped make the school famous in *High School Musical*), to the Delta Center (hosting as many as 16 teams at its peak popularity), and finally to the Salt Lake Community College for nine years. As many as 11 teams participated at SLCC's Lifetime Activities Center in 2004, but in 2008 that dwindled down to eight, including the Iranian national team, a collection of D-League players, and the Jazz. "Kind of the end of an era," Allred said. "It ran probably a lot longer than any of us expected it would."

Those who attended the event over the years—from fans to the annual gathering of agents and NBA front-office personnel interspersed throughout the crowd—got to see the likes of John Stockton, Karl Malone, Tim Duncan, Dirk Nowitzki, Kevin Garnett, Amar'e Stoudemire, Carmelo Anthony, and Kevin Durant in action before they became superstars at the professional level. Jazz fans got a sneak peek at their rookies—like No. 3 pick Deron Williams in 2005—months before training camp started. "You just kind of had these relationships you didn't get in the regular season," Allred told *The Tribune*. "Especially when it was two weeks, you'd spend time in the bleachers watching game after game."

The Jazz opted to fly across the country to participate in the Orlando Pro Summer League every July from 2009 to 2014. They made the long trek in part because management was miffed at Las Vegas for luring teams away from the Revue but also because, like Utah's capital city, the family-friendly central Florida location was preferred over Sin City and all of its distractions. "We will not go to Las Vegas," O'Connor said. "We felt like Orlando was a better place to play basketball."

With a changing of the guard in the player personnel department—the Jazz hired Dennis Lindsey from the San Antonio Spurs as O'Connor's successor—also came a change of heart. After traveling to Orlando for five straight summers, Utah decided to stay much closer to home and joined the majority of the league in sending a team to the NBA Summer League in Las Vegas in 2014. "Having our training camp in Orlando was difficult for us, and we felt it was time to move forward," Lindsey told the *Las Vegas Review-Journal*. "We feel there's a natural tie-in with Las Vegas, and it'll be great for our fans to follow us and be able to see our young players. We're very excited about the move."

The Las Vegas league founder, Warren LeGarie, who happens to be the agent for Lindsey and head coach Quin Snyder, was excited, too. The Jazz drew large crowds that first summer as fans were excited to watch first-round picks Dante Exum and Rodney Hood, along with returning players Rudy Gobert and Trey Burke. "It's a lot easier to get to Vegas than it is the East Coast," Lindsey said, citing convenience for Jazz fans as one reason for making the move.

"Las Vegas has always supported the Jazz, and it was clearly a consensus among my staff that Utah needed to be included," LeGarie told the *Review-Journal*. "It was just a matter of being persistent, and persistency won out."

That turned out to be the case for bringing summer league action back to Salt Lake City, something Jazz management hoped would eventually be the case after the Revue's demise.

In 2015 the Revue was revived but with a brand-conscious new name: the Utah Jazz Summer League. This four-day exhibition could eventually grow bigger, but the same four teams—Boston Celtics, Philadelphia 76ers, Spurs, and Jazz—were the only participants for three summers. Those squads have all gone from Salt Lake

City to Sin City for an extended summer run. Then-Jazz president Randy Rigby couldn't wipe the smile off his face after 31,500-plus fans attended the first UJSL at EnergySolutions Arena. "Fantastic," Rigby said. "The fans responded."

Other than an ankle injury to Exum, the revived event went off without a hitch and without a loss for the 3–0 Jazz. Hood gave fans a show with a 23-point, 10-rebound game. "Utah fans always, regardless of what time of year it is, they're always going to come out and support," the second-year shooting guard said. "They really pushed us over the hump tonight. It was fun just being out there in front of them."

Utah's summer league had two locations in 2016—its arena and the Huntsman Center—because of a previous event booking. It returned to the University of Utah in 2017 as construction workers rapidly renovated Vivint Smart Home Arena. The 2017 UJSL featured the dazzling debut of Jazz rookie sensation Donovan Mitchell.

74 The Longest Loss

Enes Kanter was only 19 years old when the Utah Jazz took the Philips Arena court against the Atlanta Hawks on March 25, 2012. By the time the game ended, the Jazz center's grandkids were helping him apply for social security benefits. Or at least it seemed like the game lasted for decades.

In reality, it only lasted for 68 minutes, which is a full 48 minutes of regulation play plus four overtimes. It felt even longer for those who watched the teams miss 136 shots between them and only score a combined four points in the first overtime. It remains the longest game in Jazz history and is the only other quadruple-overtime contest in the NBA since an extended Phoenix Suns and Portland Trail Blazers bout in 1997.

It wasn't long enough if you ask Gordon Hayward, who had 19 points and eight rebounds. The third-year player would have preferred to keep going until the Jazz won. "I played 57 minutes, and, man, that's a lot of basketball. I could've played 10 more overtimes if I had to," he said. "You're just out there competing, and that's all there is to it. Tomorrow morning will probably be tough, but

Longest Games

NBA Overtime Record
Six Overtimes
Indianapolis Olympians 75, Rochester Royals 73 (1/6/51)

Five Overtimes
Syracuse Nationals 125, Anderson Packers 123 (11/4/49)
Milwaukee Bucks 155, Seattle SuperSonics 154 (11/9/89)

Four Overtimes
Nine instances

Jazz Record—Overtime

Time	Opponent	Date	W/L	Score
3:16	@ Atlanta	3/25/12	L	133–139 (4OT)
3:16	Dallas	4/16/12	W	123–121 (3OT)
3:13	@ Toronto	11/12/12	W	140–133 (3OT)
3:11	Chicago	2/3/92	W	126–123 (3OT)
3:10	L.A. Lakers	12/1/05	L	101–105 (OT)

Jazz Record—Regulation

Time	Opponent	Date	W/L	Score
2:49	Cleveland	1/14/10	W	97–96
2:46	@ Denver	4/2/09	L	104–114
2:44	@ Sacramento	2/6/09	W	111–107
2:42	@ San Antonio	12/7/07	L	98–104
2:42	Boston	2/19/09	W	90–85

we're professionals, so you have to just keep playing hard no matter how long it takes."

Joe Johnson, who joined the Jazz four years later via free agency, led the Hawks to a well-earned 139–133 win with 37 points. His big night helped Atlanta prevail despite it being the team's third game in three days thanks to the league's quirky revamped schedule in the 2012 lockout-shortened season. "It was unbelievable," Johnson said. "I just had to laugh it off. I've never played in a game like that."

Very few have. It's the third longest game in NBA history. It lasted for three hours and 17 minutes. "It was tiring, but these kind of things you've got to enjoy if you love competing," Jazz coach Tyrone Corbin said. "It's a great game to be a part of. It would have been a greater game to win it."

Hayward saw the most action for the visiting team: 57 minutes and 28 seconds. Starters Al Jefferson (28 points, 17 rebounds), Paul Millsap (25 points, 13 rebounds), and Devin Harris (11 points, 10 assists) each logged 50-plus minutes. C.J. Miles had the shortest stint of the starting group with 49 minutes and 33 seconds. "I'd be lying if I said I wasn't fatigued out there a little bit," Millsap said. "But you've got to fight through that, try to figure a way to win the game. The monkey got on our back a little bit, obviously more than them, and we just couldn't finish out like we wanted to."

The end of the final five periods—counting the fourth quarter and all four overtime sessions—was frustrating for Utah. Millsap had a chance to end it in regulation but came up short on a 10-foot attempt. The Jazz then believed Millsap was fouled on a missed dunk late in the first overtime. Harris missed a desperation game-winning attempt on his old court in the second OT. That came 15 seconds after he put the Jazz up by three before Johnson knotted the score again with a triple.

Utah, which rallied out of a 17-point first-half deficit, had a chance to win in the third overtime after Millsap grabbed a late offensive rebound, but he missed another shot at the buzzer. Johnson finally put the Jazz out of their misery in the fourth overtime with a long jumper over Miles with 16 seconds remaining. It helped Atlanta's cause that both Jefferson and Millsap fouled out with the game on the line in the fourth overtime. "I was so happy when they fouled out, man, you wouldn't even believe it," Johnson said.

Coach Corbin didn't make any personnel moves in the overtimes until he was forced to when players fouled out. Guys were dead tired, but they wanted to be out there. "We fought. We're going to take a moral victory out of this one," Millsap said. "This is a good ball team we played tonight. They play excellent defense. We just didn't get it done. We've got tomorrow to make it up."

Big Al said it was almost harder to watch from the bench after he fouled out. "Of course, I wanted to stay out there," Jefferson said. "My leg was cramping. I got fatigued, but…every timeout we had, I took advantage of it. I wanted to play…It was hard to sit and watch. I wanted to be out there."

That "tomorrow" game Millsap referred to wasn't a problem. Despite the grueling marathon loss and a long flight to New Jersey, the Jazz cruised to a 105–84 blowout win against former Utah star Deron Williams and the New Jersey Nets. Utah did, however, lose its next three games. The Jazz then won a triple-overtime duel at home against the Dallas Mavericks 123–121 three weeks later. That was a piece of cake after what they went through in Atlanta.

75 Rookie Rituals

The league tried to squelch the time-honored tradition of rookie initiations in 2013, reminding all 30 NBA teams that bullying and hazing were no-nos, but the playful ritual still exists. That's why you shouldn't be surprised if you see tall young men sporting Jazz gear and pink backpacks.

Prompted by ugly hazing incidents in the NFL, that memo came two weeks too late for Rudy Gobert and Ian Clark. As part of their rite of passage, the Jazz newbies were forced to get their fingernails done in a Salt Lake City mall kiosk at the behest of veterans John Lucas III and Derrick Favors. Gobert, a first-year center from France, ended up with glittery pink nails. Undrafted out of Belmont, Clark sported a coat of sparkly purple paint over his cuticles.

Filmed by the team's video crew, both rookies were good sports. Gobert smiled but unconvincingly said, "I feel good. I like them." He also told his buddy Clark, "Very cute." The 22-year-old Clark laughed at the experience. "This is part of the process, man. You've got to do what the vets tell you to do or the punishment's worse. It's not that bad."

Some teams took extra steps to eliminate even innocent-seeming hazing acts, but Jazz players continued their traditions. Even while tearing it up on the court in a sensational rookie season, Donovan Mitchell was expected to carry on the Jazz's most popular ritual: the donning of pink backpacks. The gregarious rookie obliged and wore his pink tote with large fairy wings as instructed. Fellow rookies Tony Bradley and Royce O'Neale also received pink backpacks.

Welcome to the NBA, rooks.

Mitchell did have a complaint, though. "I'm not too fond of mine because it's a little small," Mitchell told *The Salt Lake Tribune* at the beginning of the 2017–18 campaign. "I wish it was a little bigger."

Gobert was victim of a messier prank later in his first year. He forgot to bring the team pastries—a daily rookie requirement—and was punished. One of the veteran players, allegedly, filled his new Range Rover with bags of popcorn from the arena. When "The Stifle Tower" opened the passenger door after a shootaround session, an avalanche of buttery kernels spilled out onto the parking lot. With its camera rolling, a TV crew happened to be there to film the mess and the custodial staff's ensuing leaf blower-led cleanup efforts. "I knew something was coming," Gobert said, cracking a grin. "I could feel it, but I didn't know what. I was surprised."

Gobert knew why it happened, though, and admitted he was guilty as charged. He also said he had no doubt who was responsible for the popcorn prank. "Rich Jefferson," he said after admitting he made a mistake by not supplying doughnuts that day. "I know it's him."

The same thing happened in 2017 to Weber State's Joel Bolomboy at the end of his rookie year. He tweeted out photos of the corny mess in—and out—of his car with a mea culpa message: "I learned a lot this past year…and one of those things [was] to always do what your vets asked."

In recent years Jazz rookies have been required to do a variety of mildly embarrassing or subservient tasks as part of the initiation process. They sing "Happy Birthday" to each player and coach. Doughnuts, bagels, and an occasional Crown Burger meal have been part of paying their dues. Raul Neto, Trey Lyles, and Tibor Pleiss had to do a hula dance in the 2015 preseason in Hawaii. Deron Williams instigated the Rookie Dance-Off in 2008, and the Jazz arena might've never seen a more entertaining performance than Ukrainian rookie Kyrylo Fesenko briefly breakdancing followed by Ohio State product Kosta Koufos busting out some funky moves before smoothly dropping to the court and pulling off a well-executed worm. The dancing went on for years before fading away after coach Quin Snyder temporarily ended the public scrimmages.

There's always more to do, though. Enes Kanter had to hand out jerseys. Alec Burks was expected to fetch Al Jefferson a 5-hour ENERGY drink before every game. Gordon Hayward and Jeremy Evans had their own pink princess backpacks to wear on road trips and to games and practices. Favors carried bags for vets Joe Smith and Stephen Graham and serenaded strangers celebrating birthdays at restaurants while with the New Jersey Nets.

C.J. Miles woke up early on the road to deliver shoes and a newspaper to Greg Ostertag's hotel room in 2005. "He'd be like, 'Thanks,' and throw them on the floor and go back to sleep," Miles said. "He did that to me twice and then left me alone. I did whatever he said. He just left me alone. It wasn't fun [for him] because I didn't fight it."

Earl Watson said Gary Payton was his assigned veteran with the Seattle SuperSonics in 2001, and "The Glove" kept him busy as a rookie. He had to pick Payton up at all hours of the day and night, pull his bags off the plane, and give him Gatorade with ice at practice, which was easier said than done. "Where you going to find ice during the middle of practice?" Watson said, smiling. "It's always something difficult." But a lifelong friendship emerged. "He was good with me," Watson said. "He ended up becoming my mentor—one of my big brothers still to this day."

Miles thought that the Rookie Dance-Off in 2012 was hilarious. Burks showed some decent moves, but Kanter was caught off-guard in front of 10,000 strangers. His dance moves oddly resembled off-rhythm shoulder shrugs. "Turkish people don't know how to dance," fellow Turkish player Mehmet Okur joked.

Andrei Kirilenko outsmarted his vets. When he was a rookie in 2001, buying doughnuts came with the territory of being a new guy. The young Russian pretended he conveniently couldn't understand teammates, he admitted in a streamed Q&A with the Timberwolves after he joined Minnesota in 2012. "So every time they ask me to bring doughnuts, I say, 'What? What?' And finally, somebody say, 'Okay, Jarron Collins, come over here. You gonna bring doughnuts.'"

Collins relayed to *The Salt Lake Tribune* that he got off easy another time during his rookie season. When the bill for a group breakfast at the Four Seasons hotel in Toronto arrived, the rookie was surprised to hear Karl Malone proclaim, "Young fella's paying for it." Dilemma: the Stanford grad hadn't cashed his first NBA paycheck. John Stockton, sitting next to him, whispered, "Just put down my room number." Collins said, "That was the one I got away from, and I appreciated it."

Another Jazz rookie, who remained anonymous, teased Malone for how many shots he took. The Mailman made the rookie carry his bags to his hotel room, turn on his lamp, and turn down his bed.

Jerry Sloan told *The Tribune* that he even had some rookie chores after joining the Baltimore Bullets in 1965. He had to carry shot clocks in the exhibition season and arrange cab rides on the road. Veterans might have heard an earful of colorful language if they'd tried to get him to participate in a Rookie Dance-Off, though.

76 Hood and Johnson

Rodney Hood grew up in Meridian, Mississippi, learning how to play basketball at four years old at the local Boys & Girls Club where his dad worked. Hood needed a second basket to shoot at because his older brother (by nine years) tore down the hoop their granddad built in their driveway while in high school, leaving the younger Hood stuck shooting on a bent rim for much of his childhood when he played at home. Hood had some successful Mississippi-made NBA role models to root for: Al Jefferson, Travis Outlaw, and Monta Ellis. "I wanted to be like those guys," Hood said.

Hood's favorite NBA player, though, was from a neighboring state: Arkansas' Joe Johnson. Drafted 10th overall by the Boston Celtics in 2001 following his sophomore season at the University of Arkansas, the 6'7" Johnson took a couple of seasons to get going in the NBA. But once he got going, *wow*, he really got going. A rookie starter for the Celtics, he was traded to the Phoenix Suns later that season. He averaged about 17 points for the Suns in his final two seasons and helped the team advance to the Western Conference Finals, though a cheekbone fracture limited him in the playoffs.

Johnson took the next step after signing with the Atlanta Hawks. He was named an All-Star six times—of his career total seven times—with the Hawks from 2005 to 2012. He played a similar position as Hood and was a versatile scorer who patiently wore down opponents before striking at the opportune time. (Jazz president Steve Starks later compared his on-court movements to Pro Bowl running back Le'Veon Bell because of their elite vision, crafty footwork, and ability to pick apart defenses.)

It's no wonder Hood took a liking to Johnson, who picked up nicknames like "Iso Joe" (which he doesn't love) and "Joe Jesus" (which he does). "He was real smooth," Hood said, "could shoot the ball, could score the ball—somebody I could pattern my game after."

Hood was in New Orleans when he actually spotted Johnson in July 2005. "I was too shy to say something," said Hood, who was 10 years old at the time. "I was tapping my mom, 'There goes Joe Johnson!'" Hood's mom wasn't as shy as her young son. "She was bold enough to go up there and say something to him," Hood recalled, smiling.

Unabashedly, she made Hood come over and meet Johnson. As a bonus, she snapped a now-cherished picture with Hood standing next to his favorite All-Star. Johnson also signed the back of an envelope for a kid whose head didn't even reach his shoulders yet. Years later, Hood got to meet his childhood idol a second time, but this time he had joined him in the NBA and was a rookie with the Utah Jazz. Hood showed Johnson the photo of the meaningful moment before they played against each other for the first time in Brooklyn in 2014. "It was a great thing," Hood said.

A couple of years later, it became even greater. In the summer of 2016, the Jazz desperately needed veteran leadership to complement a youthful Utah squad that included young up-and-comers like third-year Hood, Gordon Hayward, Derrick Favors, and Rudy Gobert. Johnson bought in. The 35-year-old signed a two-year deal with Utah with the understanding that he'd come off the bench behind Hayward. Though he'd been a starter since December 9, 2003, Johnson was ready for a new challenge.

In his 16th NBA season, Johnson provided the Jazz with just what they wanted and needed in 2016–17—a valuable locker room presence, a dependable scorer off the bench, a player who could play both forward positions to give Quin Snyder multiple options, a mentor for Hood and youngsters, a hard worker, and an advocate of hot yoga (which became the rage for coaches and players alike).

Old Man Joe stunned some by scoring 29 points while filling in for Hayward in the season-opener. Then, his deft late-game drive and well-executed floater, which just went over 6'11" DeAndre Jordan's fingertips, rattled around the rim before plopping in to give Utah an unexpected Game 1 road win in the first round of the playoffs against the Los Angeles Clippers. It was his eighth buzzer-beating game-winner in 10 years, an NBA best, according to ESPN. Johnson played well all series, including a 28-point effort in a Game 4 victory. He was the unofficial series MVP as the Jazz finished off the Clippers 4–3, winning Game 7 at the Staples Center for their first playoff series win since 2010.

Nobody was wondering why Johnson would go to Utah toward the end of his illustrious career anymore. "I've never questioned my decision. Maybe people thought this was a little out of the norm," he said. "But I just looked at it that they had a lot of great young pieces and adding and sprinkling in some veteran talent could help these guys, and obviously it paid off."

77 Donate to a Jazz Charity

Shortly after Larry H. Miller passed away in 2009, then-LDS church president Thomas S. Monson shared a story about a gift he received from the generous Utah Jazz owner. Visitors to the late President Monson's office in downtown Salt Lake City would be shown the gift—a sculpture depicting one of his favorite poems—and encouraged to read Will Allen Dromgoole's "The Bridge Builder." As the poem goes, a traveler questioned why an old man would build bridges he'd never use. He was informed a younger man would be coming by soon: "Good friend, I am building the bridge for him."

While sharing this story, the church leader told the *Deseret News* he was touched how Miller, a man with strong Christian convictions, had given one of the beautiful pieces of artwork to each of his children so that they would remember the ultimate bridge builder—Jesus Christ. "Everywhere we go, we'll have an opportunity to pay tribute to Larry if we will just remember to not overlook the forlorn, not shun the person who has no friends, but rather, open wide our hearts and our souls to all those who need a little help up the ladder," President Monson said. "Larry Miller was one who always reached down and helped another person up."

Service was indeed an integral part of Miller's life, whether he performed the charitable acts himself, donated personal or business funds for worthy causes, or inspired others. Miller's deep-seated desire to build bridges, as the poem referred to charitable acts, is reflected in the late Jazz owner's oft-quoted mantra: "Go out into the world and do good until there is too much good in the world." Nearly a decade after his death, the organization he left behind continues to act on that mantra. Here are some of their charities.

Day of Service—Each spring on his birthday, April 26, the Miller family and his companies' employees carry on his legacy by volunteering in the communities where they live and work. Between 2010 and 2016, 5,664 employees, including Jazz staff, had donated 22,656 hours of service to 92 organizations across seven states. The volunteers assist local Boys & Girls Clubs, food and clothing banks, emergency shelters, and other community agencies in need. "Our mission is to enrich lives," Gail Miller said, "and serving is just one of the many ways we can work to enhance the quality of life for those around us."

Jazz Dental Day: The Jazz and TeamSmile, a non-profit organization that helps pro sports teams promote the importance of dental care, have provided local youth in need with complimentary dental care during this event since 2015. Sponsored by the Crown Council, underprivileged kids from the Salt Lake City School District have received free cleanings, X-rays, fillings, sealants, extractions, and dental hygiene tips. In 2015 dentists and hygienists performed $98,000 worth of dental work for free.

Leapin' Leaners & Low Tops: For more than 20 years, the Jazz have hosted this popular fund-raising event that allows fans to interact with players and coaches. Activities on the arena court have included shooting contests, ping pong, foosball matches, and video game competitions. Admission, proceeds of which go to charity, includes dinner, locker room tours, autographs, and other fun activities. Silent and live auctions also help raise money for Larry H. Miller Charities, which serves communities where the organization does business. Guests and Jazz personnel are invited to wear dressy clothes with low-top sneakers for the fun event.

Community Courts: The Larry H. Miller Court at Vivint Smart Home Arena isn't the only Utah Jazz court around town. The organization has helped build or fund 18 different courts around Utah for public use since 2001. In 2017 the Jazz opened their newest community court at Bingham Junction Park in Midvale. The outdoor court featured 5,600 square feet of playing surface with stripes in team colors and a Jazz logo at center court, six basketball goals with adjustable heights, backboards, nets, and rims. Former Jazz president Randy Rigby described why the team built and donated these courts: "Giving back to the community is part of the Jazz organization's DNA. The Jazz and Larry H. Miller Charities began building community basketball courts in 2001 in an effort to enhance local neighborhoods and provide places for children and families to enjoy for years to come. The game of basketball is not only fun, but it also helps to instill important values that extend to life off the court."

The Jazz also sponsor an annual "We Care—We Share" Thanksgiving dinner at the arena with meals for 3,000 people in need; Christmas hospital visits to brighten the spirits of ailing youth and their families at local children's hospitals; a Martin Luther King Jr. Day scholarship; Jazz Math Hoops to help youth learn basic education; a Newspapers in Education series that addresses relevant issues with youth; a ticket donation program for nonprofit organizations, schools, and community groups; the Bear Hugs for Kids Christmas shopping event; charitable auctions; Commitment to Service in honor of Veterans Day; the Jazz Fit program to promote fitness; a Pass It Along program that awards five charitable organizations with $25,000 each; Junior Jazz youth basketball league and an annual summer tour around the Intermountain West to provide basketball clinics; the Wheelin' Jazz wheelchair team; and a "Game Night with the Jazz" fund-raiser to benefit 5 for the Fight, the cancer research organization and jersey patch sponsor.

78 Sloanisms

During his career Jerry Sloan said what he felt and felt what he said—to everybody. He barked and swore at referees. He defended and called out players in interviews. He even let media have it on occasion. And he always seemed to have a classic one-line response to any situation. He was genuine. He was blunt, folksy, funny, and grumpy—sometimes all in one answer. As this sampling of classic Sloanisms suggests, there wasn't a P.R. spin machine between his mouth and his mind.

- **"At his resignation press conference on February 20, 2011:** "I'm not looking for another job. My wife has a job for me when I get home."

- **After the Jazz lost a second game to the 14-win Minnesota Timberwolves:** "Minnesota has given us trouble from Day One for whatever reason. I don't know if we're scared of wolves or what."

- **A training camp message:** "Hope they realize they can feed their family a lot easier playing this than playing bingo."

- **To emphasize the importance of desire and effort:** "Size doesn't make any difference. Heart is what makes a difference."

- **When someone was goofing off instead of giving 100 percent:** "You can't jackpot around."

- **When he thought his players were playing in cruise control:** "Basically what we've been doing is playing in tuxedos."

- **When he wanted harmony on and off the court:** "Hey, get your ice picks out. Get all your stuff solved. Go out in the parking lot. Do whatever you have to do to get all the nonsense taken care of, so we can play basketball. Let's get back to the business of basketball."

- **On his team rallying to beat the Los Angeles Clippers, Miami Heat, and Orlando Magic after trailing by double digits at halftime, something no other team had done since 1954:** "That'll get you a toothpick and a glass of water."

- **His message to 19-year-old C.J. Miles after a lackluster performance:** "He came out kind of soft. I mean, I don't care if he's 19 or 30. If he's going to be on the floor in the NBA, he's got to be able to step up and get after it. We can't put diapers on him one night and a jockstrap the next night."

- **On Michael Jordan:** "In my prime, I could have handled Michael Jordan. Of course, he would be only 12 years old."

- **On trying to win games, not popularity contests:** "I don't need my players to like me. I need them to play for me."

- **Upon advancing to the NBA Finals for the first time:** "The most important thing in sports is to keep trying."
- **On his longtime relationship with Karl Malone:** "Eighteen years—even in a marriage, that's a long time."
- **His assessment of his players' fitness levels at the beginning of the 2010 training camp:** "I'd say in shape for shaking hands, but to play a basketball game…some of them [are] not ready."
- **On why he didn't always call timeouts to bail his players out of rough stretches:** "That's like giving them a handful of candy. As soon as they eat it, they come back and want more."
- **His philosophy on shooters:** "I'm looking for a 'making' guard, not just a shooting guard."
- **A stern response to yours truly in front of other media members:** "Are you always perfect? Have you ever had a bad day?"
- **On the importance of being in shape:** "Whenever you're always bent over grabbing your pants, it's pretty hard to think about what you're doing."
- **Paul Millsap, who'd only hit two three-pointers in his NBA career, had just scored 46 points and three three-pointers in a huge comeback win against the Heat. On whether Millsap had a green light from three-point range:** "He does now."

79 Trading Places

The Utah Jazz and Boston Celtics pulled off a creative trade. In 1986 the Jazz sent former BYU player Fred Roberts to the Celtics in exchange for a 1987 third-round draft pick and future considerations. Those future considerations: two preseason games with the Celtics at the Marriott Center. The Jazz knew Boston's championship-caliber roster—featuring stars like Larry Bird, Kevin McHale, and Robert Parish, and ex-BYU standouts Danny Ainge, Greg Kite, and now Roberts—would help pack the Cougars' large arena in Provo. That happened in October 1987 as 23,000 attended. An events promoter convinced the teams to move the second game to Cincinnati, Ohio, in 1989 after those three BYU players moved on from Boston. (That move was made before the Celtics selected BYU star Michael Smith 13th overall in the summer of 1989.) "It kind of scared us that we would be going down there with Boston without any BYU players," Jazz official Kim Turner, who organized the exhibition schedule, told the *Deseret News*.

The Roberts trade also resulted in this comical quote from teammate-to-be McHale, via the *Hartford Courant*: "Dead Fred Oral Roberts is going to be a good player. I played against him yesterday. He's got a funny-looking haircut. We'll forgive him for that, but I think he's going to help us out. He runs the court well. He's a great player. But we're getting overrun with Mormons."

Best trades: Losing Dominique Wilkins to the Atlanta Hawks was a big blow, but the Jazz needed the $1 million they received to meet payroll demands and keep the franchise afloat. Utah also got valuable sixth man John Drew—and guard Freeman Williams—and Wilkins was open about not wanting to play for the Jazz, so the trade was a necessity. Acquiring Adrian Dantley, the first star of the

Utah Jazz era, from the Los Angeles Lakers for Spencer Haywood in 1979 helped establish the franchise in its new home. Utah lost a nice scorer in Jeff Malone in a 1994 trade with the Philadelphia 76ers, but the Jazz picked up the perfect complementary player to John Stockton and Karl Malone in sharpshooting Jeff Hornacek. Trading for Pete Maravich before the team even knew what its name was going to be in New Orleans was costly but gave the Jazz star power it needed in the early years.

Worst trade: Some will argue that trading Wilkins, a future Hall of Famer and dynamic scorer, for little in exchange was the worst trade. Being forced to trade the 1979 No. 1 pick—who turned out to be a guy named Earvin Johnson—as part of the Lakers' compensation package after New Orleans signed free agent Gail Goodrich was a blow. Monster rebounder Truck Robinson (1979) and offensively gifted big man Enes Kanter (2015) both forced the Jazz into trades that resulted in very little in return, though Kanter's departure did free up playing time for Rudy Gobert.

Best exception: The Carlos Boozer era/saga ended in 2010, but the Chicago Bulls-bound power forward did the Jazz a favor by signing off on a sign-and-trade that allowed Utah to use the trade exception to bring in a much-needed scorer, center Al Jefferson, while only losing Kosta Koufos and two mid-first-round picks.

Worth the wait: On February 1, 2004, the reloading Jazz acquired Tom Gugliotta, some cash, and a few future draft picks from the Phoenix Suns (via the New York Knicks) while giving up Keon Clark and Ben Handlogten. The most important part of the transaction—and the part that makes the deal one of the best in franchise history—was acquiring the Knicks' 2010 first-round pick. Six years later general manager Kevin O'Connor used that selection to nab a spindly sophomore who blossomed into a muscular, well-rounded All-Star: Gordon Hayward.

Thank you, Denver: The Jazz have the Denver Nuggets to thank for their two brightest young stars. Utah acquired Gobert and Donovan Mitchell in seemingly lopsided draft-day trades with Denver. The Jazz gave up just $3 million and a second-round pick (Erick Green) for "The Stifle Tower" in 2013 and then sent seldom-used power forward Trey Lyles and the No. 24 pick (Tyler Lydon) for the dazzling shooting guard in 2017. In an interesting twist, Green actually played for the Jazz a few years later on a 10-day contract in January 2016. The guard was excited to be Gobert's teammate after constantly hearing about being traded for him. "The fans were giving me a lot of stuff," he said. "But I'm happy, man. Rudy turned out to be a great player."

Biggest (surprise!) blockbuster: Less than two weeks after the Jazz lost their Hall of Fame coach, the organization followed the shocking mid-season resignation of Jerry Sloan by pulling off an equally stunning trade that sent franchise player Deron Williams to the New Jersey Nets for Devin Harris, Derrick Favors, and two future first-round picks (Kanter and Gorgui Dieng, who was dealt to the Minnesota Timberwolves as part of the 2013 Trey Burke deal).

80 Joking John Stockton

Some accused John Stockton of being a dirty player. He could be prickly and dismissive with media. He developed a reputation for being distant. He refused to sign autographs. But there was a side to Stockton that the public and press didn't often see during his 19-year NBA career. He could be dang funny.

Stockton's sharp wit has become more prominent publicly in his retirement. Once a guy who would stay in the training room or sneak out the back door to avoid interviews, he even hosted a

press tour for his book *Assisted* and willingly participated in com-
memoration events for the Jazz, including the 20th anniversary of
the franchise's first NBA Finals appearance in 1997.

Here are some funny Stockton stories and jokes.

- **At his retirement ceremony:** "Thanks to all of you for coming
  out tonight, even if you had to be bribed with hot dogs to do
  it."
- **On advice Frank Layden, Stockton's first NBA coach, gave
  him early on about never changing who you were when you
  entered the league:** "I haven't changed a thing…I haven't even
  changed the length of my shorts."
- A segment of a Dream Team documentary that Stockton
  helped make while in Barcelona in 1992 highlighted his dry
  sense of humor—and his ability to blend in with a crowd
  unlike other members of that megastar cast. Stockton got tired
  of waiting on the team bus one day, so he hopped off and met
  his family. While his wife, Nada, pushed a stroller, Stockton
  held a camcorder in one hand and one of his children's hands
  in the other as they strolled through the busy and famous La
  Rambla street just like everyone else. Karl Malone and other
  players, meanwhile, were stuck on the bus. They would have
  attracted quite the scene had they hopped off. Not Stockton.
  He wore shorts—mid-length ones—a T-shirt, sunglasses,
  calf-high white socks, and sneakers. He looked like an average
  tourist and was treated as such.

  Stockton stopped one man decked out in a red, white,
  and blue outfit; patriotic hat; and jacket. He was from
  Massachusetts. Stockton asked, "You been watching the Dream
  Team at all?"

  "Yeah."

  "They're pretty good, aren't they?"

Uncle Sam had no idea who he was talking to. The delightfully uneventful walk continued. At one point, Stockton stopped a woman with a U.S. flag draped around her neck. She was also American and a big fan of the Dream Team. She proudly told him, "We met Charles Barkley the other night."

Stockton played along. "Did ya? He's a hell of a player," he said, pointing to the cartoon caricatures of Team USA players. "I see you've got all the players right there on your shirt..."Is Charles the only one you've ever seen?"

"He's the only one I've ever met."

Stockton asked his kids if they knew anybody on her shirt. "Daddy," one said. His oldest son, Houston, a toddler, pointed at his image and said, "That's my dad."

"Too bad he's not here," Stockton joked.

In addition to being one of the best ballhandlers of all time, John Stockton has a good sense of humor, a trait he rarely shows to the public. (AP Images)

It suddenly donned on the woman that the white dude standing in front of her was on the greatest basketball team ever assembled. "Do you play on the team?"

"I do."

"*Oh, no way!*"

The video cuts away to the Stockton family strolling down the large sidewalk together while again being recognized by…nobody. "I hate this. I can't go anywhere without being bugged," Stockton said sarcastically. "I'm really not that much different from Michael Jordan walking through here."

- Chris Webber developed a deep admiration for Stockton over the years. As a guest on Dan Patrick's radio show, the power forward shared a story about the time he made rookies wait on the Sacramento Kings' bus in the players' parking lot behind the Delta Center before a playoff game. Webber wanted them to see the point guard drive into the lot. He told them, "Watch the baddest man in the world pull up," Webber said. "John Stockton would come to the game literally in [a] minivan, pop his kids out, and come in there and bust us up. He's a bad man. Wherever he is right now, he's still a bad man."

- **Karl Malone's wife, Kay, told *The New York Times* about how Stockton used to tease The Mailman for being the only dad on the Jazz team without a son.** "John told Karl, 'I'll tell you how you have a boy…Take Kay out for a nice dinner, give her a couple glasses of wine, get her happy, take her home, and call me. I'll be over.'" Malone and Stockton both howled. "Then we had a baby boy," Kay said. "And, no, it wasn't John's. We did it all by ourselves. And as soon as we got the news, the first person Karl called was John. He said, 'I'm going to have a boy, so there.'"

81 Let Jeremy Dunk

That "Let Jeremy Dunk" plea added some fun to the lockout-shortened 2012 season for Utah Jazz fans. It also led to the bouncy Jeremy Evans jumping into the national spotlight and winning the dunk contest. It took a fun grass-roots campaign and an injury to the original invitee, New York Knicks guard Iman Shumpert, for the NBA to accommodate the #LetJeremyDunk movement.

To boost his bid, the Jazz sent the NBA a video of him soaring over 6'1" teammate Earl Watson for one alley-oop and slapping a #LetJeremyDunk sticker on the backboard in another slam. Watson joked that he was Evans' "dunk agent" and sounded like it while marveling how he had 10 dunks that season in only 59 minutes. "His dunk percentage is unreal," Evans said. "He might have the most dunks per minute."

Jazz fans suggested submitting a sensational dunk Evans had in the preseason over Gerald Wallace of the Portland Trail Blazers, editing out the questionable charging call, of course. Turns out, the Jazz gave the league all it needed to see for Evans to be considered a slam-dunk choice.

Evans didn't disappoint. He enlisted his best Jazz buddy, Gordon Hayward, for help in what turned out to be his most spectacular dunk. The 6'8" small forward sat in the key and lobbed up two basketballs, which Evans simultaneously caught and threw down one after the other. Comedian Kevin Hart, dressed as a mini-Mailman, delivered a Karl Malone jersey to Evans to wear for the final dunk. This No. 32 soared over the diminutive Hart, put his hand behind his head with elbow flared out a la Malone, and easily completed his jam session. He was pronounced champion over Chase Budinger of the Houston Rockets, Paul George of the Indiana Pacers, and Derrick Williams of the Minnesota Timberwolves.

Not surprisingly, Evans thanked the fans around Jazzland for their assistance. "I feel like without the fans I didn't have a chance," he told the *Deseret News.* "With them campaigning and pushing so hard, I think they were the biggest help."

Evans was the sixth Jazz player to participate in the dunk contest, but he became just the third one to be invited back for an encore, following in the high-flying footsteps of Blue Edwards (1990, 1991) and Darrell Griffith (1984, 1985). Evans, though, is the only one to get his own day in Utah. Governor Gary Herbert proclaimed February 29, 2012, as Jeremy Evans Day in the Beehive State.

During the 2013 contest, Evans impressively pulled off a reverse dunk after jumping over a seated 7'4" Mark Eaton, who tossed him the ball. In the championship round, Evans jumped over a covered portrait that he'd painted of himself jumping over a covered portrait in which he jumped over…*well, we could do this for an entire chapter.* Evans deserved more artistic points for that dunk than he received. Evans, a talented artist who occasionally sketches and paints teammates and coaches, even did a last-minute touch-up so the basketball in his painting would match the one being used in the contest. Judges, however, crowned Toronto Raptors leaper Terrence Rose champ this time around.

Though Evans jumped over quite a few things in his Jazz career for fun—Hayward, Wallace, Ronny Turiaf, the portrait he painted of himself jumping over a portrait, and his Camaro—jumping into a regular rotation spot was something he was never able to do. His slender frame (6'9", 194 pounds), some holes in his game, and a glut of big men were among his obstacles. Jazz fans would have loved nothing more than for him to become a regular in his five seasons with Utah. The amicable Western Kentucky alumnus ranks among the nicest, most athletic, and easiest-to-cheer-for players in franchise history. One fan thought so highly of him she baked fresh cookies and delivered them to him at the arena before every home game after he jumped into her heart.

82 Karl's Odd Jobs

Almost every year, you could seemingly count on two off-court traditions from Karl Malone: a publicly negotiated contract dispute with Jazz owner Larry H. Miller and a new dream job capturing his fancy. *Deseret News* columnist Doug Robinson called it "Karl Malone's years-long quest to find Something Else To Do."

In 2006 Malone's statue was unveiled, and his jersey was retired from his day job. Life was just beginning, though. "I've always said when I retire, 'I just want to take a couple years and just do things I wanted to do,'" he said. "I get to play in a big sandbox every day and play with my Tonka toys and build things and see the kids' games and just be me. I'm enjoying retirement."

Here are some of the professions a guy, who's had more odd jobs than a hired handyman—the only vocation he hasn't tried—has dabbled in or dreamed of doing.

State trooper: Malone wanted to be a state trooper if basketball didn't pan out after college. He even spent a summer as a deputy sheriff in Louisiana after his rookie season. In 2001 Malone was named an honorary colonel by the Utah Highway Patrol and pushed the state legislature for increased funding for troopers. Much was made in the 1998 NBA Finals when he revealed that an Illinois State Police trooper he'd befriended in the 2002 Olympics took him for a spin between Games 4 and 5. "Weighed some trucks," Malone said, evoking laughter from media. "I know it sounds corny to you guys. Go ahead and laugh."

Bodybuilder: It's unlikely the NBA has ever had a player who could pump as much iron as Malone. He came into the league weighing 260 with 10.5 percent body fat. An infatuation with weightlifting and working out helped him trim that down to 4.8 percent on a 256-pound, 6'9" frame. He was like Arnold Schwarzenegger with a jump shot. *Men's Health* ranked him No. 40 on its 100 Fittest Men of All Time list. It helped him put the power in the power forward position, punish opponents, and improve and prolong a hoops career that lasted 19 years. Malone told *Muscle & Fitness* magazine, "If I didn't lift weights, I don't think I would've had the career I had."

Jane Fonda: In the late 1990s, the muscularly sculpted basketball player created a total fitness workout video series called *Karl Malone's Body Shop*. The program included exercises you likely already do: the Dying Bug, Donkeys, and, of course, Mountain Climber Sumo Combo. "That concludes our bun-busting series," Malone tells his audience, assuming they aren't hospitalized following his routine by this point. "And if you do this exercise and do it consistently, it will be the best bun exercise you ever did. Guaranteed." *Sports Illustrated* gave the program, which includes four VHS tapes and busted buns, a rating of "7 abs out of Karl Malone's 8-pack."

Politician: For a while Malone talked about running for governor of two different states—in his NBA home of Utah and in Arkansas, where he has a cattle ranch. If we're lucky, he'll throw his home state of Louisiana in there and simultaneously go for the trifecta. "It do interest me, matter-of-fact," Malone said in 2002. "It really do." Malone's interest in politics piqued after visiting with president George W. Bush in the White House before the All-Star Game. Malone figured if a former pro wrestler like Jesse Ventura could win in Minnesota, then why not him? The Republican's platform: fund police, firefighters, schools, and speak the truth. "I ain't gonna sugarcoat it or b.s.," he said. Media back then asked Jerry Sloan for his thoughts on a possible Governor Malone. "I think he better worry about basketball first," Sloan said.

Hunting guide: No, this is not in reference to the controversial tidbit about Malone supposedly jokingly saying he'd like to give a "down on his luck" Vietnam vet $500,000 and a half-hour head start before hunting him down, a quote that appeared in the book, *To The Brink*. (Malone adamantly insisted he didn't say that.) The Mailman, an NRA member and avowed wildlife conservationist, enjoys sharing his passion for hunting. He still offers personal fishing and deer hunting trips on his 270-acre ranch in northern Louisiana.

Trucker: This is another profession Malone said he would've done if the NBA hadn't worked out—and not just for toy trucks in sandboxes. Turns out, it didn't work out after the NBA did. Malone's seven-truck outfit, Malone Enterprises Trucking Inc., shut down in 2004 after 18 months on the road. Malone's drivers delivered potatoes and poultry, among other items. Being a truck driver had been a dream of Malone's since he grew up in the backwoods of northern Louisiana. *The Deseret News* asked his attorney if Malone lost money on the enterprise. Randall Call replied, "He sure wasn't making any." Malone kept his personal 18-wheeler.

Rancher: Malone has retreated to one of his ranches, the one in El Dorado, Arkansas, since his NBA playing days. It's where he worked out, hauling around bales of hay, in the offseason. It's also where he was a cattle breeder. "Eight years from now when they say, 'Where is he now?'" Malone once told *Ebony*, "this is where I'll be."

Media personality: During the lockout of 1998, Karl Malone had time on his hands, and an L.A. sports radio station had an open mic. The Mailman hasn't stopped talking long enough for a commercial break since then. Well, he might still be talking if the NBA

Karl Malone's Companies and Properties

- Ownership in four restaurants in Louisiana, Idaho, and Utah
- Car dealerships in Draper, Sandy, and Heber City
- A car accessories business (Sandy) and body shop (Draper)
- Three oil change-service stores
- Cattle ranch in Louisiana
- Two condos at Green Valley Resort
- Thousands of acres of Louisiana property used for tree harvesting and mineral rights
- Commercial development business and 12,000-square-foot building in Ruston, Louisiana
- Deer-raising venture and hunting guide business

hadn't reconvened. And despite his on-air demand to be traded and claim he'd played his final game in a Jazz uniform, he was back in Utah when the league and players resolved their situation. Always one who's got something to say about any subject you can think of, don't want to think of, or hadn't thought to think of, Malone co-hosted his own show in Salt Lake City on ESPN700 in 2012. He also pondered having his own TV talk show to interview athletes. Malone told the *Deseret News*, "I could let people find out that there are more interesting things about [players] than just running up and down a court."

Haberdasher: In the 1990s Malone owned a sports merchandising shop that sold, among other things, trademark KM Western apparel. Unfortunately, Mailman's at the Sugar House Center in Salt Lake City closed after five years. Two of Malone's shirts were listed for $64 apiece in Western wear retailer Miller Stockman's 1995 winter catalog.

Coach: During his career Malone said he'd be honored to become a coach. That happened in 2008 when the Ruston, Louisiana, resident, returned to his college roots to become the Louisiana Tech assistant strength and conditioning coach. When the subject of Malone possibly coaching for the Jazz was raised in a radio interview with Brad Rock four years later, The Mailman offered a response fitting of his rural upbringing. "You can't beat the fart out of a dead mule," he said. "[That's] a no for you city slickers." Malone predicted Sloan would coach again after resigning the previous year and admitted he would love to be his assistant. Though he was certain the Jazz "ain't gonna call," Malone accepted a temporary position in 2013 as a part-time big man coach with the Jazz to tutor Derrick Favors and Enes Kanter.

Pitchman: Over the years, Malone got paid to endorse quite a few companies and products, including appearing in commercials for Rogaine, Hardees, and Skechers. In a rather hilarious spot for Foot Locker, he walks in holding a tray of grilled meat and overhears Damian Lillard say he didn't want to be like one of those basketball legends who lost in the NBA Finals over and over. "Burgers are ready," Malone said while dejectedly walking away.

Car salesman: Assisted by Miller, his first NBA boss, Malone now has three dealerships in Utah.

Logger: Long before it happened, Malone hinted that it was a possibility. After an ugly in-game spat with Byron Scott in 2001, Malone insinuated that the then-New Jersey Nets coach was a "(butt) kisser" and claimed that was rampant in the league. "I'd rather be a logger or something," he said. Malone's Arkansas-based logging company made headlines after helping clear 118 ravaged lots in Pascagoula, Mississippi, free of charge after Hurricane Katrina. He told *USA TODAY*, "Everything about this just felt right."

Pro wrestler: Malone teamed up with buddy and World Championship Wrestling star Diamond Dallas Page to battle Dennis Rodman and Hulk Hogan in the 1998 Bash at the Beach. "Basketball phenom and all-around good guy Karl Malone took a Chicago Bull by the horns and got speared again at the Bash held in sunny San Diego," *SLAM! Sports* wrote. "Rudimentary headlocks, slams, and clotheslines chewing up the dull 23-minute match time had the unenthusiastic crowd in attendance dispensing the 'b-o-r-i-n-g' chants at regular intervals."

Basketball player: That job worked out well until he shifted career gears at 40.

Mailman: Nah, but it might make for a good nickname.

83 Miller vs. Denver Fans

Larry H. Miller had a rough two-month stretch in the spring of 1994. On March 10 he was vilified after selling the Salt Lake Golden Eagles hockey team. On March 14 he got into a shouting match with Elden Campbell after the Los Angeles Lakers big man hit John Stockton. And on May 19, with a private family matter causing turmoil behind the scenes, Miller made national news after scuffling with a couple of Denver Nuggets fans in the Delta Center stands during the playoffs.

Before Miller engaged with the Nuggets fans, the late Jazz owner stormed out of his courtside seat toward the end of the first half and yelled at Jerry Sloan from behind the bench. He was particularly upset at Karl Malone's performance. Along with some choice words, Miller yelled to Sloan a couple of times, "We've got some guys that didn't show up tonight! They should be on the bench."

Miller was still fuming at halftime and, as he entered the locker room as he usually did, the emotional owner was met by John Stockton, who told him, "If you're too mad to be here, don't." Miller heeded his advice and took a detour to the training room to get water and Advil for a headache. Feeling calmed down, Miller listened to the end of Sloan's halftime speech and returned to the arena. That's when his run-in with the Denver fans happened.

Miller noticed some Denver fans, including a man in a "Mt. Mutombo" shirt, standing in front of his children's seats. He said he politely asked him to move, even saying "please." Miller described the incident in his autobiography, *Driven*: "I asked them to move. One of them said something like, 'Is this your seat?' And I said, 'They're all my seats!' Anyway, things got ugly. We yelled some bad things at each other. There was some pushing and chest bumping and name-calling. I lost it. [Oldest son] Greg and one of our security people restrained me. It was silly and stupid for me to get caught up in all that. It became a national story—the owner of an NBA team gets in a fight with a fan." The NBA and Miller agreed that he should stay away from the next two games, and he didn't attend the Game 7 at home on his own volition.

Greg described in *Driven* what happened when he saw the incident while talking to a friend next to the court: "Tom [LaPoint] said, 'Uh-oh, that's not good.' I turned and saw Dad getting into a verbal altercation with a Denver fan. I handed the Cokes to Tom and ran over there. By the time I got there, Dad was fully engaged with the fan. It was getting physical. I got Dad in a headlock. 'There are cameras everywhere,' I told him. 'You don't want to do this.' That's what got him to relax. Later, one of the TV guys told me, 'We got all that on audio. That was wise counsel you gave your dad.'" A photo in the newspaper the next day made it appear that Miller was going to punch the fan, but he told reporters the thought never entered his mind.

Miller apologized that night at the arena after the game while they were filling out a police report, Rich Babich, one of the Denver fans in the brouhaha, told *Driven* co-author Doug Robinson. Babich had a friendly conversation with Miller at a Jazz–Nuggets game in Denver a year later, and Babich and the other fan involved in the fight, Al Leiberman, were guests of the Millers at a later Jazz home game, even sitting courtside. "Other than those 10 minutes," Babich said, "he was always a gentleman."

In a televised press conference 40 hours after the incident, Miller took responsibility, apologized profusely, and explained his side of the story. "The general thing is: I made a stupid mistake. I feel badly that I have embarrassed the franchise, the city, the state, and my family. I'm embarrassed myself," Miller said. "To our players, our coaches, our fans, my family, or any others, including those from Denver that I have offended, I apologize. Perhaps the fact is I just shouldn't be doing what I'm doing."

Miller said he didn't intend to be as involved in the future to avoid any further situations, but his wife, Gail Miller, said that was short-lived. He was just too passionate and invested in the Jazz to stay away. "After the incident with the fan, Larry said he needed to pull back and not get so emotionally involved for everyone's sake," Gail said. "It didn't really last too long before he was right back out there with the team before the games, etc."

84 Team Uniforms

Combined with the new team's jazzy name and the Mardi Gras-themed colors—purple, gold, and green—the J-Note struck a perfect chord as the logo of a team located in the jazz capital of the world. (New Orleans that is, not Salt Lake City.) But the popularity of the eighth note and basketball meshed together to form the "J" has ebbed and flowed over the years.

Ownership kept the logo the same when the franchise moved from Louisiana to out West, eventually putting Utah above the ZZs where New Orleans was from 1974 to 1979. The simple but effective logo and uniforms remained a staple for the franchise for two-plus decades. Players wore white at home and purple on the road (after a green experiment).

The Jazz toyed with the idea of changing names and logos in 1983, even informing the NBA of their intentions, Larry H. Miller Group executive vice president Jay Francis told *The Salt Lake Tribune*. Market research revealed that the musical name, the Mardi Gras colors, and the J-Note didn't resonate with Beehive State fans. Utah, however, embraced all that Jazz after the success of the 1983–84 team. Francis noted that people were no longer asking if he was part of a musical group. Others were taking note of the seemingly misplaced Jazz.

The original look lasted until the mid-1990s when the NBA, hoping to boost merchandise sales, suggested that Larry H. Miller's organization modernize their logo and colors. They might as well have asked John Stockton to wear capris instead of short shorts. He liked what the Jazz had used from the beginning and said that when Miller asked for his input before the franchise finalized a style change in time for the team's two trips to the NBA Finals in 1997 and 1998. "I didn't want to change anything," Stockton said. "The Yankees don't change their logo. That was my attitude. So why do the Jazz have to change theirs?"

Despite his feedback, Stockton, Malone, and Co. debuted the team's updated appearance, which was designed to reflect Utah's famous peaks, in 1996. So long, J-Note. Say hello to a scenic logo backdrop with towering mountains, jazzier font, and a "J" that sort of resembled a saxophone. The team also opened up a different crayon box. Purple remained, but gold and green were replaced as trim colors by the trendier teal, light blue, copper, and black.

While attending a celebration for the 20th anniversary of the Jazz's first NBA Finals run in 1996–97, Stockton did admit the mountain design held some nostalgic and sentimental appeal. "You look back on it, and that's the logo we went to the Finals in and had some of our greatest experiences and memories as players," he said. "So I'm kind of torn now, but I do like the original."

The Jazz bucked tradition even more when they debuted an all-black uniform with copper trim in 1998. Those threads did not include the mountain silhouettes. Stockton wasn't the only one who preferred the classic style. The team consulted with national focus groups for three years before bringing the J-Note out of retirement as a secondary logo to the mountains. The Jazz wanted to bridge the old with the new. The green throwback uniforms with the classic logo wordmark—similar to the road uniforms from 1981 to 1984—hit the right note after being re-introduced as part of the NBA's Hardwood Classics program in 2009–10. Fans loved them, especially as the team went 10–1 in the green jerseys that season. "This logo is what Jazz fans around the world identify with," Stockton said at the time. "Having the note back puts a smile on my face. As the team moves forward toward bigger and better things, it reminds us where we came from."

The Jazz introduced another new, old uniform inside the arena that season. Jeff Hornacek's retired No. 14 jersey in the rafters was switched from the purple mountain design to the classic J-Note— a la Stockton and Malone. Jazz president Randy Rigby said Hornacek wanted the change. Jerry Sloan and Frank Layden both preferred tradition, too. "I've always associated the music note with the Jazz, so I am glad to see the logo return," Sloan said. "It was here when I arrived and it is the only logo many of the players I coached ever wore." Added Layden: "I'm a sentimental guy and I think the fact that we are bringing the music note back is wonderful."

The J-Note logo has been the primary look since 2011, but the Jazz have introduced some funky designs as alternate choices since then. In 2016–17 they occasionally wore navy pride uniforms, which featured horizontal green, gold, and white stripes and sleeved jerseys.

The team really got radical in 2017–18 when Nike took over the contract from Adidas. Along with traditional home and road uniforms, the Jazz first rolled out a solid gold statement edition uniform to mixed reviews. They brought the fire and a southern Utah flair with their massively popular city edition uniforms, which were bolder than anything the organization had ever worn. The uniforms featured cascading bands in a bright gold, orange, and deep burgundy color gradient to represent the state's colorful

While shooting a free throw in 1994, Karl Malone wears a classic home jersey, which remains popular with fans. (USA TODAY Sports Images)

arches, canyons, and vistas. "UTAH" is arched across the front of the jersey. These uniforms were also adorned with a stylish and colorful secondary state logo with basketball lines from the original logo inside of a Utah outline. Squiggly lines down each side of the uniforms represented routes from Salt Lake City to Moab and St. George.

Sales of city uniforms at the team store set a new franchise record during their January 30 debut, a night in which the Jazz clobbered the defending NBA champion Golden State Warriors 129–99. The game was played on a new court that complemented

History of the Jazz Logo

1974–79: New Orleans was on top of ZZs in JAZZ. J was the musical note merged with the multi-colored basketball. Team colors were purple, green, and gold.

1979–96: Utah replaced New Orleans on top of ZZs for obvious reasons. Everything else remained the same, including the Mardi Gras-inspired colors.

1996–04: The Jazz broke away from the J-Note design, opting for a design more fitting of the franchise's locale at the base of the Wasatch Front range. The team's mascot wordmark stretched over a circle with a merging of mountains and basketball and the word "UTAH" bending over the peaks. The J resembled a saxophone if you use your imagination, and trendier colors were selected, including teal because of its popularity in Charlotte. Team colors were purple, teal, light blue, copper, and black.

2004–10: The Jazz had the same logo but different crayons. The team colors were navy, powder blue, purple, and silver.

2010–16: The Jazz still had the mountain logo but featured another change of hues. The team colors were navy, dark yellow, dark green, and gray.

2016–present: What's old is new again. The Jazz brought back the classic design with a few minor tweaks and minus the purple. The team colors are navy, gold, and green.

the uniforms. The court also had a gradation of colors, a large delicate arch, and an arching "UTAH" in the middle of the court. Also in 2017–18, the Jazz wore an advertisement for the first time. They opted to take a charitable route with a "5 for the Fight" patch that promoted a cancer-fighting organization.

85 Jazz vs. Kobe

During a 2015 Lakers–Jazz preseason game in Hawaii, Rodney Hood got an earful from Kobe Bryant. Hood had a nice 21-point outing against Bryant, including a stretch in which the Jazz shooting guard hit a three-pointer, watched the Los Angeles Lakers star drain a deep one, and then got a bit animated after drilling another shot beyond the arc. Bryant had a message for Hood after he thought the young player was trying to show him up. "We had a little talk," Hood said, smiling. "He was just about [giving me] his resume."

That resume for Bryant includes a 20-year pro who finished as an 18-time All-Star, 11-time All-NBA first teamer, and five-time NBA champion. "Very impressive," Hood said of Bryant's resume. "Very impressive."

Kobe also told Hood, "I can shoot it 30 times. You can shoot it 10 times. Don't try to go there with me." Jazz coach Quin Snyder, who developed an excellent relationship with Bryant as a Lakers assistant in 2011–12, laughed when told what the superstar said to a young player who doesn't have the same green light. "Kobe's right, probably," Snyder said. "If he isn't, then Rodney should just tell him he's right."

Bryant couldn't rattle off his entire resume to Hood, but here's one thing that will make Jazz fans cringe: he retired as the all-time leading opponent scorer against Utah with 1,549 points (most of which seemingly came in his career finale). He averaged 25.82 points in 60 games against the Jazz, the eighth highest opponent average.

This was a rivalry that included numerous intense moments and a handful of playoff battles—but, boy, did the pendulum swing from the Jazz to the Lakers. Utah won the first two meetings en route to the NBA Finals, and then Bryant's team returned the favor three years in a row during the Deron Williams era.

There was also the game when Andrei Kirilenko blocked Bryant's shot three times, the time Kyrylo Fesenko got a technical for tossing the ball at him on the floor, the night he efficiently scored 52 points on 19-for-26 shooting in a 2006 win in L.A., the time Mehmet Okur mimicked a mildly vulgar gesture Bryant made after the Money Man followed the star's three-pointer late in a 2009 regular-season game with an even bigger long ball in that Jazz win, the time in 2004 when the Jazz were fined and ticked off Lakers convert Karl Malone by making a humorous video mocking Bryant and alluding to legal issues he was facing from his sexual assault case, and the time Bryant was hounded defensively by Gordon Hayward, who was sporting a farmer's sunburn from a SoCal beach trip, and bobbled away an opportunity to put up a last-second game-winning shot in an 86–85 Jazz win. (He complimented the Utah rookie for being "a more talented Jeff Hornacek.") "I can remember just the first time we played against him. Jeremy Evans and I were sitting at the Staples Center, and he walked over and said, 'What's up?' to us," Hayward said. "Both of us were smiling pretty big. Jeremy was giggling a little bit…Both of us looked up to him and watched him for so many years, and then to be there in that moment was cool for us."

Bryant faced the Jazz more than any other player: 84 times in the regular season and playoffs. He usually had the upper hand, beating the Jazz 47 times in his two-decade career, but the San Antonio Spurs were the only team in the NBA who beat his Lakers more (48 times) than Utah (37 times).

One of those wins came in Bryant's final trip to Utah. It happened to be the worst loss of his career—a 48-point drubbing (175–123) on March 28, 2016. One fun aspect was how Bryant requested to defend Hood in the second half—and held him scoreless—after the Jazz guard lit the Lakers up for 30 points in the first half. Like in Hawaii, trash talking was involved—but no resume swapping. "He was just congratulating me on the season," Hood said. "I just told him he was the greatest of all time, a guy I've been looking up to since I was a little child."

The Jazz honored Bryant before that final game in Salt Lake City with a video that highlighted the love-hate relationship and mutual respect between Kobe and Utah fans (not including the bandwagon jumpers who always cheered for him). Bryant pounded his heart several times, waved to the cheering crowd—which later gave him a standing ovation on his way out and gave him some boos for old time's sake—and jogged over to give owner Gail Miller a courtside hug. The Jazz also gave Kobe a Utah-centric set of gifts: passes to state and national parks, a framed picture of Delicate Arch, a Snowbird season pass, a pair of skis with a custom fitting, and one "Play soft defense and watch me in awe in my career finale" coupon. (At least it seemed like they might've given him that last one.)

The Kobe game Jazz fans love the most happened at the Delta Center in the 1997 Western Conference Semifinals. Bryant was a rookie and helped the Lakers force overtime in Game 5 of a series they trailed 3–1. The 18-year-old had a chance to win the game, but his fading mid-range shot fell short of the rim at the buzzer. That was a sign of things to come. In overtime Bryant went on an

air-ball spree from three-point range, including critical misses with
39.7 seconds left and then again with 4.0 to go while trailing by
three.

The Jazz eliminated the Lakers with a 98–93 win. Fans have
often gotten after him with "Air-ball!" taunts, but that four-air-ball
game helped shape him as a basketball player. Jerry West, the NBA
logo model and former Lakers executive, told media members, "I
really felt that was the defining moment in his career. You know
why? If somebody would've shot an air-ball on our team and then
shot a second one, they wouldn't shoot a third one. He was fearless.
I think that's one of the things that supported him to greatness. He
wouldn't allow himself to fail."

Bryant agrees. During his season-long farewell tour, he was
asked about that four-air-ball game nearly 20 years after it happened. He turned a negative into a positive. "It was an early turning
point for me, being able to deal with adversity, being able to deal
with public scrutiny and self-doubt," he said. "At 18 years old, it
was gut-check time. I look back at it now with fond memories.
Back then it was misery."

Bryant gave Utah fans everlasting misery—and NBA fans one
last fond memory—in his grand finale. Not only were the Jazz the
last team to lose to Kobe, but he went out in style by scoring 60
points and sparking a wild one-man rally in the Lakers' 101–96
win. Utah, which found out earlier in the day it had been eliminated from the playoffs, led by 10 points with 2:16 remaining when
Kobe channeled his inner Black Mamba. He struck for 13 straight
points, including the go-ahead jumper. "He's the most competitive
guy that's been in this league in a long time, and every opponent
that played against him knew it," Lakers coach Byron Scott said.
"They hated him. The arenas he played in most of the time hated
him, and I think he really loved and relished being the villain."

If it makes Jazz fans feel better, Kobe did have one air-ball
against Utah that final night, completing a full career circle. His

teammates didn't care. They sprayed him with champagne in the locker room after a finale that was as grand as possible outside of the playoffs. "The perfect ending would have been a championship," Bryant said, smiling. "But tonight was [me] trying to go out, play hard, and try to put on a show as much as I possibly could. It felt good to be able to do that one last time."

86 Visit Jack & Dan's

Bar X, Beer Hive Pub, Twilite Lounge, Desert Edge Brewery, and The Red Door are considered among the top spots to nab an adult beverage in Salt Lake City. Bout Time is a fun spot to nosh and watch sports. The most well-known sports bar for Utahns, however, might be one that is 725 miles away.

Located across the street from the Gonzaga University campus in Spokane, Washington, Jack & Dan's Bar & Grill isn't just revered by Zags faithful. It is also a cherished part of Utah Jazz lore and a must-visit establishment for fans of the late Jack Stockton's famous son, John. *Sports Illustrated* ranked Jack and Dan's as the sixth-best sports bar in America. "This bar, located a couple of blocks from the Gonzaga campus, is best known for being co-owned by the father of Spokane's greatest sports hero, John Stockton," Chris Ballard wrote in his *S.I.* bar rankings piece. "Jack Stockton, a part-owner since 1961, knows his son's fame is good for business, but he reminds people, 'I was here before John ever bounced a ball in the pros.'"

Jack Stockton passed away at age 89 in May 2017. He'd sold his share of the bar a decade prior to that, but this place will always be linked with Utah's Hall of Fame point guard. He even mentioned it during his enshrinement speech in 2009. "Out here in the crowd are lifetime family friends who never missed the call to raise money for trips or for uniforms," Stockton said. "Then they'd support the family by going down to my dad's tavern, Jack & Dan's, and expertly critique our performance game in and game out. They continued that process for the 19 years, watching the Jazz on satellite."

You, though, wouldn't know Jack was fiercely proud of his son's accomplishment by simply frequenting this bar. "I've been working in this place 42 years," Jack Stockton told the *Seattle Post-Intelligencer*. "He's never worked a shift here. If anybody's picture should be up in here, it's mine."

Even at the height of the point guard's NBA playing days, the tavern only had a modest display of Stockton memorabilia (for John, not Jack) and Jazz paraphernalia despite Jack's deep love for both. "Anyone looking for a Jazz/Stockton shrine in the bar was disappointed...Even when I returned in 2002, stopping in town during vacation, the only basketball artifacts were a small drawing of Stockton and Malone above the bar and a hanging rug with a Jazz logo," wrote *The Salt Lake Tribune* columnist Kurt Kragthorpe. "Anything more would have violated the Stocktonesque code of not bringing attention to yourself even if the owners welcomed the fans who liked to watch Jazz telecasts at Jack & Dan's."

Even Jack & Dan's website doesn't boast about its most famous patron's accomplishment. "But," *Deseret News* columnist Brad Rock noted, "there is a picture of someone named Ed Eschenbacher being named Bartender of the Year."

Jack Stockton ran the bar, now listed as one of Spokane's official historical landmarks, for 45 years before passing the torch. John's old Gonzaga teammate, Jeff Condill, was by his side for more than a decade. Though Utah games are not televised like they used to be and employees don't all occasionally wear Jazz shirts anymore, the Stocktons' legacies proudly live on in the bar.

The bar was within a jump, hop, and a skip of where John Stockton honed his basketball skills. His parents' red-and-white brick home was only 150 yards away from the bar's back door.

Fellow Spokane-bred sports legend Mark Rypien, the Super Bowl XXVI MVP, told *Sports Illustrated* that he'd drive by the Stocktons' home while in high school only to see John out there playing at all hours. "Ten, 11:00 at night," Rypien said, "and he was out on the driveway, dribbling a basketball."

John, though, would head over to the bar to meet his hero—his dad—after playing in the afternoon. Jack would then pedal his second oldest son home on the handlebars of his bike at dinnertime.

Another Spokane sports hero has a connection to Jack & Dan's. The late Sandy Sandberg occasionally sat in the seat in front of the first TV above the bar and watched his Hall of Fame son, Ryne, play for the Chicago Cubs. Jack's establishment was one of the things that impressed Frank Layden about John. He often joked, "He has a lot of things going for him. He's Irish Catholic, he laughs at my jokes, and his dad owns a bar."

87 From Hot Rod to Boler and Locke

After 35 years of having every on-the-court move described by a beloved colorful character who turned "You gotta love it, baby!" and "Stockton to Malone!" into Utah household phrases, a new era of Jazz broadcasting began on October 28, 2009. So long, Hot Rod Hundley.

Hello, David Locke.

The transition was as weird for the charismatic and confident Locke as it was for Jazz fans after Hundley exchanged the play-by-play airwaves for warmer winter air in Arizona. The sports talk show host predicted it would be "strange" and "hard" for listeners to hear his broadcasts compared to his predecessor's. Though he has Bay Area roots and lived in Seattle for about a decade, Locke, like many Utahns, had listened to the late Hundley since childhood. "I grew up a Jazz fan, and that's the guy I'm used to," Locke said. "So, I miss him, too."

When Locke filled in for Hundley for a Jazz game at the Toronto Raptors in 2008, one of the broadcaster's co-workers, 1320 KFAN's Ben Bagley, aptly described the changing of the guard. "You're really good," Bagley told Locke, "but, boy, was it weird."

Craig Bolerjack has partially replaced two Utah broadcasting mammoths, including Hundley as the Jazz's lead TV personality (when the simulcast was split up in 2005) and former Channel 5 sportscaster/BYU voice Paul James upon his semi-retirement. "My only advice, and I've talked to [Locke] about it," Bolerjack said, "is just go do the game, be yourself."

Bolerjack calls Hundley "an icon" and he warned Locke to ignore the catcalls and use it as motivation to work harder—a formula that's worked for him. "You can't take [criticism] personally. You just have to keep pushing through," Bolerjack said. "He has to be patient and understand that Hot Rod's a Hall of Famer, and it takes time to achieve those heights."

Because of his opinionated personality, Locke expected to be doubted and dissed. He counted on his hard work to win over fans—and Locke's detailed statistical analysis and player breakdowns leave no room to question his work ethic. For what it's worth—and to Locke it's worth a whole lot—Hundley gave his replacement his blessing. Locke has the full support of his bosses at the Jazz, too—both through the awkward-by-default transition and then again when his contract was renewed a few years later.

The vernacular and voice of the Jazz have been vastly different. Fun Chick Hearn-inspired phrases—like "belt-high dribble" and "hippity-hop"—are no longer part of the broadcasts. Instead, Jazz fans get an earful of researched data, visceral sound effects (Locke growled on occasion when Paul Millsap grabbed rebounds), interviews with NBA experts (i.e. Thurl Bailey and Pace Mannion), TV-like cut-ins from other NBA games, and signature calls like "He buys one and gets one free!" (for old-fashioned three-point plays). Jazz executive vice president of sales and marketing Chris Baum described Locke's style as "the new world of broadcasting." Locke calls it "a real rock-and-roll NBA arena feel" with passion, a vibe, and a heartbeat. Locke said his crack staff spend eight to 10 hours to prepare for each "out-of-the-box" call.

Locke prepped for this opportunity his whole life even if he had a difficult time envisioning getting a gig that Hot Rod had for three-and-a-half decades. Locke announced moves while playing Strat-o-matic and other sports games when he was as young as five. For years he tweaked his talent even when he was his only listener. He also called the action at random games—high school baseball, the Jazz, and the Seattle Seahawks—and described what he saw out loud.

Locke also called live action for real audiences. He was the voice of the Seattle SuperSonics. He was a WNBA broadcaster for two teams—one year for the Utah Starzz and seven for the Seattle Storm. He called University of Washington football and basketball games on Fox Sports Northwest TV for a year. He occasionally called pro baseball games for the Ogden Raptors and Salt Lake Buzz when he worked in Utah radio in the 1990s.

Getting let go by the Sonics in 2007 proved to be a blessing in disguise for Locke. He returned to Utah for work, initially as a drive-time sports talk host and then with an additional moonlighting broadcasting position with the Jazz. Eventually, Locke left the sports talk show and focused solely on calling games and hosting a daily *Locked on Jazz* podcast.

Locke's love for Utah grew as a kid when he traveled from the Bay Area to the Beehive State while his dad did business in Salt Lake City. He moved to Utah to begin a sports radio career after graduating from Occidental College in 1992. That career eventually led him to the Northwest, but Locke's wife jokingly claimed she always knew he still had one foot in Utah. "This is where I feel most comfortable. It feels like home to me," the Park City, Utah, resident said.

Hall of Fame coach Jerry Sloan admitted the transition was odd for him, too, but he joked that his wallet would benefit after picking up the dinner tab a time or 200 over the decades. "I'll save some money…Hot Rod's not a big spender," Sloan said, laughing. "We loved Hot Rod. He was great to work with, and we certainly will miss him a lot."

With his booming baritone voice and affable personality, Bolerjack has become a beloved part of televised Jazz broadcasts. When he took over for Hundley as the TV voice of the Jazz in 2005, Bolerjack was moonlighting as a national play-by-play announcer for CBS Sports and calling NFL, college football, and NCAA basketball games. Bolerjack told the *Deseret News* that a man once approached him at one of his sons' ballgames and enviously said, "Gosh, I wish I had your job."

Like Locke, Bolerjack spends hours and hours preparing for broadcasts, getting updated on the ins and outs of the Jazz, and studying up on the opposing team. He's developed a fun rapport with his broadcast partner and color commentator, Matt Harpring. Bolerjack's famous catchphrase comes out of his mouth near the end of tight games as he bellows out, "Buckle up!" He also has an affinity for using the word "bang" and loved to shout out "Money!" when Mehmet Okur hit three-pointers.

The Kansas City native, who stands 6'3" with a broad-shouldered frame, had high hopes of a football career, but the 200-pound offensive tackle required knee surgery his senior season of high school. He walked on at Kansas State but then retired from the sport after tearing the ACL in his healthy knee. Older brother Steve prodded him to pursue broadcast journalism so he could put his love for sports to work. Bolerjack eventually got a chance to call high school football games and decided this was the career for him after calling the action from a crow's nest on the top of a telephone pole. He had to climb up metal spikes with his partner and then did the play-by-play as the makeshift booth swayed in the wind. "It was very windy, and I was thinking What the hell are we doing up here?" he told the Doug Robinson of the *Deseret News*. "That proved to me that this is what I want to do. I was proud to be there…That night was kind of an epiphany for me."

Bolerjack ended up with KSL-TV as the weekend sports anchor after a Utah sportscaster, Don Judd, saw him on TV and alerted him of an audition while they were both in Wichita, Kansas. The 26-year-old was excited to come to the Beehive State in 1985. "BYU had just won the national championship [in football], and there was the Jazz and the U," Bolerjack said. "They had it all."

And 30-some-odd years later, they still have Boler.

88 Big Al and His Big Bed

Al Jefferson was one of the Utah Jazz's best players during his three seasons with the franchise from 2010 to 2013. A much-coveted scoring center whom they acquired to pair with rising point guard

Deron Williams, Big Al remains ranked in the top 10 in four categories in Jazz history: scoring (sixth, 18.5 points per game), rebounds (fifth, 9.5 rebounds per game), blocks (sixth, 1.55 blocks per game), and minutes (sixth, 34.4 minutes per game). The most memorable stats of Big Al's time with the Jazz might be: 10' x 12'. Those were the dimensions of the 6'10" center's bed. That's bed, not bedroom. *King-sized?* Try kingdom-sized.

This became public knowledge in October 2012 when point guard Mo Williams posted a photo of himself on Jefferson's mammoth-sized mattress set while he visited his teammate's home. The 6'1" Mo Williams looked like a toddler on his parents' California King while sprawled out on the light brown duvet and white fluffy pillows. Mo Williams was stunned by its enormity, so he did what friends do: took a photo and posted it on social media to tease his buddy. The photo and tweet went viral, appearing on major sports websites—at least those that with enough bandwidth to show a bed that size.

The price tag was also a biggie. Jefferson reportedly paid $23,287 for the bedroom set, according to some shrewd detective work by Jazz fan blog Salt City Hoops, which procured and posted the itemized invoice. Though the 265-pound veteran's sense of humor was large like him, Jefferson couldn't figure out why people cared so much about him having a costly customized bed that gave him plenty of room to toss and turn at his leisure. "It's really silly," Jefferson said. "There's more important things going on in this world than me buying a bed that I can afford."

To his point Jefferson made $15 million that season. If you were to compare that to a person with a $50,000 salary, it'd be like spending $77.62 on a bed—a price you might find at a yard sale for a twin-sized box spring. Jefferson knew he was buying a big bed but didn't realize it was darn near the size of the key on a basketball court until it filled his bedroom. "Talking about it and actually seeing it is two different things," Jefferson admitted.

Mo Williams found that out, but he had to carefully answer reporters' questions about his buddy's bed after starting a media frenzy with his post. "I can't talk about it. I'm sorry. I got my big fella mad at me," he said, trying but failing to suppress his laughter. "I apologize publicly to Al Jefferson."

Big Al, also trying not to smile, said he wasn't quite ready to forgive a fellow Mississippian. He wanted to exact some revenge first. "I'm going over to his house today, taking a bunch of pictures of everything," Jefferson said. "I don't have a Twitter account, but I'm going to start me one and I'm going to put it on Twitter."

Jefferson might never hear the end of it about his bed. Two seasons later—after Jefferson signed with the Charlotte Hornets—his young, Turkish friend Enes Kanter couldn't resist teasing Jefferson in their first meeting since Jefferson left Utah in free agency. He crafted a handwritten love letter for the ages and had a ballboy deliver it to Big Al's locker at Time Warner Cable Arena.

Here's what the (partly censored) letter said:

Dear Big Al,
My Boy! I'm gonna pump fake you all night.
Jeremy (Evans) said he is gonna dunk on you.
Airport was closed but thank you for letting us land on your bed.
Biggie says you're a (not-fit-for-print inside joke).
Love XOXOXO
Your Boy Big Turk

Moments later, Jefferson strolled over to the Jazz locker room and asked his former coach, Ty Corbin, for permission to enter. "As long as you don't do nothing crazy," Corbin jokingly told him. The sweaty athlete then waltzed in and shared a good laugh about the note and reminisced with Kanter and his old Utah friends. "He showed me some love," Jefferson said. "I thought it was funny."

"He was just like a big brother," Kanter said. "He was a really nice guy."

The Jazz got the last laugh, though. With his Bobcats trailing by one, Jefferson missed two tip-ins in the final 13 seconds. Trey Burke got the rebound and hit two free throws to help Utah win 88–85.

Jefferson expressed his appreciation for his time in Utah, which came after an unfortunate ending (a DUI arrest and suspension) with the Minnesota Timberwolves. "Utah really changed me as a person, on and off the court," he said.

For the record, Big Al left the big bed in Utah. Considering he'd just signed a three-year, $40 million deal with Charlotte in the summer of 2012, he could afford a new one. And, oh, Jefferson did not write Kanter back when he returned to Utah on December 30 of that year.

89 Rodney King Riots

The first round of the 1992 playoffs was progressing as expected between the favored Utah Jazz and upstart Los Angeles Clippers. Utah cruised to a pair of wins at the Delta Center and was in control of the best-of-five series even after dropping Game 3 at the Los Angeles Memorial Sports Arena. And then all hell broke loose.

The day after that 98–88 Clippers victory, the Rodney King trial verdict was announced. Four Los Angeles Police Department officers were acquitted of beating King in spite of the incident being videotaped. Chaos erupted around Los Angeles as angry people lashed out after the jury's surprising decision. Over the next 24 hours, rioting resulted in 1,000 structural fires, 600 injuries, 23 deaths, $1 billion in damages, and a lot of looting with much of the mayhem happening within a few miles of the Sports Arena. "I'm used to going to the video store and getting a video and seeing that kind of stuff," Karl Malone told the *Los Angeles Times*. "It was incredible and it was sad."

Originally scheduled for April 30, Game 4 was postponed as a city under curfew and hazy skies dealt with more important matters. "For the next six days, Los Angeles was a war zone," former Jazz beat writer Steve Luhm of *The Salt Lake Tribune* recalled in a 2012 column. "The Jazz lived, practiced, and played on the fringe of the insanity."

Jazz coach Jerry Sloan described the scene to Luhm as "mind-boggling" and "scary." Former Utah media relations director Kim Turner said the team hotel in Marina Del Ray "was like a jail." Jazz players Mark Eaton, John Stockton, and Ty Corbin hopped in a rental car and drove to Eaton's family condo in Orange County just to have a change of scenery.

The Jazz considered returning to Utah until things settled down—and even offered to host Game 4 at the Delta Center—but they remained in L.A. The team even got out for one practice at Inglewood High School, which wasn't too far from the worst of the rioting. Tensions were high, though. The Jazz received police escorts. Armed guards secured the vicinity. Chained doors to the gym shut once players, team personnel, and media entered the building for practice with the smell of smoke and the sound of sirens in the air. *Deseret News* columnist Brad Rock, who was there covering the playoffs, recalled how "a feeling of eeriness and fear gripped the city." One Jazz office staffer took the first available plane home, telling Rock, "I gotta get out of here." A Salt Lake City sportscaster, Wesley Ruff of ABC-affiliate Channel 4, had his Geo Metro rental car surrounded at a red light after exiting an

L.A. freeway while driving toward a satellite truck to broadcast a segment. Inexplicably, he managed to escape with no harm. His TV truck was later shot at twice. "The people looked at me like, 'What the f--- are you doing here?'" Ruff told *The Tribune*. "I thought I was going to be dragged out and beaten. And there was no helicopter here. I thought, *I'm going to die, and nobody is going to know*."

Clippers executives turned down the Jazz's offer to relocate the game to Utah. They wanted to keep as much of a home advantage as possible. After a frantic search, they settled on playing at the Anaheim Convention Center on May 3. The Clippers rented a U-Haul truck to transport their court, baskets, and benches to their makeshift home arena. A Clippers team that featured Danny Manning, Doc Rivers, Ron Harper, and Olden Polynice—playing in the franchise's first playoffs in 16 years and its first postseason appearance since relocating from Buffalo—used a late 11–2 run to even the series at 2–2 with a gutsy 115–107 victory. "It was like, for the people of L.A., the first time they could actually come out of their houses and rejoice and have fun again," Rivers said.

"We knew we were playing for more than that game," Polynice, who later played for Utah, told ESPN. "We were trying to help the city recover and heal."

The teams returned to Utah for Game 5, which the Jazz easily won 98–89 en route to their first ever trip to the Western Conference Finals. "They escaped," Luhm wrote. "From the Clippers. From Los Angeles."

90 Places to Eat

With 1,700 restaurants around Salt Lake City, there are plenty of dining options for Utah Jazz fans before games. Friendly warning: SLC is not NYC, so most places won't be open late enough for postgame meals.

Crown Burgers is one popular spot near the arena that has some unofficial history with the Jazz and gives fans free parking spots if they eat there on gamedays. Located on the northeast corner of North Temple and 300 West (which becomes John Stockton Street in front of the arena), this well-known Utah eatery features charbroiled burgers, including the unique pastrami burger, onion rings, fries, and fry sauce, salads, ice cream, and Greek offerings like kebabs, gyros, and souvlaki.

For years Jazz rookies were expected to buy a Crown Burgers lunch for teammates and team staff on Locker Cleanout Day, which was held at the arena the day after their season ended. In 2012—the day after the Jazz were swept out of the first round by the San Antonio Spurs—Enes Kanter and Alec Burks did the lunch run. The final bill was $340. "You've got to do what you're told," Burks said. The shooting guard said Crown Burgers knew it was coming, so it didn't catch employees off guard to make dozens of burgers and enough baskets of fries to feed, well, an NBA roster.

In recent years, the Jazz have relocated the Locker Cleanout Day festivities to their practice facility, now called the Zions Bank Basketball Campus, and everything has kind of changed. Reporters are no longer welcome in the locker room. Athletes do their exit interviews with management and then sit at a podium for a press conference-style interview instead of the traditional scrum. And Crown Burgers is no longer on the menu. The Jazz have their own caterers who provide lunch, even for the media, so no complaints here. It was a fun tradition while it lasted, though.

In addition to Crown Burgers, here are some other great dining options.

Valter's Osteria: This fine-dining establishment is Golden State Warriors coach Steve Kerr's favorite spot on the NBA circuit. The Warriors reserve a private room and enjoy a delectable meal together whenever they're in town. "It's amazing food," Kerr said during a 2018 shootaround. "I told the coaches last night that there is not a better restaurant in the country than Valter's. We let him bring whatever he wants."

The Park Café: This is the place, as they say in these parts, for breakfast—or lunch—if you ask basketball players familiar with this café. Earl Watson eats there. Former Ute forward Kyle Kuzma stopped by for his favorite dish—Michigan hash with a side of French toast—when the Los Angeles Lakers visited Salt Lake City during his rookie season. Former University of Utah standouts Delon Wright and Jakob Poeltl also dropped in for the same specialty when the Toronto Raptors came to Utah in November 2017. Wright even brought some Raptors teammates with him to experience the breakfast.

Cheesecake Factory: This chain might be the most frequented restaurant by NBA players, and that's no different in Salt Lake City. Al Jefferson and Rudy Gobert are among the big guys who filled their big appetites on the chicken and perhaps one of their signature desserts.

Red Iguana: This place looks run down but offers some of the best Mexican grub in Utah, which used to be part of Mexico. There are three locations in the Salt Lake area, but the North Temple spot is the original.

Bruges Waffles & Frites: Just across the street from Pioneer Park—at 336 West 300 South—this hot spot serves up authentic Belgian food.

Caputo's Market & Deli: This deli, also across the street from Pioneer Park, is known for its tasty sandwiches with Italian meats and cheeses, pastas, and salads, but it closes at 7:00 PM so don't show up too late.

Cucina Toscana: Located on the same SLC block as Caputo's and Bruges, this dinner-only restaurant serves fine Italian, including its signature dish, *La Lasagna Classica Alla Bolognese* (translation: yummy lasagna).

R&R BBQ: Less than a mile south of the arena on 300 West, this award-winning restaurant features the slow-cooking creations of competitive BBQers Rod and Roger with some of the best smoked meat, succulent sauces, and lip-smacking sides this side of Texas. It also has a spot in the arena.

91 Enjoy the #Nightlife

Some Golden State Warriors caused a stir leading up to the 2017 Western Conference Semifinals by admitting they would've rather played the Los Angeles Clippers than the Jazz. Not because of basketball. It was because of the entertainment options in Los Angeles compared to Utah. "There's no nightlife in Utah," Warriors forward Matt Barnes complained in an ESPN interview. "Obviously, as players, you want to be able to have a little bit of a nightlife."

Teammate Andre Iguodala might've been convinced the Jazz name has two ZZs because Salt Lake City induces snoozing. "The problem with Utah is that you're just sitting there and your mind is, like, dead…[When] you're in L.A., you're like, 'Man, this is just the vibe in L.A.' But in Utah, it can kind of lull you to sleep."

Jazz forward Joe Ingles knows all about the loud Utah nightlife. Truth be told, the happily married 29-year-old Australian, who is father to twins, admitted he was the wrong guy to ask. "I haven't thought about nightlife for about 12 years," he said. "I couldn't tell you one place to go in America." And that's coming from a bloke who lived in L.A. before SLC.

Always one to crack a joke, Ingles came up with a solution that could benefit both the nightlife-seeking Warriors and the Jazz: "They can still go to L.A. between the games if they want. They've got enough money to pay for a jet to go over for a night and come back on gameday." He liked the idea of the Warriors being worn out from nightclub action so much that he offered another option. "If they want entertainment, they can drive to Vegas if they really want," Ingles said. "I'll hire the car for them."

Some Utahns were offended by the Warriors' statements, and others offered touristy suggestions. When the series shifted back to Utah, local media members stoked the flame of this controversy, of course. In one particularly awkward interview at Vivint Smart Home Arena the day before Game 3, Steph Curry was peppered with silly questions about the topic. His first response—"Business trip"—didn't deter sound-byte seekers. One TV interviewer even asked if he'd be interested in an indoor trampoline park, trolley rides, or a downtown bookstore. "All three of those," Curry said, perhaps wishing he was at any of them instead of in this interview session. "Can you send me the address?"

Hopefully, the reporter sent the address of historical Temple Square, which attracts three to five million visitors a year; the Utah Olympic Park in Park City; the Oval in Kearns; some of the popular hiking and mountain biking trails along the Wasatch Front; or the Discovery Gateway Children's Museum, which is No. 1 on the featured listings at VisitSaltLake.com. There are also some fine mattress stores if sleeping is your idea of a good night.

Local leaders and tourism officials had fun with the fuss being made over the city being full of fuddy-duddies. They sent messages to the Warriors, made a catchy promo video, and even built a new website: theresnothingtodoinsaltlake.com. Among the many nightlife (and daylife) suggestions: 1,700 restaurants, 120 hotels (sleep!), 30-plus museums, seven world-class microbreweries, theaters, concerts, ballets, fireworks, ethnic celebrations, dudes decked out in Swiss attire blowing alpenhorns on top of a nearby mountain (don't knock it 'til you try it), and—get this—NBA games.

And the Warriors had the gall to call Salt Lake City boring! Just get a load of what GSW guard Klay Thompson had the nerve to say about his night off in Utah between Games 2 and 3: "I'll find something to do. I go by the saying, 'Only boring people get bored.'" He even mentioned that there's a nice movie theater in the city.

The Jazz also went to town, so to speak. President Steve Starks brainstormed a clever idea to make thousands of T-shirts with the rallying cry: #nightlife. The Jazz donated $1 from each sale to their cancer-fighting "5 for the Fight" charity partner.

The Warriors swept Utah in four games in that second-round series, so there wasn't too much time to catch everything Salt Lake has to offer. But in the team's first trip back to the Beehive State the following season, a group of Warriors players went to The Escape Key, an adventure that forces participants to use teamwork to find a way out in less than an hour. Curry humorously mocked the backlash by posting a photo of his teammates—who escaped—and a one-word caption: #nightlife. "That," he said while smirking the next morning, "was a little subtle dig."

The Warriors did not enjoy the #nightlife on the night of this game. The Jazz jabbed back with a not-so-subtle big dig—a 129–99 blowout win that gave their fans quite the show and night. Iguodala might tell you his team was lulled to sleep.

92 International Roster

Having international players on the roster used to be a foreign concept for the Utah Jazz. That's certainly not the case anymore. In recent years, in fact, the Jazz locker room has had somewhat of a United Nations feel to it. Forget New York. Utah has welcomed more immigrants than any other team in the NBA in recent years.

During the 2017–18 season alone, the Jazz employed players from eight—nine if you count Joel Bolomboy—different countries. The power forward, originally from Ukraine, played his rookie season (2016–17) in Utah after being drafted in the second round out of Weber State, but he was waived at the end of the 2017 training camp. Other countries represented by Jazz players in the 2017–18 campaign: Australia (Dante Exum and Joe Ingles), Brazil (Raul Neto), Canada (Naz Mitrou-Long), France (Rudy Gobert), Spain (Ricky Rubio), Sweden (Jonas Jerebko), Switzerland (Thabo Sefolosha), and the United States (10 players). Bonus: Utah's lead assistant coach that season, now Phoenix Suns head coach Igor Kokoskov, hails from Serbia.

Utah led the NBA with most international players in the 2016–17 (seven) and 2017–18 seasons. "It's not something we set out to do. It's not by design," Jazz coach Quin Snyder told the *Deseret News*. "We just try to get good basketball players."

In 1992 the Dream Team captured the imagination of basketball fans and players across the globe, sparking worldwide interest in a sport that was already growing in popularity. The NBA has seen a steady influx of foreigners since then, going from 23 international players at the beginning of the 1991–92 season to a record 113 on opening night in 2016.

The Jazz didn't have an international player on their team for their first 15 seasons. That changed when the franchise drafted Puerto Rican star forward Jose Ortiz with the 15th pick of the 1987 draft. Utah had high hopes that the 6'11" Ortiz would help bolster the frontcourt with Karl Malone and Mark Eaton, but the former Oregon State standout never panned out as an NBA player. The

International Players in Team History

Jose Ortiz (1988–89), Puerto Rico
Olden Polynice (1999–01), Haiti
John Amaechi (2001–03), Great Britain
Andrei Kirilenko (2001–11), Russia
Carlos Arroyo (2002–05), Puerto Rico
Raul Lopez (2002–05), Spain
Raja Bell (2003–05, 2010–13), U.S. Virgin Islands
Gordan Giricek (2003–08), Croatia
Aleksandar "Sasha" Pavlovic (2003–04), Serbia and Montenegro
Mehmet Okur (2004–11), Turkey
Aleksandar Radojevic (2004–05), Serbia and Montenegro
Rafael Araujo (2006–07), Brazil
Kyrylo Fesenko (2007–11), Ukraine
Francisco Elson (2010–11), Netherlands
Enes Kanter (2011–15), Turkey (born in Switzerland)
Rudy Gobert (2013–present), France
Andris Biedrins (2013–14), Latvia
Dante Exum (2014–present), Australia
Joe Ingles (2014–present), Australia
Raul Neto (2015–present), Brazil
Trey Lyles (2015–17), Canada
Tibor Pleiss (2015–16), Germany
Boris Diaw (2016–17), France
Joel Bolomboy (2016–18), Ukraine
Thabo Sefolosha (2017–present), Switzerland
Jonas Jerebko (2017–18), Sweden
Ricky Rubio (2017–present), Spain
Naz Mitrou-Long (2017–18), Canada

1987 Pac-10 Player of the Year started his first 15 games with the Jazz—after playing in Spain for a year after being drafted—but struggled and quickly fell out of the playing rotation. Ortiz was waived by the Jazz partway through his second and final NBA season after suffering from mononucleosis and playing in only 13 games for just 64 minutes. "It's been a really tough situation for him," Jazz coach Jerry Sloan said at the time.

Ortiz had a successful international career after that. One of his shining moments included playing on the Puerto Rico national team that upset Team USA in the 2004 Olympics. Perhaps leery from that experience, the Jazz didn't have another international player on their roster until adding Olden Polynice of Haiti in 1999. Utah has had at least one international player every year since then—from Great Britain's John Amaechi (2001–03), Russia's Andrei Kirilenko (2001–11), Turkey's Mehmet Okur (2004–11) and Enes Kanter (2011–15), France's Rudy Gobert (2013–present) and Boris Diaw (2016–17), to Australia's Dante Exum and Joe Ingles (2014–present), among others.

In all, the Jazz have had 26 international players from 19 different countries over the years. Some have been busts, like Ortiz, Brazil's Rafael Araujo, Latvia's Andris Biedrins, and Canada's Trey Lyles. Some, such as Kirilenko, Okur, Gobert, and Ingles, have been solid if not stellar contributors. And some, like Polynice, Croatia's Gordan Giricek, and Kanter, fall somewhere in between.

The year he played in Utah, Diaw laughed and jokingly threw his hands up in the air, celebrating with a "Whoo! Whoo! Whoo!" when told that the Jazz topped the league in international diversity. "It's good," the French big man said. "That means it's a global competition. It's still called the National Basketball Association... but it's not just national anymore. It's global."

93 JP Gibson

Not only did the Utah Jazz make a surprise player acquisition during the 2014 training camp, they also saved their best free-agent signing for last. In a transaction that even met the approval of talk show host Ellen Degeneres, the Jazz signed JP Gibson to a one-day contract at their intrasquad scrimmage in early October. Then a spunky five-year-old guard who'd battled acute lymphoblastic leukemia since 2012, Gibson signed his new deal using a purple crayon before conducting a pregame interview. "We are a young team and we decided that we'd go even a little younger," Jazz president Randy Rigby said. "JP Gibson is the newest member of the Utah Jazz team for the day."

And what a heartwarming day it turned out to be. Gibson instantly won over players, coaches, and fans alike with his personality, charisma, and a *SportsCenter* Top 10 worthy play of the game. Gibson held his own during the media session, too, revealing that he plays *NBA Jam* on his iPad at home, that he scores "a lot" of points when he plays basketball, that he beats his dad, Josh, when they play soccer, and that Gordon Hayward and Trey Burke were his favorite players.

The blond toddler stole the show during this memorable event. Sporting a very baggy green Jazz uniform with his last name on the back, No. 1 warmed hearts during introductions, the Rookie Dance-Off (Dante Exum and Rodney Hood didn't have a chance), and warm-up stretches. The grand finale came when he was subbed in for the last play of the scrimmage. After taking the inbounds pass, Gibson made fans erupt as he dribbled by Exum and Steve Novak. Once Gibson got into the lane, 7'1" Rudy Gobert gave him a big assist by lifting the toddler up for a two-handed slam dunk like no other. JP's dad called the experience a "dream come true." Coach Quin Snyder said it was special. "To have him come out there and then for Rudy to lift him up and to dunk was pretty cool," Hayward said. "It was a special moment for all of us."

Gibson continued to support his old team after his contract expired. His family even makes an annual trip to watch the Jazz play in the NBA Summer League in Las Vegas. "It's great to plan a family vacation that's centered around basketball. That's every dad's dream, right?" said JP's father, Josh Gibson. "It's nice to have an excuse that, 'Oh, JP wants to go.' You can't say no to the kid who had cancer."

After passing a two-year benchmark in May 2017 of being cancer free, the Gibsons were hopeful that JP was in the clear. His mom said she experiences "scanxiety" every time he's examined or blood is drawn. Sadly, just a couple of weeks after she said that and JP had cheered the Summer Jazz on in Las Vegas, Josh Gibson posted a heartbreaking handwritten letter from his son on July 29, 2017: "I'm JP. My cancer is back. Wish me luck! [Heart] JP."

The Jazz organization, players, and fans rallied around him. Rudy Gobert tweeted out a photoshopped picture of Gibson busting a backboard while slamming on his own. Gobert also put his initials on shoes as a tribute and wrote "JP" on his hand as part of the Jazz's "5 for the Fight" cancer-fighting fund-raiser. University of Utah coach Larry Krystkowiak, a former Jazzman, and his wife Jan visited the Ute fan in the hospital. A Jazz fan created a JP Strong shirt to raise money for the Gibson family. In November of 2017, Gibson made it to a regular-season game and started the second grade while continuing to undergo treatment for leukemia. He kept tabs of the Jazz from home, too. During a game on December 23, 2017, his dad tweeted out that JP didn't like that a whistle wasn't blown when he thought Donovan Mitchell was fouled. His dad said JP yelled, "Hey, refs! You watch the game with your eyes, not your ears!"

JP has loved sports from Day One, his dad said. At 12 months old, he climbed up on the couch and watched full basketball games with him. JP insisted on shooting hoops for an hour every night before bedtime when he was just 15 months old. He patiently waited until he was six to join a local Jr. Jazz team and he's had a ball doing that since then. "He'll have to work his way back up [to the NBA]," his dad joked. "But he's excited. He'll probably get more playing time."

94 Follow the Jazz on Social Media

When social media platforms like Twitter started catching on and athletes began tweeting out their thoughts and daily itineraries like everyone else, the reactions of Utah Jazz players were varied. Matt Harpring, 32 at the time, said he was too old for that modern form of tech-based communication. (Harpring has since joined Twitter.) Paul Millsap said he'd need to be careful of not incurring the wrath of his coach. (He's also on Twitter.) And his coach, Jerry Sloan, was perplexed when the subject of social media use was broached at a practice in the spring of 2009. "I don't know anything about websites. I don't follow that," Sloan said, earnestly. "I don't even have a computer. I don't know how to turn one on."

Okay, but what would he do if a player tweeted during a game as had happened elsewhere? "I don't know what you're talking about," Sloan said. "I'm being totally honest. How would you do that?" Reporters began to explain that you do it on your phone when the old-school coach interjected, "I have a phone, but I don't know how to use it."

Some whippersnappers who've donned Jazz uniforms have been quite adept at using the fancy gadgets. If it makes Sloan feel better, it's highly unlikely any of them know how to operate a John Deere tractor, though. Here's a collection of some of the more entertaining social media interactions by Jazz players.

- A month after Oklahoma City Thunder big man Enes Kanter said mountains were the only thing he'd miss about Utah, he lamented a 94–89 OKC loss to his former Jazz teammates: "We cannot just let a team not even in the playoffs spot beat us like that." Trevor Booker fired back on Twitter: "Wouldn't go to war with any other guys! Helluva season Jazz Nation!!! And oh yeah, glad we didn't lose to a non playoff team @ Enes_Kanter"
- When everything was good in Utah in 2012—well, except his feeling of loneliness—Kanter tweeted: "Eating dinner downtown, looking for a blonde to eat dinner with me at my table. Does anyone wanna join me?" Next came this tweet: "Just finished dinner. Thanks Twitter <3 Now need a massage. BRUNETTES WELCOME ;)" Not surprisingly, Jazz management was not thrilled with those messages.
- Shortly after news broke on July 4, 2017, that Gordon Hayward chose the Boston Celtics over Utah in free agency, Jazz center Rudy Gobert posted an Instagram video of him singing the NSFW lyrics "These hoes ain't loyal" from a Chris Brown hip-hop song about loyalty. Asked about it the next day, Gobert smiled and said, "I was just listening to music."
- Joe Ingles and Ricky Rubio were teammates in Spain, and it didn't take long for them to start busting each others' chops when Rubio joined Utah. Rubio started one particular tweet-a-tweet encounter by asking Ingles if the new practice facility he'd tweeted about touring was big enough that he wouldn't have to see him. Ingles, whose hair isn't quite as thick as it used

to be, wrote: "They have a ponytail room off to the side for you." Rubio, whose flowing hair is often pulled up into a man bun: "Don't start that game. Don't be jealous. You wish you had my hair. A year from now you won't need a haircut ever again. #BaldJoeIsComing."

- A fan (@madkidpalmcity) asked Booker to dunk on Gobert when his Brooklyn Nets played the Jazz in November 2017. Booker's reply: "He's too scared to play." Gobert didn't take it sitting down, though his injury forced him to sit out: "Yes I got scared when I saw your (bald) head..."

- Gobert tried to influence Gordon Hayward's free-agency decision while his teammate was taking recruiting trips to the Miami Heat, Boston Celtics, and Utah Jazz. His emoji-filled tweet on July 1, 2017, was an instant classic. It consisted of six emojis in this order: a palm tree (Heat) and trashcan, a sham-rock (Celtics) and the poop emoji, and a saxophone (Jazz) and trophy. The clever tweet was so popular in Utah some Jazz fans made T-shirts and posters for summer league games out of the design. It was inserted into Twitter handles. Isaiah Thomas, then with Boston, and Heat center Hassan Whiteside both hoped to entice Hayward to join their teams and responded in hilarious fashion to Gobert with tweets that included trophies and rings next to their teams' emojis, and people shrugging or angrily gesturing next to the Jazz's emoji. Welcome to the NBA's emoji era.

95 Trevor Booker

Though the reserve power forward, Trevor Booker, only played for Utah for two seasons, averaging just 6.5 points and 5.4 rebounds, few short-term players have endeared themselves to Jazz fans like Book did. They loved his enthusiasm and energy, his hustle and drive, his spunk and feistiness. They loved how much he loved them. Many Jazz fans will not soon forget the crazy shot he made against the Thunder in Oklahoma City, the way he mixed it up with Los Angeles Clippers star Blake Griffin, the way he smacked Los Angeles Lakers big man Roy Hibbert, and how he humorously went after Enes Kanter on Twitter multiple times after the young Turkish player demanded a trade and insulted just about everything Utah-related.

Booker's Harlem Globetrotters-worthy shot will likely be one that appears on highlight videos again and again. With 0.2 seconds on the shot clock at the end of the first half of a game at Oklahoma City in January 2015, the Jazz were set up to inbound the ball on the far sideline. The only shot that can even be completed in that amount of time, per NBA rules is a tip, and that's what Utah coach Quin Snyder called for. The power forward headed to the hoop, thinking Gordon Hayward would throw a lob, but when that didn't materialize, Booker rushed back toward the small forward and stopped with his back to the basket.

Craziness ensued.

Hayward made a bounce pass to Booker, who instinctively tipped the ball with both hands up and over his head. The ball plopped right into the net in time. It looked like Booker was playing volleyball or hot potato or, as OKC announcer Brian Davis exclaimed, "Are you kidding me?…That defines 'Grandma Shot!'"

Booker lifted his hands up, shrugged his shoulders, and flashed a huge smile. Hayward said he was just trying to make sure the Thunder didn't steal the ball. He had no idea how it actually went in. "You should ask him about that," Hayward said. "Honestly, I have no clue."

Booker and his cousin, Lakers forward Jordan Hill, did. "I know you won't believe me, but we practiced those shots all the time growing up," said Booker, who received a text from Hill after the video of the shot went viral. "I guess you can say the hard work finally paid off."

In the years since moving on to play for the Nets and Sixers, Booker has continued to speak glowingly about all things Jazz and playfully interact with his former teammates, especially Rudy Gobert, on social media. "If the opportunity ever came about, I'd definitely love to play in Utah again," Booker said in a July 2017 HoopsHype.com podcast while still under contract with Brooklyn. "Their organization is great. The fans are great. My family and I loved it out there."

Booker had an incident with a large man from L.A. in each of his two preseasons with the Jazz. In October of 2014, Booker fouled Griffin hard as the Kia hurdler drove to the basket on a fast break. Griffin immediately approached Booker, and the two players became entangled for a brief moment before referees and teammates quickly intervened. Booker was mystified after being assessed with a Flagrant 1 foul for his role in the fracas. He said he wasn't mad until Griffin grabbed the back of his head and pulled him closer. "We have our history," Booker said. "We've gotten into it before." That by itself might have been enough to win over Jazz fans, some of whom have loved to hate the L.A. big man. Booker sprained his ankle during the brouhaha, requiring him to sport a walking boot.

A year later, Booker became embroiled in a heated series against two Lakers big men in an exhibition game in Hawaii.

First, Booker responded to getting bumped by Julius Randle by pushing the L.A. power forward. That merited technical foul No. 1. Hibbert, who'd generously shared his elbows with Jazz players all night, then bumped into Booker's chest. That didn't go over well. The 6'8" Booker reacted by smacking the 7'2" Lakers center in the head with the open palm of his left hand. That merited technical foul No. 2, an ejection, and a suspension from the first regular season game. "Trevor's an emotional guy," Snyder said. "He's competitive."

96 Funny Frank Layden

Thurl Bailey smiled while referring to the early days of the Jazz in Utah when the franchise was simultaneously trying to figure out how to win games and win over fans. Now a studio analyst for Jazz broadcasts, Bailey said his old coach had an accommodating way to answer fans when they'd ask what time games started at the Salt Palace back then. Frank Layden's response: "What time can you be there?"

During the 1997 NBA Finals, *Deseret News* columnist Lee Benson accurately described Layden's importance to the Jazz organization and the team president's use of humor in the process. "There was a time, and it wasn't that long ago, when Frank Layden was not just the franchise's coach and general manager, but also the person who positioned himself on the front lines and provided comic cover," Benson wrote. "For years the Jazz rode Layden's sense of humor. He was always the master of deflection. They can't make jokes about you if you make them first."

Layden never lost his sense of humor as the Jazz improved, but it wasn't as necessary to draw attention to himself anymore while the spotlight shined on John Stockton, Karl Malone, and Jerry Sloan. Game-winners, not one-liners, captured the interest of fans and media. As Benson pointed out, though, Layden might have been the funniest man in Utah—at least this side of then-University of Utah basketball coach Rick Majerus and his array of jokes about his excess weight and the ski team makeup (read: white) of his college roster. We could fill an entire book with gut-busting Layden jokes, but we're limited to one chapter.

- To a fan getting on a referee's case: "Who are you calling a fool? You paid to watch this game."
- "When I coached at Niagara, I had a player who was such a poor foul shooter that when he went to cross himself he missed his forehead."
- "I never get into politics. I'm not a member of an organized political party myself. I'm a Democrat."
- "As a teenager I played in a Catholic Church league. We couldn't afford uniforms, so we had to wear choir robes. It really slowed down our fast break, and the choir smelled funny on Sundays, too."
- "Even Jesus had trouble with 12 guys."
- "One veteran reported for training camp so out of shape that his stomach crossed the mid-court line three steps before the rest of his body."
- "Our team has a great bunch of outside shooters. Unfortunately, we play all our games indoors."
- "I stepped on a scale that gives fortunes. The card read: 'Come back in 15 minutes alone.'"
- "They'd worship this body in India."
- "It used to take me two years to do what Jerry [Sloan]'s doing now in one."

- "One sportswriter suggested that we rename our team the Opossums because we play dead at home and get killed on the road."
- "We're a team in transition. We've gone from bad to worse."
- "I was down in the lounge one evening, enjoying a glass of wine when a beautiful, vivacious, tall, young lady approached me at my table and invited herself to sit down with me. After some introductions, she made the most unbelievable proposal

Known for his self-deprecating humor, Jazz head coach Frank Layden patrols the sidelines in 1988. (USA TODAY Sports Images)

to me. She said that she would do anything—anything—that I
wanted for $300. So she painted my condo."

- "We had a point guard who was so short that he had to stand
on a stool while showering. Otherwise, the water would be cold
by the time it reached him."

- "I coached a team that was so bad. We couldn't win at home.
We couldn't win on the road. I failed as a coach because I
couldn't figure out where else we could play."

- "The worst team I coached lost nine straight, and then we went
into a slump. On our days off, we had a victory celebration."

97 Utah Stars

Less than a year after relocating to Salt Lake City from Los Angeles
and following a midseason roster overhaul, the Utah Stars claimed
the American Basketball Association title by beating the Kentucky
Colonels 131–121 in Game 7 on May 18, 1971. Willie Wise and
Zelmo Beaty were carried off the Salt Palace floor during the wild
celebration that night. Nearly 50 years later, it remains the state's
only professional basketball championship. "I think that's something that should go down—at least in the history of Utah—as
the greatest sporting event or greatest sporting team," Wise, who
believes the ABA champs would've beaten Lew Alcindor's NBA
champion Milwaukee Bucks that year, claimed in a retrospective
piece by Dirk Facer of the *Deseret News*. "Not taking anything away
from Stockton and Malone, of course, but still the fact remains that
they haven't won anything and we did."

Years before paving the way for the Jazz in Utah, the Stars
announced they were moving to Salt Lake City after failing to

establish a solid base in Lalaland. They only averaged 1,461 fans in 1969–70 at the Los Angeles Coliseum after struggling for two years as the Anaheim Amigos, an ABA charter member since 1967.

Utah embraced its new basketball team, as was noted in a catchy team song:

"Here come the Stars, here come the Stars, here come the Stars.

Pro basketball is here at last, here come the Stars.

Now we've got to see them, we've got the action,

Utah's first major league attraction.

Here come the Stars, here come the Stars from Utah, here come the Stars."

The Stars came and so did the fans. Utah set an ABA attendance record by averaging 6,246 fans that first season in the 12,166-seat Salt Palace.

Former Boston Celtics bench boss Bill Sharman coached the Stars that season, and the team rewarded its loyal new fans with a 57–27 record. Beaty, a two-time NBA All-Star, Wise, Red Robbins, and mid-season acquisitions Glen Combs and Ron Boone were among the guys who became household names in a state that was known for its love of college basketball. The Stars swept the Texas Chaparrals 4–0 in the opening round that year. In Round Two they upset the Indiana Pacers, who'd finished one game ahead of them at 58–26—thanks to a 108–101 road win in Game 7 that the *Deseret News* called "The Miracle On 34th Street."

The Stars were welcomed back to Salt Lake City by thousands of fans at the airport. Utah went on to give them even more to cheer about by knocking off the Colonels in seven games in the ABA finals. An overflow crowd of 13,260 fans showed up at the Salt Palace for a magical Game 7. As the buzzer sounded, the Stars were joined on the court by a deluge of fans, who carried Wise and

Beaty off the floor on their shoulders. "It happened so fast that we couldn't get off the floor," Beaty said. "It was just wonderful."

The Stars never repeated that championship feat, but they continued to draw big crowds, played entertaining and competitive basketball, and seemed to have an exciting future after drafting star Moses Malone in 1974. Even so, the carpet was pulled out from under them on December 2, 1975, when owner Bill Daniels folded the franchise and partially merged with the Spirits of St. Louis.

That signaled the beginning of the end for the ABA, which fizzled and merged with the NBA following that season after the Baltimore Claws, San Diego Sails, and Stars ceased operations. "I was personally crushed when the team was disbanded," Stars coach Tom Nissalke told the *Deseret News.* "The fans understood what we were doing. That's what made it a super situation because Stars fans are knowledgeable basketball people."

If there was a bright side, the Stars' success in Salt Lake City set the stage for the NBA and all that Jazz four years later. That transplanted team from New Orleans had two familiar faces from the old ABA team: Nissalke, the Jazz's first head coach in Utah, and the durable Boone.

98 The City of Utah

Karl Malone might never live down calling Utah a bad city, but he isn't the only one who's incorrectly identified the Beehive State. During the 2001 playoffs, Dallas Mavericks big man Dirk Nowitzki rankled Jazz fans and geography teachers alike when he explained to a cameraman at the airport why the Mavericks traveled back to Texas between games at the Delta Center. The young Nowitzki blurted out: "Well, Utah is a bad city."

At least Derek Harper knew he was insulting a state and not a city in his infamous "You go play in Utah" dig. Later in his career, Nowitzki explained himself. He says he meant that the Mavericks simply wanted to go home and sleep in their own beds, and they could do it with two full days off between Game 1 (April 21) and Game 2 (April 24). Of course, this explanation would've made more sense if he'd said, "Well, Utah is a bad city to sleep in." Instead, Nowitzki claims he said that because "it's the playoffs, and we shouldn't spend too much time there. It's hostile."

And, yes, he meant hostile, not hostel.

But the feisty German—who had several run-ins with people from The Bad City: Andrei Kirilenko, Matt Harpring, Earl Watson, the mayor of Utah—said what he said and said it to a guy with film rolling, no less. It was on the news that night in Salt Lake City. Town criers sounded the persecution alarm. Damage done.

Tar, feather, and pitchforks were apparently all on back order, so Jazz fans had to make due with screaming, booing, and attempting to call his hotel room when the Mavericks came back the day before Game 2 tipped off. They'll show you bad city! The second-year player entered the Delta Center arena to warm up long before tip-off the next day and was greeted with a Jazz fan holding an all-time great sign that read: "Germany is a bad city."

Nowitzki—or "Dirty Dirk" as some Jazz faithful call him—laughs about it now. "They got me good," the Dallas star said at a 2014 shootaround in The Bad City (of Utah, not Germany). "They booed me with 90 minutes on the clock. We got off on the wrong foot."

It didn't help the relations between sister cities Utah and Germany that the seven-footer added elimination to insult in 2001, using his wrong foot to boot the Jazz out of the playoffs. The Mavericks overcame a 2–0 deficit, John Stockton and Karl Malone, and his geography faux-pas to rally for three straight wins and a best-of-five, first-round victory. Nowitzki called Jazz fans' reaction "awesome," for what it's worth. Get this: he even offered a belated, albeit mild, endorsement of Utah's capital. "Actually, I like the city," Nowitzki said. "I don't mind it. It's nice with the mountains. I don't mind being here."

The Wasatch Front mountains are exquisite. Just ask Enes Kanter.

Jazz fans should probably cut Nowitzki some slack for the part in which he misspoke about Utah being a city. (Except for geography teachers—they can remain irked.) Only a couple of months apart, two respected players in the organization made accidental references to "the city of Utah." Veteran Joe Johnson referred to it as such at his exit interview in May 2017. That came after his age-defying heroics led the Jazz past the Los Angeles Clippers in the first round, so you know there was no ill intent. Then in July, beloved rookie Donovan Mitchell said, "Utah is a beautiful city" during a Channel 5 interview with sportscaster Rod Zundel on the night he was drafted and traded to the state of Salt Lake City.

Al Jefferson, who had a great relationship with Jazz fans in his three seasons, also called it "the city of Utah" at locker cleanout in 2013. Kris Humphries did, too. Which brings us back to Malone, who started the trend in 1985 when the Louisiana native was interviewed after the Jazz drafted him. The Mailman was teased for decades for delivering this famous line in his Southern drawl: "I'm glad to be in the city of Utah." But know that Malone has learned his (geography) lesson. During his 2006 statue unveiling, he said, "I realize now, 20 years later, that it's a state."

99 Truck Robinson

Only 6'7", Truck Robinson was an undersized power forward who more than made up for his size deficit with a powerful motor and a nose for the ball. He was a Paul Millsap type player before Paul Millsap was even a twinkle in his parents' eyes. "If you ever had the opportunity to see Leonard 'Truck' Robinson play basketball at Tennessee State University or in the NBA, then you know exactly how he earned his nickname," Robinson's Tennessee Sports Hall of Fame biography reads. "Even as a pro, he stood out as a strong power forward and a rebounding specialist."

New Orleans ended up being merely an extended pit stop for this Truck, but the Tennessee State product had one of the best seasons in the history of the Jazz franchise during his short tenure. Robinson's NBA career began in 1974 with the Washington Bullets after being drafted 22nd overall, which at the time was in the second round. He then played for the Atlanta Hawks and developed a reputation for being a versatile player who could score with the best of them while also being able to rebound better than most.

Robinson really shined with New Orleans after signing a contract as a free agent with the Jazz in 1977. But if Robinson was a star in NOLA—and he was—then Maravich was a supernova, and that caused some well-publicized friction. "I came into a situation where Maravich was all the people knew. Pete, Pete, Pete," Robinson told *Sports Illustrated*. "You couldn't name five players on the Jazz before I got there. It was Pete and the rest of the Jazz. All of a sudden I come in—a black player in the South—and it's Pete and Truck. A lot of people didn't care for that."

Even so, things clicked for Robinson during his first and only full season with New Orleans. He averaged 22.7 points and an

NBA-leading 15.7 rebounds for an Elgin Baylor-coached Jazz team that went 39–43 and didn't qualify for the playoffs. Robinson, who became only the third forward to be the league's top rebounder, was named an All-Star and earned a spot on the All-NBA first team.

Robinson's numbers were similarly good the following season when he demanded a trade. He had become disillusioned with the Jazz at the end of his first season after Maravich was sidelined with an injury. "It was all frustration," Robinson said. "I'd come in, put on my clothes, play 45 minutes, and we'd get our tails kicked. Nobody'd give a damn. Then I'd go home and come back again for the same routine."

That frustration with Jazz management boiled over into the summer of 1978 after his attempt to restructure his contract was spurned. Management told him that's not how the organization did business, even though Maravich reworked his deal the previous offseason. "The Jazz has two sets of rules," Robinson's agent, Don Cronson, told *SI*, "one for Pete and one for the rest of the players."

Robinson's second season with the Jazz was highly productive until it was cut short because he asked to be traded to the Phoenix Suns. In what turned out to be the beginning of the end for this franchise in New Orleans, Robinson was shipped to the Suns in exchange for two players and a pair of first-round draft picks. He'd averaged a career best 24.2 points and 13.4 rebounds in 43 games before heading to Phoenix on January 12, 1979. Robinson had success with the Jazz, even though he described the situation as: "In New Orleans, we had only one option. Then it was every man for himself."

One month later, the organization announced that Maravich was out for the remainder of the year because of a knee injury. A couple of months after that happened, owners Sam Battistone and Larry Hatfield announced that they intended to move the franchise to Salt Lake City.

Robinson received one of the greatest compliments about his worth from an opposing team's executive after being traded from New Orleans to the Suns. "I'm really sorry to see Truck come into our division, especially to Phoenix because they were a good team already," Los Angeles Lakers general manager Bill Sharman said.

Robinson was an All-Star repeat in 1981, but he never again put up the numbers like he did during a brilliant year and a half with the Jazz. He retired from the NBA in 1984, having averaged 16.0 points and 9.5 rebounds in 705 games.

100 What If?

Considering the Utah Jazz have yet to win a championship going on 45 years now, there are plenty of "What if?" scenarios to go around.

What if...Pete Maravich hadn't jacked up his knee before relocating to Utah...or Rickey Green's layup had fallen in the second round of the 1984 playoffs...or Adrian Dantley and Jazz management had gotten along...or Mark Eaton's back hadn't gone out on him in the early 1990s?

What if...Michael Jordan had pursued a shoe salesman career after being cut from his sophomore high school team...or sat out his Flu Game...or not pushed off Bryon Russell...or Howard Eisley's three-pointer had counted as it should have...and Scottie Pippen hadn't planted the thought in Karl Malone's head that mailmen don't deliver on Sundays?

What if...Carlos Boozer and Deron Williams had stayed together; Andrei Kirilenko and Mehmet Okur had stayed healthy; and Jerry Sloan, Paul Millsap, and Kyle Korver had stayed around?

Or going back to their best decade, what if they'd snuck past the Portland Trail Blazers in 1992, '99, and 2000, the Houston Rockets in 1994 and '95, and/or the Seattle SuperSonics in 1996? And what if Gordon Hayward...sorry, too soon.

There are interesting "What if?" questions involving some Hall of Famers, too.

What if...the Jazz hadn't lost the pick that eventually turned into Magic Johnson...or Dominique Wilkins hadn't demanded a trade before even giving the Jazz a chance, and they didn't desperately need money to meet payroll...or Julius Erving had decided to accept Larry H. Miller's offer to play in Utah?

Those can be fun or maddening situations to think about. Even Wilkins wonders about that now that he looks back at how things came together for a team he refused to play for—the Utah Jazz—after the financially shaky franchise selected him third overall out of Georgia in 1983. Now an analyst for Atlanta Hawks broadcasts, the Human Highlight Film said he didn't want to play power forward like Utah wanted. "I was a small forward," Wilkins told Eric Woodyard of the *Deseret News* in 2018. "Power forwards in them days was some big, physical—and I'm not going to say what else—and I didn't want no part of that."

With hindsight and maturity now in his favor, Wilkins can't help wonder what if he'd ended up on the same team as John Stockton and Karl Malone. "Playing with Stockton and Malone, we probably could've won a few championships. Not probably. We would've," Wilkins said. "But again, things happen in life for a reason, and you've got to take what cards are dealt, but coming to Atlanta was a blessing for me, and I've never left."

While it's fun to imagine that trio winning a collection of NBA championship banners, they might be hanging from the rafters of an arena in a different city. The Jazz wouldn't have been able to pay the players on their roster if not for $1 million received from Atlanta in a package that also included John Drew and Freeman

Williams in exchange for Wilkins. Even after making payroll during that financially shaky era, the ownership situation remained in a precarious situation before Miller finally bought the whole kit and caboodle from Sam Battistone in 1986. Depending on how you look at it, the Wilkins trade could go down as the worst or the best deal the Jazz ever made. If you like the team in Utah, well, it unfortunately had to happen.

A decade earlier, the Jazz—in New Orleans at the time—made a transaction that fizzled for them and sizzled for the Los Angeles Lakers. Hoping to bolster their backcourt, Jazz management acquired five-time All-Star Gail Goodrich in 1976. The idea was to team up the 11-year NBA veteran with Pete Maravich and watch the scoreboard light up.

New Orleans, by the way, signed Goodrich away from the Lakers as a free agent on July 19. The NBA worked out compensation packages to soften the blow for teams that lost veteran players in free agency back then, so the league decided to award the Lakers with the Jazz's following three first-round picks and a future second-rounder. Goodrich's new team also received a couple of draft picks (a lower first-round selection in 1978 and a second-round pick) as part of the exchange. This is the same concept that resulted in Atlanta receiving two first-rounders and six draft picks overall from New Orleans after Pistol Pete signed with the Jazz as a free agent in 1974. Yikes.

Injuries to Goodrich and Maravich over the next couple of years led to the Jazz finishing an NBA-worst 26–56 in 1978–79, which resulted in the Lakers being rewarded the No. 1 overall pick of the 1979 NBA Draft. Tinsel Town, meet Earvin Johnson. Call him Magic because he pulls championships out of a hat and, well, just watch him play and you'll understand.

That's a painful what if. "They made a deal with a free agent that they thought would help their team," Goodrich told the *Deseret News*. "But the league, in an effort to discourage free agency—I'm not sure they'll admit to this even now—stepped in and awarded the Lakers those draft choices as compensation. It was a big settlement that New Orleans eventually had to agree to. But not until there had been a lot of behind-the-scenes pressure from the league."

On the bright side, the Jazz did end up with a late second-round pick (Essie Hollis), who only played in the NBA for one season, and a first-round pick (Jack Givens) they traded to Atlanta along with Goodrich. (Yes, your sarcasm detector is functioning properly.)

And then there's the Moses Malone what if. A man with a Hall of Fame name and Hall of Fame game, this Moses was picked No. 1 overall by the Jazz in a supplemental pre-merger draft of ABA players on December 30, 1975. This Malone actually was selected by the Jazz franchise after playing professionally in Utah with the Stars until the ABA franchise folded and he ended up with the Spirits of St. Louis. Malone would have played for the Jazz, but the franchise requested and received permission from the NBA to put the gifted forward into the 1976 ABA Dispersal Draft pool in order to recoup the 1977 first-round pick they'd lost from picking him up in the first place. That No. 1 pick was then given to the Lakers as part of the Goodrich transaction, which in a roundabout way only cost the Jazz both Magic and Moses.

Malone went on to have a marvelous NBA career with seemingly every club in the NBA but the Jazz, including the Buffalo Braves, Rockets, Philadelphia 76ers (twice), Washington Bullets, Hawks, Milwaukee Bucks, and the San Antonio Spurs. At least Utah got him for the beginning of his career with the Stars in 1975 when he was named an ABA All-Star as a rookie. Malone amassed 29,580 points and 17,834 rebounds in his career in the ABA and NBA.

Miller tried to work his magic in 1986 to bring a different superstar to Utah. "I tried to woo Julius Erving from the 76ers," the late Miller wrote in his autobiography, *Driven*. "We arranged to meet near Morgan, Utah—Julius had been vacationing in Jackson Hole—and we drove back to my home together. He came over to our house to share a barbecue with our family, Dave Checketts, and Frank Layden. Afterward, we chatted in the family room about the possibility of having him spend a year or two in a Jazz uniform. Eventually, he wound up in the driveway playing basketball with Greg and the other boys."

While that established a friendship, it wasn't enough to establish a partnership. Miller and his wife, Gail, flew out to Philly to make one final push, but the eventual Hall of Famer, who'd shown some interest, turned down the Jazz's lucrative two-year, $3.5 million offer and opted to play out the final year of his career with the Sixers.

Now imagine a Utah Jazz roster that included Dr. J, Magic, Moses, Dominique, John, Karl, and a healthy Pistol Pete. That's a pretty fun what if. But if you asked Sloan about that imaginary scenario, he'd probably tell you to stop jackpotting around or, "That'll get you a toothpick and a glass of water when you're hungry."

Acknowledgments

Although I will always cherish my nine years on the Utah Jazz beat, those memories came at a cost. For every fun basketball moment I experienced, there was a get-together, holiday, birthday, lacrosse game, recital, or some other sliver of unrecoverable time that I missed with my family, my friends, my church, and myself. In the summer of 2017, my bosses and I decided it was time for me to pass the beat-writing baton on to someone else.

That was not an easy thing to do. Jazz fans had been a big part of my life. I'd tried to inform, entertain, and engage you—in the paper, via email, over social media, in gas stations, and at grocery stores. I let you into my life, and you let me into yours. I loved it. I'm especially grateful for my Jazz followers and friends on Twitter. We've had quite the time over there. I'm thankful for the *Deseret News* and its readers, whose support gave me an opportunity to earn a living and travel the country to watch and report on an entertaining sport.

Over the years one conversation seemed to happen again and again—and I'm not talking about the "Can I have free tickets?" or "Will you get me so and so's autograph please?" questions I'd often hear. The other conversation went like this:

Family: "You should write a book!"

Me: "I should."

Friends: "You should write a book!"

Me: "I should."

Jazz fans: "You should write a book!"

Me: "I should."

And then one day, a terrific publisher—Triumph Books—reached out.

Publisher: "We'll pay you to write a book!"

The timing was tricky, but my wife correctly told me I'd always regret it if I didn't seize this opportunity. As usual, Heather was right. Without her help, encouragement, support, and sacrifice over the years, this book and my career would not have been possible. My four kids—Ethan, Sydney, Aidan, and Jackson—were also cooperative, supportive, and excited as I wrote this book because they knew how important it was to me. I love you all dearly. I looked at this project as a labor of love with hope that my kids will read it fondly to know more about the team their dad grew up loving and loved covering while they grew up.

Along with my mom, Patty, and my dad (RIP, Big Tom), I'd like to thank my brothers, Tommy and Kelly (aka "Chunk") and my sisters, Tami and Natalie—along with their beautiful families— for their love over the years. (Please forget about this book until after you open your Christmas presents.)

I'm grateful for the many talented sportswriters who've covered this beat before me and alongside me. I leaned on their gifted story-telling and news gathering as much as mine. Tim Buckley was my mentor and friend while I worked as his right-hand man during the 2008–09 and 2009–10 seasons. I also appreciate *Deseret News* friends Kent Condon, Brad Rock, Andrew Aragon, Mike Sorensen, and Aaron Morton for their assistance on the Jazz beat. I admire Lee Benson, Doug Robinson, Dirk Facer, Loren Jorgensen, and Linda Hamilton, colleagues who covered the team for other outlets as well, including Kurt Kragthorpe, Ross Siler, Bill Oram, Aaron Falk, Steve Luhm, Tony Jones, Jim Burton, and Andy Larsen. Also, there are a number of sharp bloggers, radio hosts, TV personalities, and team broadcast crew members who do a fine job of informing and entertaining about Utah's favorite NBA team. I've maintained that the Jazz market is spoiled with the coverage it receives.

I'd like to give a special thanks to *Deseret News* sportswriter Jeff Call, who wrote the BYU book in this *100 Things* series. His insight and tips were invaluable, and his book is really good, so I encourage Cougars fans to buy it.

I annoyed, pestered, and questioned Jazz coaches Jerry Sloan, Tyrone Corbin, and Quin Snyder at times, laughed with them at other times, and tried to fairly report on them at all times. I appreciate their professionalism and cooperation in situations that can be stressful and demanding on all involved. For the most part, Jazz players were good to work with. And the Jazz PR staff has been wonderful to me over the years, including Jonathan Rinehart, Derek Garduno, Caroline Burleson, and Frank Zang.

My journalism career began, of course, at McDonald's. Yes, really. I was an assistant manager back in the early 1990s when my boss asked me to make a newsletter for our restaurant. *The McD Monthly*, as I called it, only lasted two issues—turns out my time was needed flipping burgers more than crafting a workplace publication—but it sparked a desire in me to give journalism a try. From there I enrolled in Journalism 101 and after submitting my first actual article—a story on athletic expansion at the Salt Lake Community College—I was hired as sports editor of the school paper, *The Horizon*. The editor who gave me my first big break, Larry D. Curtis, became a good friend and a vocal writing advocate of mine. Julie Slama and Roselyn Kirk were also quite helpful back in my SLCC days. In addition, I'll always be indebted to former *D-News* sports editor John Robinson for taking a chance on "The Jodinator" 25 years ago.

I'm thankful Triumph Books gave me a chance to end my Jazz writing days with one last chapter, so to speak, about an organization that is still searching for a championship but one that has definitely found its way into the hearts of so many. A state that has divided college loyalties is united through the Jazz. It's my hope that readers will enjoy their stroll through memory lane as much as I did.

Sources

Newspapers

Deseret News
The Salt Lake Tribune
Chicago Tribune
New York Post
The New York Times
New York Daily News
Newsday
Los Angeles Times
USA TODAY
San Antonio Express-News

The Kansas City Star
The Spokesman-Review
The New Orleans Advocate
Las Vegas Sun
The Denver Post
The Orange County Register
Las Vegas Review-Journal
Hartford Courant
Seattle Post-Intelligencer
Daily Press

Magazines

Sports Illustrated
Muscle & Fitness
Ebony
The Sporting News

Websites

The Players' Tribune
NBA.com
HoopsHype
NOLA.com
Wave3.com
Basketball Reference
UtahJazz.com
Bleacher Report

GeorgiaTech.com
DanOnTheStreet.com
Greg Miller blog
ESPN.com
NotInHallOfFame.com
Cavs.com
SLAM! Sports

Books

Sir Charles: The Wit and Wisdom of Charles Barkley
Driven: An Autobiography
Assisted: The Autobiography of John Stockton
Behind the Drive: 99 Inspiring Stories from the Life of an American Entrepreneur
To The Brink: Stockton, Malone, and the Utah Jazz's Climb to the Edge of Glory
NBA List Jam!: The Most Authoritative and Opinionated Rankings
The Best of Benson: A Twenty-year Anthology of Sports Writing
Utah Jazz media guide

Wire Services

Associated Press
United Press International

Audio and Video

The Dan Patrick Show
FOX 13 KSTU
1280 The Zone
1320 KFAN
Mormon Channel